HODDER GIBSON
AN HACHETTE UK COMPANY

Jane Cooper

English

National 4 & 5

With thanks to the English teachers and students of Firrhill High School, especially Hayley Mound, Anna Brown and Rachael Erskine.

The Publishers would like to thank the following for permission to reproduce copyright material:

Photo credits p. 10 David Burton/Alamy; p. 24 Clynt Garnham Business/Alamy; p. 25 CBW/Alamy; p. 33 Fortean/TopFoto; p. 47 The Granger Collection/TopFoto; p. 174 Copyright Guardian News and Media; p. 180 Copyright Guardian News and Media; p. 186 Copyright Guardian News and Media; p. 191 Copyright Guardian News and Media; p. 201 David Stock/Alamy; p. 208 Alinari/TopFoto.

Acknowledgements Promote Shetland: extracts adapted from *Discover the Mystery of Shetland* (2013); **Patrick Collinson:** extract adapted and abridged from 'Equity release is not the answer', *Guardian* (16 March 2013), reproduced by permission of Guardian News & Media Ltd 2013; **Luke Salkeld:** 'Boy who ran up £1700 bill playing a game on his parents' iPad' adapted and abridged from *Daily Mail* (1 March 2013), reproduced by permission of Solo Syndication on behalf of the *Daily Mail*; 'Policeman father reports his own son' adapted and abridged from *Daily Telegraph* and *Daily Mail*, (25/26 March 2013) extracts reproduced by permission of Telegraph Media Group Limited and Solo Syndication on behalf of the *Daily Mail*; **Peter Reading:** 'Tryst' and 'Pace Packer' from *Collected Poems 1: Poems 1970–1984* (Bloodaxe Books 1995), reproduced by permission of Bloodaxe Books; **Lynne Truss:** extracts from 'Eats, Shoots and Leaves', (Profile 2003), reproduced by permission of David Higham Associates; **Tim Price:** extracts from 'For Once', written for Pentabus Theatre Company and published by Methuen Drama (2011), © Tim Price, Methuen Drama, an imprint of Bloomsbury Publishing plc.; **Alan Bennett:** 'A Cream Cracker Under the Settee ' extract reproduced by permission of The Random House Group and United Agents; **Anne Frank:** extracts from *The Diary of a Young Girl* (definitive edition, 1995), edited by Otto H. Frank and Mirjam Pressler, translated by Susan Massotty, reproduced by permission of Penguin Books Limited and Doubleday, an imprint of the Knopf Doubleday Publishing Group, a division of Random House LLC.; **Sue Townsend:** extracts from *The Secret Diary of Adrian Mole*, reproduced by permission of Curtis Brown Group Ltd, London on behalf of Sue Townsend © Sue Townsend 1982, and The Random House Group; **Nigel Slater:** extracts from 'Toast' (Harper Perennial 2004), reproduced by permission of Harper Collins Publishers Limited © 2004 and Gotham Books, an imprint of Penguin Group USA LLC.; **Bill Bryson:** extract from *The Life And Times Of The Thunderbolt Kid* (Black Swan, 2007), reproduced by permission of Bill Bryson and The Random House Group; **Caitlin Moran:** extracts from *How To Be A Woman* (Ebury Press 2012), reproduced by permission of The Random House Group and Harper Collins Publishers © 2011; **Mark Kermode:** extract adapted from *The Good, The Bad and the Multiplex* (Arrow 2012), reproduced by permission of The Random House Group; **Martin Luther King Jr:** extract from 'I have a dream' speech, reprinted by arrangement with the Heirs to the Estate of Martin Luther King Jr., c/o Writers House as agent for the proprietor New York, NY. © 1963 Dr Martin Luther King Jr. Copyright renewed 1991 Coretta Scott King; **Amelia Hill:** 'Autism doesn't hold me back. I'm moving up the career ladder', extract adapted and abridged from *Guardian* (9 March 2013), reproduced by permission of Guardian News & Media Ltd 2013; **Jonathan Gilbert:** 'Paraguayan landfill orchestra makes sweet music from rubbish', extract adapted and abridged from *Guardian* (26 April 2013), reproduced by permission of Guardian News & Media Ltd 2013; **Jane Thynne:** "I set my daughter a computer curfew', extract adapted and abridged from *Guardian* (27 April 2013), reproduced by permission of Guardian News & Media Ltd 2013; **Zoe Williams:** 'Has Liz Truss tried looking after six toddlers? I have', extract adapted and abridged from *Guardian* (2 February 2013), reproduced by permission of Guardian News & Media Ltd 2013; **Eric Schmidt and Jared Cohen:** extracts adapted and abridged from *The New Digital Age*, (John Murray 2013); **Deborah Orr:** 'Children are sent to school too young in the UK', extract adapted and abridged from *Guardian* (9 March 2013), reproduced by permission of Guardian News & Media Ltd 2013; **Edwin Morgan:** 'Good Friday' and 'Trio' (*Collected Poems*, Carcanet 1996) reproduced by permission of Carcanet Press Limited ©1996.

SQA material is © Scottish Qualifications Authority and reproduced with SQA permission

Every effort has been made to trace all copyright holders, but if any have been inadvertently overlooked, the Publishers will be pleased to make the necessary arrangements at the first opportunity.

Although every effort has been made to ensure that website addresses are correct at the time of going to press, Hodder Gibson cannot be held responsible for the content of any website mentioned in this book. It is sometimes possible to find a relocated web page by typing in the address of the home page for a website in the URL window of your browser.

Hachette UK's policy is to use papers that are natural, renewable and recyclable products made from wood grown in sustainable forests. The logging and manufacturing processes are expected to conform to the environmental regulations of the country of origin.

Orders: please contact Bookpoint Ltd, 130 Park Drive, Abingdon, Oxon OX14 4SE. Telephone: (44) 01235 827720. Fax: (44) 01235 400454. Lines are open 9.00–5.00, Monday to Saturday, with a 24-hour message answering service. Visit our website at **www.hoddereducation.co.uk**. Hodder Gibson can be contacted direct on: Tel: 0141 848 1609; Fax: 0141 889 6315; email: **hoddergibson@hodder.co.uk**

© Jane Cooper 2014

First published in 2014 by
Hodder Gibson, an imprint of Hodder Education,
An Hachette UK company
2a Christie Street
Paisley PA1 1NB

Impressions number 5 4 3 2
Year 2018 2017 2016 2015 2014

Cover photo © Michelle D. Milliman/Shutterstock.com/
Illustrations by Barking Dog
Typeset in Bembo Regular 13/15 by Integra Software Services Pvt. Ltd.
Printed in Italy

A catalogue record for this title is available from the British Library

ISBN 978 1 4441 9212 4

CONTENTS

Introduction

This book covers two courses: National 4 English and National 5 English. They fit quite closely together. Both courses exist to give you an opportunity to develop your skills in the four keys areas of English: *reading*, *writing*, *listening* and *talking*. Both courses will give you chances to work with literature, language, and the media.

Schools tackle these courses differently. You might be in a class where some students are working towards National 4 while others are working towards National 5; you might be in a class where everybody sets out to aim for the same qualification.

Even then, things may change as you work your way through the courses. You might start on National 4 but find that you are doing very well, in which case you and your teacher might decide that you should tackle National 5 instead. Some students might start off aiming for National 5 but realise that it is a better idea to do National 4 first. Because of all of this, it makes sense for this book to cover both courses.

There are strong similarities between the two courses:

- In each course you need to pass a unit called Analysis and Evaluation, which tests your knowledge of what you *read* and what you *listen* to.
- In each course you need to pass a unit called Creation and Production, which will get you to *write* and to *talk*.
- Each course also has a Literacy Unit. You must pass this to get National 4. You do not have to do this unit for National 5, but your school or your teacher may decide that you will do it.

All these units will be assessed in school by your teacher. You do not have to do any exams for these units, or send anything away from school to be marked. The units will not be graded, but you will know if you have passed or failed.

There are some differences between the two courses:

- In National 4 there is an Added Value Unit. This will be assessed in school by your teacher. To pass this unit you need to choose a topic, and then find and study at least two texts that allow you to explore this topic. Finally, you have to present your findings either orally or in writing, and be able to answer questions about what you have done.

- In National 5 you will send away a Portfolio of two pieces of writing to be marked by someone outside your school.
- In National 5 you will also sit an exam (sometimes called the Question Paper) that assesses different aspects of your reading skills. One of the tasks will test your ability to read something you have never seen before under exam conditions, and answer questions on it. You will also write a critical essay about a text you have studied in class, and you will answer questions on a set Scottish text that you have studied in class.

To help you to see as clearly as possible that you are covering all the skills and tasks you are meant to tackle, this book is arranged in chapters that go with each of the units or assessments. DON'T PANIC if that is not quite how your teacher tackles your course. Because the units are based on skills, your teacher may teach you something, or get you to do an activity, or complete a task or challenge, in such a way that you are learning or improving one of the skills and then proving that you have done so.

So, here are some questions that you might sometimes want to (very politely!) ask your teacher:

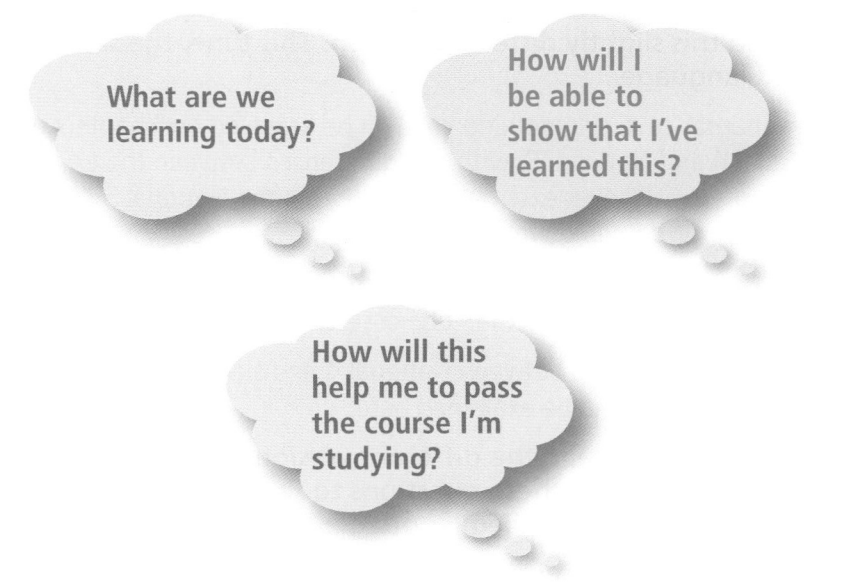

What are we learning today?

How will I be able to show that I've learned this?

How will this help me to pass the course I'm studying?

If you don't understand what you are doing, or why you are doing it, just ask!

How to use this book

Each chapter of this book covers something you will be assessed on. The chapters on the units cover both National 4 and National 5. Any differences between the two levels are made clear. Some of the chapters cover the parts of the National 5 course that are assessed outside school. Every chapter begins by telling you what you will be assessed on.

On some pages of this book a 'Combined assessment' box will let you know if the task you are doing could be used to help you pass more than one assessment.

One of the differences between National 4 and National 5 comes up very often. It is mentioned in almost all of the tasks and assessments. We are going to look at this now.

Straightforward and detailed language

At National 4, you are expected to be able to understand, and use, *straightforward* language. At National 5, you are expected to understand, and use, *detailed* language. You need to know the difference between them.

Active learning

Work with a partner. Together, read over the three paragraphs in the section called 'How to use this book' again. They are written in **straightforward** language.

Now, read this slightly different version. This time, the same information has been written in **detailed** language.

Each chapter covers something you will be assessed on: chapters on the units will cover both National 4 and National 5, with any differences between the two levels being made clear. Some of the chapters will cover external assessment in the National 5 course. Every chapter of the book will commence by detailing what is assessed.

On some pages a 'Combined assessment' box will explain whether the current task can be used to provide evidence for more than one assessment.

One of the differences between National 4 and National 5 comes up in almost all of the tasks and assessments, and will be examined here.

You might need to read the different versions of the information more than once. When you are ready, answer these questions to show you understand the difference between **straightforward** and **detailed** language:

- What do you notice about the lengths of sentences?
- What do you notice about the number of sentences?
- What do you notice about the vocabulary?

Try to get used to spotting straightforward and detailed language. Newspapers such as the *Sun* or *Metro* are more likely to use straightforward English. A paper like *The Times* or the *Guardian* is more likely to use detailed language. Books written for children and teenagers are more likely to use straightforward language. Books for adults are more likely to use detailed language.

Active learning

Read this paragraph. It is written in detailed language.

The effects of the extreme weather were experienced throughout southern Scotland, areas within the Forth and Clyde valleys being most severely affected. The Police, Fire Service, Coast Guard and Mountain Rescue all worked ceaselessly to preserve life and to aid in securing property. Numerous residents were accommodated in a sports centre after a suburban street in Glasgow flooded. A local authority spokesperson praised the efforts of the emergency services and of municipal staff, while reminding the public that further inundations were predicted.

Use a dictionary if you need one. Rewrite the paragraph in straightforward language. Then compare your version with someone else's.

Don't panic if you found that task tricky. Whenever this book is dealing with National 4, it will use straightforward language.

Mark schemes and answers

In many places in this book, there are tasks for you to do. These will help you check your understanding of what you have learned. For some of these tasks, there are mark schemes answers at the back of the book. Your teacher might get you to mark your own work, or another pupil's work, or your teacher might decide to mark it. DO NOT look at the answers until you have tried the task or you just will not learn anything.

CHAPTER 1 The Analysis and Evaluation Unit

This unit, like the Creation and Production one covered in the next chapter, is in both National 4 and National 5. You must pass this unit to pass the National 4 or National 5 courses. In this unit you will be assessed on your skills in *reading* and *listening*. This chapter covers these two skills separately, starting with *reading*.

First, however, we are going to look at two linked ideas that are highly important in the National 4 and 5 courses — *purpose* and *audience*. It makes sense to work on these now, because the easiest way to understand them is by seeing how they come up in what we read or listen to. Note too that these ideas also apply to what we write or say.

Purpose and audience

- **Purpose** means **WHAT a text is for** – why somebody said it, or wrote it.
- **Audience** means **WHO a text is for** – who is supposed to read it or listen to it.

To pass the unit assessments in National 4 and 5 Reading and Listening, you need to be able to identify the purpose and audience of texts produced by someone else. To pass the unit assessments in National 4 and 5 Writing and Talking, what you write or what you say must fit your given purpose and be right for your target audience.

Here are some possible purposes:

- to entertain
- to persuade
- to inform
- to explain.

1   How many more purposes can you think of?

Possible audiences include people from a particular:

- age group, e.g. children, teenagers
- place, e.g. Americans
- profession, e.g. doctors
- interest or hobby, e.g. birdwatchers.

2   How many more audiences can you think of?

Sometimes two texts can have the same purpose but different audiences. The *Sun* and *The Times* are both newspapers. Their purpose is to inform. They are even produced by the same company. But they are aimed at very different audiences. Radio 1 and Classic FM are both music radio stations. Their purpose is to entertain. Again, they aim at very different audiences. BBC 3 and BBC 4 are both digital television channels. Each channel produces some programmes that aim to entertain, and some that aim to inform. But they aim at very different audiences.

3   For each of the examples above, can you explain who the two different audiences are?

4   Try to think of other examples of two texts that have the same purpose but different audiences.

Active learning

This task will help you to think about texts that have the same purpose but different audiences. You – or your teacher – may need to do a little preparation for this. Alternatively, if your classroom is set up with a good Internet connection and a data projector, you should be able to do the task straight away.

First, go to the website of your nearest multi-screen cinema.

Then, make a list of all the films currently showing at that cinema.

Next, watch the trailer for each of these films. The cinema's website may have links to these, or you may have to look them up separately.

Now decide who the target audience is for each film. It will help if you think about their age, their interests, and perhaps their social class or educational background.

Finally, decide the purpose of each film. You can start by assuming that any film on at your local multiplex has a main purpose to entertain. But, do any of these films have another purpose too? Are they perhaps examining a theme or a subject?

Active learning

This second task will get you thinking about both purpose and audience at the same time and definitely needs some preparation.

Homework: every person in your class, and also your teacher, needs to collect all sorts of paperwork. Try to collect as many different examples as you can of the following texts:

- junk mail
- newspapers – both free and paid for
- magazines – both free and paid for
- leaflets and flyers
- takeaway menus
- brochures
- catalogues.

Basically, if it is printed on paper and you can bring it into school, bring it.

Classwork: working in a group, share all the texts you have brought in. For each text, decide the purpose and the target audience.

Active learning

This third task will get you to show that you can write to fit certain purposes and audiences. It also takes some preparation.

First you, or your teacher, should prepare lots of small coloured cards. Each card should have a purpose written on it. You need at least as many cards as there are people in the class. It is fine to repeat the same purpose more than once.

Next you, or your teacher, should prepare lots of small coloured cards in a different colour. Each card should have an audience written on it. You need at least as many cards as there are people in the class. It is fine to repeat the same audience more than once.

Third you, or your teacher, should prepare lots of small coloured cards in a third colour. This time each card should have a subject written on it. You need at least as many cards as there are people in the class. Try to make all the subjects different.

Now shuffle the cards, give each person one card of each colour, so that everyone gets, at random, a purpose, an audience and a subject.

Then write a paragraph that fits all of these. For example, here is what happened when someone got the purpose *to persuade*, the audience *elderly people*, and the subject *marshmallows*.

Marshmallows are a wonderful sweet if you have false teeth. They're not too chewy, they're not too hard. You can enjoy them without ever worrying that they'll do any harm to your dentures.

If you are absolutely sure it is impossible to write a paragraph based on the cards you have been given, tell your teacher. If he/she agrees that your combination cannot be done, then swap one card for a different one.

Finally, read your paragraph to a partner who does not know what was on your cards. Ask this person to guess the purpose, audience and subject.

You can shuffle all the cards and play again if you like.

You will be asked to identify purpose and audience in your reading and listening work. In National 4 assessments you may get some hints, perhaps by being asked to choose from a short list of possible choices. At National 5, you will probably be expected to work out the purpose and audience by yourself. You will usually also be asked to give some evidence to show how you identified the purpose and audience. National 5 students might be asked to give more evidence.

You will also be expected to write, and to talk, to suit your chosen purpose and your audience. This will be covered in the next chapter on the Creation and Production Unit. For now, it is time to get on to the main work for this chapter and this unit.

Reading

What you will be assessed on

In the end, whether you are sitting National 4 or National 5, you have to show all the appropriate reading skills by **understanding, analysing and evaluating** at least **one written text**. This text should use **straightforward** language if you are a National 4 student. If you are sitting National 5, you should be reading texts that use **detailed** language. (Look back at the Introduction to this book to find out more about what 'straightforward' and 'detailed' mean here.)

You will show your ability to understand, analyse and evaluate what you read by doing the following:

- Identifying the **purpose and audience** of the text. National 5 students will also be able to *explain* the purpose and audience.
- Identifying the **main ideas and supporting details**. National 5 students will also be able to *explain* these ideas and details.
- Applying your knowledge of language to explain the **meaning and effect** of the text. National 5 students will also apply their *understanding* of language, and will be able to use appropriate *critical terms*.

Combined assessment

The work you do for the reading outcome of the Analysis and Evaluation Unit may help you with another part of the course.

- It might be possible to use this work as evidence of reading for the National 4 Literacy Unit (or the National 5 one, if your school or college teaches this). Remember that literacy assessments should be based on non-fiction reading. If you are a National 4 student, your literacy reading assessments should be based on texts of at least 500 words. If you are a National 5 student, your literacy reading assessments should be based on texts of at least 700 words.
- It might also be possible to pass the reading part of the Creation and Production Unit by reading some of the sources you research for your National 4 Added Value Unit.

Ask your teacher if he/she is hoping to combine assessments in this way. Your teacher must be sure that you have covered all the skills each unit asks for.

Warning

There is one thing you need be careful of. You probably **cannot** provide evidence of passing your reading outcome by basing this on a text you have studied in class. This is because, if your teacher has taught you a text, you will not really be able to show that you have identified the purpose and audience or that you have identified the ideas and supporting details. It will not truly be you explaining the meaning and effect of the text. These will all have been covered by your teacher as you studied the text. If it is not your own work, you cannot use it to pass the unit assessment.

Main ideas and supporting details

As we saw above, you will be assessed on your grasp of the main ideas and supporting details in the text. We are going to use some short texts to get you working on this now.

First, here is a worked example. Read this extract from a tourist brochure about Shetland.

Blown away

Shetland is one of the windiest places in the UK, with an average speed throughout the year of force 4. In the winter, speeds of hurricane force 12 are regularly recorded. Very few months of the year are gale-free and some have near–continuous gales.

We can see the main idea of this paragraph right at the start:

> **Shetland is one of the windiest places in the UK …**

This is backed up by a four supporting details:

1. … [the] average wind speed throughout the year is force 4.
2. In the winter, speeds of hurricane force 12 are regularly recorded.
3. Very few months of the year are gale-free …
4. … some [months] have near-continuous gales.

Active learning

You are going to work on finding main ideas and supporting details in some more short texts. The texts, and tasks, will become more challenging as we go on.

1 Read these paragraphs from the Shetland brochure:

The treeless nature of the islands is due at least in part to the salt spray from the sea thrust ashore by these winds.

The winds have also shaped the built landscape. The buildings along Lerwick's long narrow main street are huddled together for protection from the elements. All the islands' many harbours are either natural shelters or else have been given substantial breakwaters. At Sumburgh Airport the runway has giant rock defences at either end to protect it from the huge seas. The spectacular power of the sea in strong winds is nowhere better witnessed than along the Eshaness coastline. At the end of the road a lighthouse sits high on a cliff, but stones from the rolling sea below have from time to time broken its windows.

The main idea of this passage is:

Wind has a huge effect on Shetland

Now find the supporting details that prove this. You have been given a clue word to help you with each one. Try to use your own words as far as possible to show your understanding.

    1 TREES
    2 STREET
    3 HARBOURS
    4 AIRPORT
    5 LIGHTHOUSE

2 A tourist brochure about Fife included two pages about local food. Here is the first paragraph from those pages:

With rich farmland and blue waters, **the Kingdom of Fife is the perfect environment for producing the most delicious natural produce** from mouth-watering berries to succulent meats and the freshest seafood.

Look at the bit in bold. It's the main idea of these pages. Can you put that idea into your own words?

Now read the following paragraphs, which also came from these two pages. Pick out **at least three** supporting details that back up the main idea. Remember to put them in your own words.

The East Neuk is home to a number of fishing boats that bring home their daily catch of prawns, crabs and lobsters ready to be turned into beautiful dishes. Sample mackerel, which has been freshly line caught in the Firth of Forth, or try lobster and crab from the local fishermen who land their daily catch in the harbour of Anstruther itself. Wherever you eat on Fife, you are guaranteed fabulous fresh seafood.

You can savour excellent cooking in Fife's Michelin-star restaurants at the Peat Inn near St Andrews and Sangster's in Elie. Or, sample Fife's delicacies at one of the farmers' markets that take place almost every Saturday.

B. Janetta's ice cream parlour in St Andrews offers more than fifty varieties of ice cream, including an Irn Bru sorbet and millionaire's shortbread frozen yoghurt.

3 The following extract is a more complex text, with more than one set of ideas in it. The writer, a journalist specialising in writing about money, has one overall main idea for the article. His main idea is that older people should sell their houses and move into smaller, cheaper properties.

First, read the article:

What we should be doing is radically rethinking the sort of properties we wish to live in as we get much older. We should no longer support a world in which four-bed homes remain occupied by single pensioners using unearned cash gifted them by the property boom, while young families are squeezed into ever-smaller flats and paying ever-higher rents.

Here's a simple, and financially sensible, solution. Downsize. Got a £300,000 house as in the example above? Sell it to a younger family, and buy a good-sized flat or smaller home for £210,000. You will be releasing £90,000. And you can still leave something to your offspring, should you wish.

We prize the idea that grannies and granddads must stay in their family homes all their life. Why? So they can close off rooms, as they become too expensive to heat?

It's understandable that people have an emotional attachment to their homes, and no one should be forced out. The idea of one's final years in a poky one-bed flat with nightmare neighbours horrifies me as much as anybody else. But a decent-sized, well-managed two-bed mansion block flat, with a lift, shops and GP services within close walking distance? No car to worry about, space for family to visit, a park close by? What's not to like?

I know a couple who, after she was diagnosed with breast cancer and her husband retired, sold their £400,000 four-bed home to buy a £225,000 two-bed bungalow and have adjusted their lives accordingly – and put more than £150,000 in the bank. They remain in financial control, and have prepared themselves for, hopefully, a long and happy retirement. It's the only sensible approach.

Remember, the writer's main idea is that older people should sell their houses and move into smaller, cheaper properties.

This is made up of two smaller ideas:

A It is a bad idea for pensioners to keep living in big houses.
B There are benefits for everyone when pensioners move to smaller houses.

Now do these tasks:

i Using your own words as much as possible, give the details that support idea A above.
ii Using your own words as much as possible, give the details that support idea B above.

Warning

In the next few pages you will get the opportunity to try four different reading tasks. These are **not** final assessment tasks. Such tasks have to be kept secure – they cannot go in a textbook. But, they will give you a chance to use and practise your reading skills.

Remember you will be asked about purpose and audience. There will be questions on main ideas and supporting detail. You will also be asked about the meaning and effect of language.

The first two tasks are non-fiction reading tasks, based on newspaper articles about similar subjects.

The first task is at **National 4** level. First, read the passage:

Boy who ran up £1700 bill playing a game on his parents' iPad

1   When their five-year-old pestered them to let him play on their iPad, Greg and Sharon Kitchen's first instinct was to say No. But faced with a house full of visitors, along with their son saying that the game he wanted to play was free, they eventually said Yes. That decision was a costly one. The next day they found out their son Danny's little game-playing session had cost them £1700.

2   Yesterday the Kitchens warned other parents of the danger of allowing children to play 'free' games which come with hidden costs. Although Apple has since refunded the full amount, the family said it has been a tough lesson to learn.

3   Danny had asked his father for a passcode to download a game called Zombies v Ninja, which involves touching the iPad screen to aim ninja-style weapons at cartoon zombies. His parents left him playing while they entertained friends at their home. But by pressing a shopping trolley icon on the screen, Danny was offered the chance to buy extra 'ammunition'.

4   His mother knew nothing about his spending spree until she saw emails from iTunes the following day listing what he had bought. 'Danny was pestering us to let him have a go on the iPad,' she said from the family home in Warmley, near Bristol. 'He kept saying it was a free game so my husband put in the passcode and handed it to him. It worried me when he asked for the password but I had a look at the game, it said it was free so I didn't think there would be a problem.

5   'We had lots of visitors in the house and were both a little busy. I woke up Monday morning and looked at my emails and had loads from iTunes. I thought it must be a mistake, so I checked my bank balance online and nothing had been taken out. I thought nothing of it until my credit card adviser phoned and told me they had allowed the payments.'

6   In ten minutes Danny had bought dozens of in-game 'weapons' and 'keys' which cost up to £69.99 a time. 'I can't believe he was able to spend so much,' said Mrs Kitchen, a mother of five who runs a children's entertainment business with her husband. 'It was far too easy a thing for him to do and more should be done to limit stuff like this from happening.

7   'I told Danny he'd better get ready for bed and run and hide before Daddy got home. Through his tears he turned back and said "But where can I hide?" Bless him – that stopped me being angry but of course, it's a lot of money.'

8   Danny said: 'I said to Dad can you put the passcode for the game, he said no and then I said it was free so he said yes. The next day it cost lots of money. I was worried and I felt sad. I was crying. I'm not sure how I did it, I thought it was free. I'm banned from the iPad now.'

9   Mr Kitchen, 44, said: 'I was livid. Not amused at all. But Danny was very sorry so I couldn't stay mad at him for long. I'm relieved that they have said they are going to give us back our money.'

10 An Apple spokesman said it was vital that parents kept their passcodes safe and said software was available to prevent children from using the iTunes store. In an email to Mr Kitchen, the company said iPads, iPhones and iPod touches have built-in parental controls to restrict access to content. The company also said parents have the option to turn off 'in-app purchases'.

Adapted from an article in the Daily Mail, 1 March 2013

Now answer these questions:

1a Who do you think would like to read this article? Choose one:
- parents
- teenagers
- computer experts.

1b Give a reason why this person **would want** to read the article.

1c Give a reason why one of the other possible people **would not** be interested in reading the article.

2a What is the purpose of this article? Choose one:

- to make readers feel sorry for this family
- to make readers laugh at this family
- to warn readers about the risk of this kind of thing.

2b Explain how you know that this is the purpose of the article. Give evidence from the text to support your answer.

3 The article shows that huge sums can be spent very quickly, and very easily. Give **two details** that prove this.

4 Look at paragraph 4. Which **two** expressions suggest that Danny nagged his parents?

5a How does Mrs Kitchen's language in paragraph 7 show us that Danny is a very young child? You should **quote** something she says and **explain** why you have chosen this quotation.

5b How does Mrs Kitchen's language in paragraph 7 show us that she felt some sympathy for Danny? You should **quote** something she says and **explain** why you have chosen this quotation.

6 Explain one way the Apple company is made to seem unfriendly or unhelpful in paragraph 10.

For mark scheme see page 252.

This next task is at **National 5** level. First read the passage:

Policeman father reports his own son

1 A policeman has shopped his 13-year-old son for fraud after he ran up a £3700 bill playing iPad games.

2 PC Doug Crossan, 48, was horrified when his credit card company informed him that son Cameron had blown a small fortune in the App Store. He claims the teenager, who now faces the possibility of being arrested and questioned by his father's colleagues, was unaware he was being charged for the in-game purchases and wants Apple to scrap the charge.

3 But the technology company has refused and his only way of recouping the money is to report the purchases as being fraudulent. So Mr Crossan, of Clevedon, North Somerset, has reported Cameron to the Action Fraud helpline – meaning it is now up to the police to decide if a crime has been committed.

4 He said: 'I am sure Cameron had no intention to do it, but I had to have a crime reference number if there was any chance of getting any credit card payments refunded. In theory the

local police station could contact me and ask for Cameron to come in to be interviewed. I could make it difficult of course and refuse to bring him in and they would have to come and arrest him.

5   'Really I just want to embarrass Apple as much as possible. Morally, I just don't understand how Apple gets off with charging for a child's game.'

6   Cameron has only owned the Apple tablet computer since December after he and other students at Clevedon School were bought them to aid them in class.

7   Mr Crossan logged the details of his MBNA Virgin credit card with Apple when he used the device to download a music album.

8   Cameron then racked up more than 300 purchases on games such as Plants vs Zombies, Hungry Shark, Gun Builder and Nova 3. Many of them are free to download but users can buy in-game extras – in one game Cameron had purchased a virtual chest of gold coins costing £77.98.

9   When his father confronted him Cameron quickly confessed, claiming he did not know he was incurring charges as the games were initially free.

10 Mr Crossnan said he had recently seen similar stories where families had been refunded under similar circumstances and given this he thought he had a reasonable chance of receiving a refund.

11 He said: 'We have asked Apple to consider our case in the same light, as the case is mirrored by him playing exactly the same free games, but Apple have refused.

12 'Apple iTunes is now refusing to speak to me or give me an idea of why it will not refund. It sent me a copy of the terms and conditions stating that all purchases are final and further contact should be by way of a solicitor.'

13 Apple has refused to cancel the charges, citing parental responsibility and pointing out that iPads contain password locks to prevent accidental or unwanted purchases.

14 But Mr Crossan, an officer with Avon and Somerset Police, believes the company has tricked his son into making purchases he was not aware of.

15 He said: 'I am a father of a studious, polite and sensible 13-year-old who has been duped after uploading free children's games on his iPod and iPad. None of us had any

knowledge of what was happening as there was no indication in the game that he was being charged for any of the clicks made within the game. Cameron innocently thought that because it was an advertised as a free game, the clicks would not cost. Our son is mortified to think that this has happened. I wonder how many others there are in the UK that have suffered at the hands of these apps?'

16 Mr Crossan only found out about Cameron's spending when he cancelled the direct debit for the credit card, believing it was clear, and MBNA Virgin contacted him to reveal more than £3000 was still outstanding.

17 He has now reported the purchases to Action Fraud, the national fraud reporting centre run by the National Fraud Authority, a Government agency.

18 Victims are issued with a police crime reference number and details are then passed to the police, who may pursue the case further. Officers decide whether or not a crime has been committed and, if so, they then give the person who has reported the crime the opportunity to press charges. Avon and Somerset Police today refused to comment on the case.

19 With more than half a billion active accounts, the App Store is the most popular online marketplace in the world. The store currently offers more than 775,000 apps to iPhone, iPad and iPod touch users.

20 Apple declined to comment on Mr Crossan's case.

Adapted from articles on the *Daily Mail* website and in the *Telegraph*, 25 and 26 March 2013

Now answer these questions:

1a Who would be likely to read this article? Think about:
- age and/or
- interests and/or
- gender and/or
- another audience you can identify.

1b Explain, by making reference to the passage, how you reached this conclusion.

2a What is the purpose of this article?

2b Support your answer with evidence from the text.

3a What has Cameron done?

3b What has been his father's reaction to this?

3c What has been Apple's reaction?

4a Identify one example of informal language from the first two paragraphs. Why has the writer used informal language here?

4b Identify one example of formal language used in paragraphs 3 and 4. Why has formal language been used here?

5 Read paragraphs 6–9. Explain, with reference to the text, two ways in which these paragraphs make Cameron seem innocent.

6 What impression of Apple is created by the final paragraph? How is this impression created?

For mark scheme see page 253.

The next two reading tasks are based on fiction texts, in fact on poems. Each poem features a young person and an accident. The first task is at **National 4** level.

First, read the poem:

Out, Out

The buzz saw snarled and rattled in the yard
And made dust and dropped stove-length sticks of wood,
Sweet-scented stuff when the breeze drew across it.
And from there those that lifted eyes could count
5   Five mountain ranges one behind the other
Under the sunset far into Vermont.
And the saw snarled and rattled, snarled and rattled,
As it ran light, or had to bear a load.
And nothing happened: day was all but done.
10   Call it a day, I wish they might have said
To please the boy by giving him the half hour

That a boy counts so much when saved from work.

His sister stood beside him in her apron

To tell them 'Supper'. At the word, the saw,

15   As if to prove saws know what supper meant,

Leaped out at the boy's hand, or seemed to leap—

He must have given the hand. However it was,

Neither refused the meeting. But the hand!

The boy's first outcry was a rueful laugh,

20   As he swung toward them holding up the hand

Half in appeal, but half as if to keep

The life from spilling. Then the boy saw all—

Since he was old enough to know, big boy

Doing a man's work, though a child at heart—

25   He saw all was spoiled. 'Don't let him cut my hand off—

The doctor, when he comes. Don't let him, sister!'

So. But the hand was gone already.

The doctor put him in the dark of ether.

He lay and puffed his lips out with his breath.

30   And then—the watcher at his pulse took fright.

No one believed. They listened to his heart.

Little—less—nothing!—and that ended it.

No more to build on there. And they, since they

Were not the one dead, turned to their affairs.

Robert Frost

Now answer these questions:

1a Who do you think would like to read this poem? Choose one:
- parents
- teenagers
- farm workers.

1b Give a reason why this person **would want** to read the poem.

1c Give a reason why one of the other possible people **would not** be interested in reading the poem.

2a What is the purpose of this poem? Choose one:
- to make readers feel sorry for this boy
- to make readers criticise this boy for being careless
- to warn readers about the risk of farm accidents.

2b Explain how you know that this is the purpose of the poem. Give evidence from the text to support your answer.

3a Read lines 1–16. The writer makes the saw sound as if it is alive. Explain two ways he does this.

3b Read lines 1–16. The writer makes the saw sound dangerous. Explain two ways he does this.

4 The boy does not seem to understand what has happened to him. Give two pieces of evidence from lines 19–27 that show this.

5a The writer, Robert Frost, often uses repetition. Give one example of this.

5b Explain why you think he used repetition in this case.

6 This poem features a number of characters. We see the boy, his sister, and the doctor. There are also other farm workers in the poem. Read lines 9–12 and 33–34. Explain one way Frost makes us feel dislike for these other farm workers.

For mark scheme see page 255.

The next task is at **National 5** level. It is about a pair of connected poems. First, read the poems.

'Tryst'

Me and Gib likes it here – always comes of a night
no one else gets here, see. That's his Great-Grandad's stone.
Gassed, *he* was; got sent home from one of them *old* wars.
       Tommy, they called him.
We sprayed HARTLEPOOL WANKERS on one of them. Great!
This is the newest one – sad it is, really, it's
some little ten-year-old girlie's. Then plastic daffs
       look very nice though.

He likes to get me down in the long weeds between
two of them marble things – I can see ivy sprout
on the cross by his head. He makes me squiggle when
    he sticks his hand up.

He works at one of them mills what makes cattle food.
He stacks the sacks. You should see them tattoos on his
arms when he flexes them. There is a big red heart
    with TRUE LOVE on it.

He runs the Packer-thing all on his own, he does.
We're saving up to get married and have a big
do like that big snob that works in our office had
    (Crystal, her name is).

I let him do what he wants – he pretends that he's
the Ripper sometimes, and gets me down on a grave;
then what he does with his hands feels like scurrying
    rats up my T-shirt.

When we've saved up enough, we're going to wed in church.
This is alright, though – at least in the summertime.
They don't pay poor Gib much, stacking them heavy sacks
    off the conveyer.

'Pacepacker'

THE *PACEPACKER* NEEDS ONE OPERATOR ONLY.
PLACE EMPTY PAPER SACKS IN RACK MARKED 'SACKS',
ENSURING THEY ARE CLAMPED TIGHT WITH SPRING CLAMP.
ADJUST CONVEYERS TO CORRECT HEIGHTS. SWITCH ON.
WHEN 'START RUN' LIGHT SHOWS GREEN, PRESS 'START RUN' BUTTON.
SACKS ARE PICKED UP BY SUCKERS, STITCHED AND CONVEYED
TO ELEVATOR, ENSURE CLOTHING AND HANDS
ARE CLEAR OF CONVEYER BELT.
The corrugated rapidly-moving strip of rubber seemed
to draw the arm smoothly, unresistingly
up through the oiled steel rollers. The 'Stop Run' light
shows red. The matt belt glistens where a smear
of pink mulch, fatty lumps, flensed skin, singed hair,
is guzzled dry by plump impartial houseflies.

Peter Reading

Now answer these questions:

1a Who would be likely to read this poem? Think about:
- age and/or
- interests and/or
- gender and/or
- another audience you can identify.

1b Explain, by making reference to the poem, how you reached this conclusion.

2a What is the purpose of this poem?

2b Support your answer with evidence from the text.

This pair of poems can be divided into three distinct sections

3a Who is narrating the first section? What is this section about?

3b Where do the words of the second section come from? What is this section about?

3c Whose 'voice' do we hear in the third and final section? What is this section about?

3d What is the connection between the first poem 'Tryst' and the second poem, 'Pacepacker'?

Neither the narrator of the first section, nor her boyfriend Gib, seem very intelligent.

4a By making close reference to the text and/or its language, give at least one piece of evidence to show that the girl is not very intelligent.

4b By making close reference to the text and/or its language, give at least one piece of evidence to show that Gib is not very intelligent.

The narrator of the first section seems to have mixed feelings about Gib.

5a By making close reference to the text and/or its language, give at least one piece of evidence to show one **positive** feeling she has about Gib.

5b By making close reference to the text and/or its language, give at least one piece of evidence to show one **negative** feeling she has about Gib.

6 By making close reference to the text, give at least one example of how the middle section of the poem ('THE *PACEPACKER* NEEDS … CONVEYER BELT') is made to sound commanding.

Think about the whole poem.

7a By making close reference to the text and/or its language, explain at least one way the author makes us feel sympathy for the girl.

7b By making close reference to the text and/or its language, explain at least one way the author makes us feel sympathy for Gib.

For mark scheme see page 256.

You have now seen four sample reading tasks. You have had the chance to work on both fiction and non-fiction texts, and at National 4 and National 5 level.

In the end, it is up to you and your teacher to decide when you are ready to be assessed for reading. Remember you will be asked about purpose and audience. There will be questions on main ideas and supporting detail. You will also be asked about the meaning and effect of language.

When the time for assessment comes, your teacher must:

- Be sure you are reading the right level of language: straightforward for National 4, detailed for National 5.
- Give you an assessment that tests you on all the right aspects of reading. This could be by using one of the Unit Assessment Support Packs produced by the SQA. Alternatively, your teacher could make up his/her own assessment questions based on a text he/she thinks you will appreciate and understand.
- Keep a record of evidence that you have passed the assessment.
- Make sure that you have answered enough questions correctly to cover each standard – purpose and audience; main ideas and details; meaning and effect.

If you do not pass first time, your teacher should give you another assessment. This must be based on a new text at the same level of difficulty, and should ask new questions. You only have to answer the questions that cover the standard(s) you got wrong in your first assessment.

Listening

So far this chapter has dealt with one of the Analysis and Evaluation skills, *reading*. Now we are going to move onto the second of these skills, *listening*.

Of all the four language skills – *reading*, *writing*, *talking* and *listening* – listening is the one you use most in real life. It is the one you get a lot of your entertainment from and the one you use most at school in your learning. Until recently though, it has not been taught or assessed nearly as much as the other three skills.

What you will be assessed on

In the end, whether you are sitting National 4 or National 5, you have to show all the appropriate listening skills by **understanding, analysing and evaluating** at least **one spoken text**. This text should use **straightforward** language if you are a National 4 student. If you are sitting National 5, you should be listening to texts that use **detailed** language. (Look back at the Introduction to this book to find out more about what 'straightforward' and 'detailed' mean here.)

You will show your ability to understand, analyse and evaluate what you listen to by:

- Identifying the **purpose and audience** of the text. National 5 students will also be able to *explain* the purpose and audience.
- Identifying the **main ideas and supporting details**. National 5 students will also be able to *explain* these ideas and details.
- Applying your knowledge of language to explain the **meaning and effect** of the text. National 5 students will also apply their *understanding of language.*

Combined assessment

The work you do for the listening outcome of the Analysis and Evaluation Unit may help you with another part of the course.

- It might be possible to use this work as evidence of listening for the National 4 Literacy Unit (or the National 5 one, if your school or college teaches this).
- It might also be possible to pass the listening part of this unit by listening to a media source you choose to research for your National 4 Added Value Unit.
- You may be able to pass your listening assessment by evaluating the group discussion you take part in for your talking assessment.

Ask your teacher if he/she is hoping to combine assessments in this way. Your teacher must be sure that you have covered all the skills each unit asks for, remembering that literacy assessments should be based on non-fiction uses of language.

⚠ Warning

There is one thing you need be careful of. You probably **cannot** provide evidence of passing your listening outcome by basing this on a media text, such as a film or television drama, that you have studied in class. This is because, if your teacher has taught you a text, you will not really be able to show that you have identified the purpose and audience or that you have identified the ideas and supporting details. It will not truly be you explaining the meaning and effect of the text. These will all have been covered by your teacher as you studied the text. If it is not your own work, you cannot use it to pass the unit assessment.

Active learning

Close your eyes and listen, in absolute silence, for 1 minute. Then write down everything you could hear.

Although the book is written to feel like it is speaking to you, it cannot actually make sounds. So, this part of the chapter will give you suggestions of what you can listen to and of ways you can work on these.

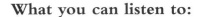

What you can listen to:

Some of the material you might listen to is audio only – purely listening. For example you could listen to:

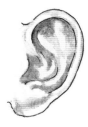

- radio news broadcasts
- famous speeches
- a film review or interview from the Radio 5 Live film programme
- a short section from a longer Radio 4 programme such as *Today, Front Row, Women's Hour, PM, You and Yours, Saturday Review*
- a short section from a longer Radio 4 programme on a particular subject area: the station has programmes about science, the environment, farming, food, books, politics, money, etc.

A lot of the material you can listen to is audio-visual – something you watch and listen to. For example you could watch and listen to:

- other students' individual presentations
- group discussions in your class
- a section of a television news broadcast
- adverts
- an individual segment of a magazine-style television programme such as *The One Show, Coast, Countryfile*
- film trailers
- film clips
- a clip from a fictional television drama or comedy
- part of a television documentary
- a chunk of *Horrible Histories.*

Another wonderful site, with material for both National 4 and National 5, is the Class Clips part of the BBC Learning Zone. If you go to **www.bbc.co.uk/learningzone/clips** you can search for clips on almost any subject you can think of.

There are two sites where you will find listening material that might be a bit tough for National 4 students, but could be helpful for National 5 students:

- TED talks – in which experts talk about a subject they understand well. Go to **www.ted.com/talks** and you can search by subject to find talks on areas you are interested in. Many of these speakers are from overseas, usually the USA.
- **http://5x15stories.com** where you will find British-based speakers giving 15-minute talks, again about topics they know well and are interested in. You can search this site by subject, or by the name of the speaker.

Active learning

This task requires some preparation in your own time. Above are three websites where you can find clips to listen to and watch.

Homework: your task is to find a clip you are interested in.

Classwork: share the clip you find with members of your class or group. You could do this via the classroom computer and data projector, or on your own smartphone, laptop or tablet.

- **Introduce** your clip by explaining how you found it.
- **Show** the clip.
- **Explain** the main idea of this clip.
- **Outline** at least two supporting details that back up this main idea.
- **Give** one reason why you like the clip.

The rest of this section will give you a number of structures for listening. These will be **generic**. This means they will not be designed to get you listening to a specific text. Instead, you will be given a series of approaches for listening to certain types – genres – of texts. You could try several of these tasks to help you develop your listening skills.

As you work through these next few pages, remember these three important things:

1 This chapter is about passing a **listening** assessment – the words you hear matter more than any visual material that supports them. It is all right if you mention visual material and media techniques in your answers, but it is up to your teacher when he/she designs any listening assessments to make sure that you could still get the answers right even with your eyes shut.

2 If you are doing a listening task to pass your unit assessment, this **must** be based on a text you have not listened to or watched before. The questions can be similar to ones you have used before – because they are designed to test the same skills – but, if you are being finally assessed on it, the text should be a new 'unheard' one.

3 When you are doing a listening task, you can listen to/watch a clip **as many times** as you like. There is no limit to how often you listen to/watch it. You can also rewind and replay smaller sections of the clip as often as you need to. You may make notes as you watch and listen, if you think this will be helpful.

Listening to a group discussion

We will start with this task as it is easy to do even if your teacher, or your school, is a bit low-tech.

Obviously, listening is a huge part of good discussion skills. Anyone who takes part in a group without listening carefully will not be able to contribute well. But, you can also step back a little and evaluate a group discussion in order to give evidence of your listening.

First, take part in a group discussion. As you do so, you must demonstrate that you are listening to others by doing at least some of these things:

- taking turns
- supporting and/or building on other group members' comments
- challenging and/or appropriately disagreeing with other group members' comments.

Now consider the group discussion you have been part of. Reflect on it and answer these questions:

1 What were the main ideas that came out of this discussion?
2 How, and how well, did group members take turns?
3 How, and how well, did group members listen to each other?
4 How well did group members contribute to the discussion?

National 5 students can also answer these further questions:

1 Comment on the language used by group members. For example, was it formal or informal? Support your answer with quotations and/or reasons.
2 How good was the evidence given by group members to support their ideas? Support your answer with quotations and/or reasons.
3 Comment on the pace and structure of the discussion. Were ideas considered thoughtfully or rushed? Were all ideas explored in enough depth?

Listening to another student's individual presentation

This again is a task that does not necessarily need a lot of technical knowledge or equipment. However, it is a good idea if your teacher bases this on a recording of a presentation, rather than one you watch happening live.

This is partly for the sake of the student who is talking. Imagine how much more nervous you would feel if you knew your individual presentation was going to be watched in this way.

The recording is for your sake too. Your teacher will be able to consider the talk and make sure that its language is at the right level – straightforward for National 4, detailed for National 5. Your teacher can also make sure there is enough in the talk for you to be able to answer the questions on. In addition, recording the talk gives you the chance to watch it over and over again, as is your right.

First watch your fellow student talking. You can make notes if you wish, and can watch it as many times as you need to.

Then answer these questions:

1　Purpose
　　a　What was the purpose of the presentation?
　　b　How did you know this was the purpose?
2　Audience. The intended audience was students who were listening, and a teacher who was assessing.
　　a　How well did the speaker make his/her talk appeal to the students in the audience? Give reasons to support your answer.
　　b　How well did the speaker make his/her talk fit the situation of being assessed by the teacher? Give reasons to support your answer.
　　c　Did the speaker interact in any way with the audience? What was this interaction? How successful was it? Give reasons to support your answer.
3　Content
　　a　What was the overall subject of the presentation?
　　b　What were the speaker's main ideas about the subject?
　　c　How well did the speaker use supporting details such as information, evidence or personal experience to back up these main ideas? Give reasons and/or evidence to support your answer.
　　d　How well did the speaker use any props, images, PowerPoint slides or video or audio material to support his/her talk? Give reasons and/or evidence to support your answer.
4　Evaluation
　　a　Overall, what was successful about the presentation?
　　b　Overall, how could the presentation have been improved?

National 5 students can also answer these further questions:

5   Comment on the language used by the speaker. For example, was it formal or informal? Did he/she use any specialised language, such as jargon or subject-specific terms? Support your answer with quotations and/or reasons.

6   Comment on the pace and structure of the presentation. Were ideas considered thoughtfully or rushed through? Were all ideas explored in enough depth?

You could also use the above questions to get you listening to a TED Talk (www.ted.com/talks) or a 5x15 talk (http://5x15stories.com) or to listen to a speech.

Listening to and watching scripted, fictional television

The most straightforward way to listen to and watch scripted, fictional television is to pick a small section from the first episode of a television drama or comedy when the writer is trying to introduce characters, and to establish a situation.

Watch the opening, then answer these questions:

1   Purpose
    a   What kind of reaction are the makers of this programme hoping to get from the audience?
    b   What things are said by characters to get that reaction from the audience?
    c   Explain how these words when spoken would create that audience reaction.

2   Audience
    a   Who would like to watch this programme? (You could think about age, gender, interests and social class.)
    b   Give evidence: explain what it is that makes the programme appeal to this audience.

3   How believable do you find the storyline to be? Give reasons to support your answer.

4   Identify three pieces of information the programme gives you. Why is each of these important in helping you understand and follow the programme?

5   Think about the main characters you have met so far. Pick two of these characters. What is each person like? Support your answers by referring to things the characters say.

6   Choose two characters who speak quite differently. What is different about the ways they speak? (You could think about dialect, accent, pace, tone, the words they choose to use and the moods they express through their words.)

7 Which character do you think will face the biggest challenge as the programme continues? What will this challenge be? Why will this character find it so difficult?

Listening to factual television or radio

Listen to your chosen programme or clip. Remember you can hear it, or parts of it, as many times as you need to, and you can make notes while you listen. **Then answer** these questions:

1 Purpose
   a What is the purpose of this programme?
   b Quote from, or make references to, the text to show how you identified this purpose.

2 Audience
   a Who would like to watch or listen to this programme? (You could think about age, gender, interests and social class.)
   b Give evidence: explain what it is that makes the programme appeal to this audience.

3 Content
   a What was the overall subject of this programme or clip?
   b What were the main ideas about this subject?
   c How well did the programme use supporting details such as statistics, evidence or experiences to back up these main ideas? Give reasons and/or evidence to support your answer.

4 Evaluation
   a Did you find this programme interesting or not? Refer to details from the programme to explain why.
   b If you were only shown an extract, did this make you interested in watching the whole programme? Refer to details from the programme to explain why you did, or did not, want to watch more.

National 5 students can also answer these further questions:

5 Comment on the language used in the programme. For example, was it formal or informal? Did the programme use any specialised language, such as jargon or subject-specific terms? Support your answer with quotations and/or reasons.

6 Comment on the pace and structure of the programme. Were ideas considered thoughtfully or rushed through? Were all ideas explored in enough depth?

7 How reliable did the speakers in the programme seem? Give evidence to support your answer. This evidence might be based on the **words and language** they use, or on the **way** they speak.

You have now seen four sample, generic, listening tasks. In the end, it is up to you and your teacher to decide when you are ready to be finally assessed for listening. When that time comes, your teacher must:

- Be sure you are listening to the right level of language: straightforward for National 4, detailed for National 5.
- Give you an assessment that tests you on all the right aspects of listening. This could be by using one of the Unit Assessment Support Packs produced by the SQA. Alternatively, your teacher could make up his/her own assessment questions based on a text he/she thinks you will appreciate and understand.
- Keep a record of evidence that you have passed the assessment.
- Make sure that you have answered enough questions correctly to cover each outcome – purpose, audience, main ideas and details, meaning and effect.

If you do not pass first time, your teacher should give you another assessment. This must be based on a new text at the same level of difficulty, and should ask new questions. You only have to answer the questions that cover the standard(s) you got wrong in your first assessment.

CHAPTER 2 The Creation and Production Unit

This unit, like the Analysis and Evaluation one covered in the previous chapter, is in both National 4 and National 5. You must pass this unit to pass the National 4 or National 5 course. In this unit you will be assessed on your skills in *writing* and *talking*. This chapter will cover these two skills separately, starting with *writing*.

Writing

What you will be assessed on

In the end, whether you are sitting National 4 or National 5, you have to show all the appropriate writing skills by producing at least **one written text**. This text should be clearly **understandable at first reading** – in other words, your teacher should not have to reread anything to try to work out what you mean. Your meaning will be this clear if you choose the right sort of **language** and **vocabulary**, and if it is **technically accurate**, which means there should not be mistakes in your spelling, punctuation and grammar.

There are some other choices you need to make too. You must choose the right **ideas and content** to include in your writing. In addition, you must choose **a format and a structure** that suit the **audience** you are writing for and the **purpose** of your piece of writing. If you are sitting National 4, this text should show your command of **straightforward** language. If you are sitting National 5, the text should be in **detailed** language. (Look back at the Introduction to this book to find out more about what 'straightforward' and 'detailed' mean here.)

Combined assessment

The work you do for the Creation and Production Unit may help you with another part of the course.

- It might be possible to use this work as evidence of writing for the National 4 Literacy Unit (or the National 5 one, if your school or college teaches this). Remember that literacy assessments should be based on non-fiction writing. For a piece of writing to count as a pass for literacy, it must be at least 300 words long at National 4 and at least 500 words at National 5.
- It might also be possible to pass the writing part of this unit by producing a written response at the end of your National 4 Added Value Unit.
- If you are doing National 5, a piece of written work might be evidence of writing for this unit and eventually also go into your Portfolio.
- Your talk work from this unit might contribute to combined assessment. You might be able to pass your assessment in listening by listening to someone else talking, or by evaluating and answering

questions about a group discussion that you have watched or taken part in. There is more information about this in the 'Listening' section of Chapter 1.

Ask your teacher if he/she is hoping to combine assessments in this way. He/she must be sure that you have covered all the skills each unit asks for.

Technical accuracy

As we saw above, your writing has to be understandable at first reading; it must be clearly expressed and make full sense. It also has to be **technically accurate**, without significant mistakes in spelling, grammar and punctuation. Because this applies to all of your writing, we will spend a little time looking at the idea of technical accuracy now.

This book cannot teach you technical accuracy. There just is not enough space. If you have difficulties with using language in this way, your teacher will certainly notice this and can recommend other books or exercises you can use. What we can do here though is show that technical accuracy matters. Getting it wrong can change meaning. Look at this sentence:

The girls like pizza.

It tells us that a number of young female people love eating an Italian foodstuff made of tomato, cheese, and other toppings on a flat, dough base.

However, if you use an apostrophe where you should not, you get this:

The girl's like pizza.

which creates a very unfortunate impression:

Or look at this example:

A woman, without her man, is nothing.

This rather old-fashioned sentence tells us that unless a woman has a man in her life, she is of no worth or value. Look what happens if we use exactly the same words in exactly the same order, but just change the punctuation.

A woman: without her, man is nothing.

Can you explain what the sentence means this time?

Active learning

Below are two letters. Each one contains exactly the same words in exactly the same order. Only the punctuation is different. Again, this totally changes the meaning. Half the students in your class should practise reading the first version out loud, the other half should practise reading the second version. Be as expressive as possible. When you are ready, get one person from each half of the class to read their letter aloud.

If you want to see some more examples of how small punctuation changes have a huge effect on meaning, look for the cartoon books *The Girls Like Spaghetti* and *Twenty-Odd Ducks* by Lynne Truss.

Dear Jack,

I want a man who knows what love is all about. You are generous, kind, thoughtful. People who are not like you admit to being useless and inferior. You have ruined me for other men. I yearn for you. I have no feelings whatsoever when we're apart. I can be forever happy – will you let me be yours?

Jill

Dear Jack,

I want a man who knows what love is. All about you are generous, kind, thoughtful people, who are not like you. Admit to being useless and inferior. You have ruined me. For other men I yearn! For you I have no feelings whatsoever. When we're apart I can be forever happy. Will you let me be?

Yours,

Jill

Ideally, you will be a skilled enough user of language that you do not make a lot of mistakes as you write. You should also be able to check over your own writing before you hand it in to your teacher, and to notice and correct any errors. If your teacher still finds mistakes when he/she marks your work, you should be able to correct these.

Some schools use a correction code. Teachers put coded marks in the margin to show that there is a mistake on that line of work. Below is an example of a correction code.

sp	spelling	**^**	something missing
caps	mistake in use of capitals	**rep**	repetition
S	sentence error	**✓**	something good
NP	new paragraph	**exp**	not clearly expressed
p	punctuation mistake	**?**	what does this say?

Active learning

You are going to see an example of work that a teacher has marked using the correction code.

1 Identify each specific mistake the student has made.

2 Correct the mistakes.

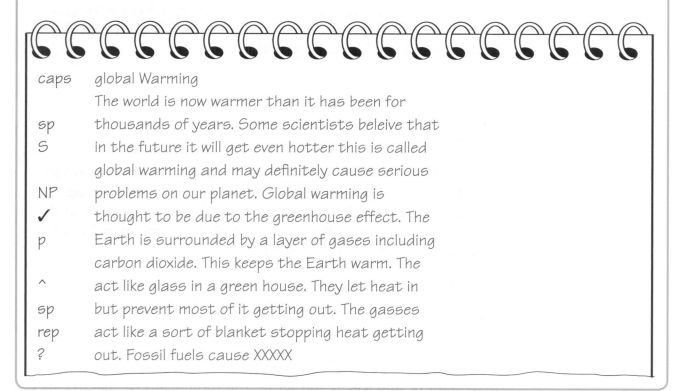

caps	global Warming
	The world is now warmer than it has been for
sp	thousands of years. Some scientists beleive that
S	in the future it will get even hotter this is called
	global warming and may definitely cause serious
NP	problems on our planet. Global warming is
✓	thought to be due to the greenhouse effect. The
p	Earth is surrounded by a layer of gases including
	carbon dioxide. This keeps the Earth warm. The
^	act like glass in a green house. They let heat in
sp	but prevent most of it getting out. The gasses
rep	act like a sort of blanket stopping heat getting
?	out. Fossil fuels cause XXXXX

Read this piece of work by another student. Decide where the teacher would mark errors. What would the teacher write in the margin each time?

Drugs both legal and illegal have their effects and risks. In this report I will discuss how bad the risks can get in to some drugs.

Paracetamol is used commonly as a pain releever, but if used incorrectly, can lead to long term liver damage in some cases of the drug, it can contain a drowsiness drug too.

caffeine, although not recognised as a harmful drug, can leave you with brown teeth and the shakes. It is placed in almost 99% of energy because of it's ability to keep people awake and stop them falling asleep.

Penultimately, cocayne and ecstasy, even though not the same drug, have similar long term effects of depression and mental illness and similar risks of dependency on it and permanent damage to the body. And finally, anaesthetic, both local and can be very dangerous as if you were to be given an overdose you could die.

In conclusion, drugs both legal and illegal have their risks. It just depends on how personally you are wanting to use them.

Now that you have a better idea about what technical accuracy means, we will go on and look at one other important idea.

How your work will be assessed

Some of your written work might be self-assessed and some of it might be assessed by another member of your class. However, some of your writing will be formally assessed by your teacher. If you are using any piece of writing to pass your unit assessment, you have to follow these guidelines:

- The work has to be done under controlled conditions. This means it will be done in school or college so your teacher knows it is your own work and sees how you have done it.
- Your teacher can give you advice and guidance.
- Your teacher can support you as you prepare and plan. He/she can discuss your ideas with and give you advice and support in making notes.

- Your teacher is not allowed to give you key ideas, specific wording, or a detailed plan or structure.
- Your teacher cannot correct your work in detail. This means he/she cannot show you exactly what your mistakes are or how you should fix them.

If you do not pass the assessment first time round, you can have another go. But, this might mean starting again with a whole new task. Your teacher will make clear what you should do to be reassessed.

Let us go on now to look at some specific types and genres of writing.

> ⚠ **Warning**
>
> Some of the most common genres of writing that you might tackle in school are NOT going to be dealt with in this chapter. Short story writing, personal writing, two-sided argumentative writing and one-sided persuasive writing are all covered in depth in Chapter 5. You can look there to find advice about them.

Writing newspaper articles

Newspaper reports follow a particular set of rules and guidelines shown in the table below. Some of these cover the way the piece is written, others the layout.

Writing guidelines	Layout guidelines
• The headline above the article may use alliteration, rhyme or a pun to grab the reader's attention. • The first paragraph gives the key points of the story. • Later paragraphs tell the story in more detail. • Quotations tend to come later still. Those with the closest personal connection to the story are quoted first. Experts, commentators, and people with less strong personal connections are quoted later.	• There is a headline above the article. • There may also be a subheading. • The text is set in columns. • The article may be illustrated with a photograph or some other graphic such as a map or diagram. • If there is a photo or other graphic, a caption will explain what this shows. • The journalist's name (known as the by-line) appears at the start or end of the article.

Active learning

Read the following article. How many of the features listed above can you spot?

MONSTER MYSTERY

Edinburgh eel worries walkers

Walkers in Holyrood Park were astonished yesterday to see what appeared to be a monster rising from the waters of Dunsapie Loch.

A group of ramblers on an organised walk were passing the loch, which is at the Meadowbank end of the park, just as it was getting dark around five o'clock, and heard splashing at the water's edge.

Next, as they looked on in horror, a head appeared above the surface of the loch. The beast, which they later described as looking rather like an eel, but of vast size, thrashed about for some minutes before submerging again.

One of the walkers, Graham Gibb, said later, 'It certainly wasn't a swan or anything else you'd normally find in the park. It was at least ten metres long. I'm sure I saw fangs too. My wife managed to get a picture of it on her phone.'

A spokesman for the park authority later said, 'We know of no unusual creatures in the park or its waterways. A full investigation will be carried out. In the meantime we urge visitors to the park to take care, but not to be afraid.'

Robin Mackenzie

The monster, snapped by one walker

As the **first paragraph** of a news story is so important, let us focus on that in a little more detail.

The first paragraph should deal with the **five Ws**:

Who **What** **Where** **When** **Why/How**

The story about the Edinburgh eel does this.

1 **Who** – a group of ramblers.
2 **What happened** – they got frightened.
3 **Where** – in Holyrood Park.
4 **When** – yesterday.
5 **Why** – because they saw a monster.

Go back to the news article you were annotating. Label the start of the article in more detail to identify the five Ws.

Watch a television news broadcast or listen to a radio news broadcast. Pick three news stories. For each one, using the five Ws, write the opening paragraph for a newspaper item on the same event.

News **headlines** also use certain types of language. The purpose of the headline is to attract the reader's attention. A front page headline may even convince someone to buy a particular paper, and headlines on other pages are there to make you want to read the article that follows. Headline writers, especially those working for tabloid papers, love using word tricks to achieve this effect.

The story about the monster in Holyrood Park uses alliteration in both the headline and the subheading. This is a common tactic. For example, a football story about an Edinburgh derby game could have the headline:

HAPPY HEARTS HAMMER HOPELESS HIBEES

Headline writers are also found of puns, i.e. jokes based on the sounds of words. One of the most famous headlines of all time went with a report of a genuine football match in which, against all odds, Inverness Caledonian Thistle beat Celtic in a Scottish Cup match. The headline, based on the song 'Supercalifragilisticexpialidocious' from the film *Mary Poppins* said:

SUPER CALLY GO BALLISTIC CELTIC ARE ATROCIOUS

Letter writing

In this era of emails and text messages, people do not write nearly as many letters as they used to. But, there are still times when only a letter will do. When you need to be taken seriously, a letter has more weight than an email. When you want your words to last, something physical on paper can feel more real than something you could delete at the touch of a button.

There are certain strict rules about letter style.

Active learning

To see whether you know the rules for letter layout, answer the questions below. Your teacher will be able to tell you the answers.

- All letters should start with the sender's address. Where does it go?
- What else would go just beneath the address?

Now let us think about the greeting at the start:

- How do you start a letter to your friend Ryan?
- How would you start one to the Head Teacher of your school?
- How would you start one to an important stranger if you did not know his/her name?

Finally, you need to know how to end your letter. Match the proper ending to the person receiving the letter:

Yours sincerely	the Head Teacher
Yours faithfully	a friend or relative
Lots of love	an important stranger

Some letter-writing tasks will make you write **formal** letters, while others are about writing **informal** letters. You must be able to tell them apart, because this affects the content of the letter.

Active learning

Look at the following letter tasks. Which are formal and which are informal?

1 Imagine you are a new recruit to the army. Write a letter to your family or to a close friend describing you first week's experiences.

2 Imagine you live on the top floor of a bock of flats. Write a letter to your local housing authority complaining about the breakdown of the lift and the lack of security.

3 Imagine you have had the opportunity to swim with a dolphin. Write to a close friend to describe the experience.

4 Write to a pen friend, explaining the ups and downs of British weather and how it plays a huge part in our lives.

5 Write a letter to your local Director of Recreation and Leisure suggesting better facilities for sports in your area.

6 You disapprove of circuses because you think they are cruel to animals. Write a letter to your local newspaper to explain your objections.

The body of the letter will vary depending on whether it is informal or formal. Informal letters should be friendly and chatty. Formal letters, depending on the task, will usually either be giving information or putting across an opinion.

One common reason for writing a formal letter is to complain. If you have been given bad service, or if something you bought broke down, then writing an effective formal letter will often make the reader put right that situation.

Active learning

Read the letter below. As you do so, look for the answers to these questions:

1 What two things did the letter writer expect Furnitureland to do for her?

2 How did the company fail in these two matters?

3 What does she expect the company to do for her now?

Third Floor Left
27 Marwendale Street
Edinburgh
EH10 9CA
18 March

The Deliveries Manager
Furnitureland
Straitongate Retail Park
Lasshead
Midlothian
EH22 1NN

Dear Sir or Madam,

1   My husband and I recently visited your shop and purchased three 'Shakespeare' bookcases. As these were supplied in boxes too large to fit in our car we paid an extra £25 to have them delivered to our home. We signed a contract in which you guaranteed a delivery on Tuesday, 15 March. Furthermore, you undertook to deliver at our convenience, between the hours of 7 and 9pm

2   Unfortunately your staff neither arrived on time, nor did they actually deliver the bookcases to our flat. I therefore now wish to make a complaint.

3   Firstly, the bookcases arrived late. Although they should have been brought by 9pm at the latest, the Furnitureland lorry eventually reached our street at 10.15pm, causing considerable noise and disruption to our neighbours at this late point in the evening. Although we had given you our phone number when we arranged the delivery, at no time did anyone call us to explain that they were running late, or to advise us of an updated arrival time.

4   Secondly, your staff did not complete the delivery. Upon seeing that we lived three floors up in a tenement block without a lift, the driver and his assistant refused to carry the bookcases up our stairs on the grounds that this might hurt their backs. Eventually my husband and a neighbour carried the items up, your driver having abandoned them in the downstairs hallway of our building.

5   Our address details, as shown above, and as left by us when we booked the delivery, make it quite clear that ours is not a ground floor property. Also, it is surely the responsibility of a delivery driver to deliver the goods ordered: any such person should be fit for his job.

6   The service we received from your company was clearly unsatisfactory. In order to amend the situation, I would appreciate a full and immediate refund of the delivery charge.

Yours faithfully,

Joanna Sharp

Active learning

Now answer these questions:

1 Give three examples of formal words the writer uses.

2 Give three examples of formal phrases the writer uses.

3 Which other new detail did you notice about the layout of a formal letter to a business?

4 The letter is in six paragraphs:

   a What is the purpose of paragraphs 1 and 2?
   b What is the purpose of paragraph 3?
   c What is the purpose of paragraphs 4 and 5?
   d What is the purpose of paragraph 6?

Let us focus a little more on making the right choice of formal language.

Look at the group of phrases in the box below. Which are formal? Which are informal? What makes these phrases informal?

I wish to complain about …	I'm totally raging.	This is unacceptable.
I am very annoyed that …	I want you to …	To sort this out …
This won't do.	It was not appropriate.	I expect you'll …
In order to amend this …	I wish you to …	I'm complaining about …

Active learning

Now it is time to try writing your own formal letter of complaint.

First, decide what you want to complain about. Did you get terrible service in a shop or restaurant? Did you order something that arrived late, or damaged? Did you go on a holiday where the accommodation and facilities were not as the brochure suggested? Did you buy something that fell apart or broke down shortly afterwards?

Next, like the letter writer above, think about the difference between what you reasonably could have expected, and what actually happened. This will help you to structure your letter.

Now write your letter, following these steps:

Step 1. Write your address correctly at the top right of the page. Follow this with the date. If you are writing to a business whose address you know, put this on the left side of the page, below your own address, as you saw in the example letter.

Step 2. Begin with a formal greeting below this on the right.

Step 3. Write a paragraph to explain who you are and why you are writing.

Step 4. Write **several paragraphs** to explain clearly what the problems were. For each problem explain what you expected and what actually happened. You could use some of these phrases to introduce the problems:

Another problem was …	I am also concerned that …	A further difficulty was …
I was also upset that …	One issue was …	In addition to this …
It is also worrying that …	Furthermore, …	

Step 5. Finish off with a paragraph to explain politely but firmly what you would like the reader of the letter to do to put all of this right.

Step 6. Finish your letter with a suitable signing off and your name.

Check over your letter before you give it to your teacher.

- Does it have the right ideas and content?
- Does the letter fulfil its purpose to complain?
- Is it written to reach its target audience?

- Have you followed the guidelines for layout as well as those for content?
- If you are aiming for National 5, have you used detailed language?
- Is it technically accurate?
- Is the meaning clear at first reading?

You could also choose to write a more informal letter – perhaps one tied in to a text you have been studying in class. This kind of letter could allow you to show not only your letter-writing skills, but also your understanding of the characters, plot, and themes of the text. For example, after studying J. B. Priestley's play *An Inspector Calls*, you could try to imagine that you are either Eric or Sheila Birling and that you are writing to a friend to explain what happened the night the Inspector came.

If you would like to look at a text that uses informal letters, *The Curious Incident of the Dog in the Night-time* by Mark Haddon contains a number of letters written to the main character, Christopher, by his mother.

Script writing

Like letter writing and writing news stories, script writing has some clear guidelines about layout.

Active learning

Ask your teacher to get copies of lots of different plays out of the English Department book cupboard. It does not matter what they are, as long as you have as many different ones as possible. Get into groups so that each person in your group has a different playscript to look at. Examine your scripts and answer these questions:

A What do we call the sections a play is divided into?

B How do playwrights show that a character is about to speak?

C How do playwrights show what the stage set looks like and how it is laid out?

D How do they indicate any actions or gestures an actor should make, or the way an actor should speak?

Of course, although we do study them in school, playscripts are not written for audiences to read. They are there to help actors know what to say and to show directors and production staff how the play should go and what it should look like.

Look at the opening page of the print version of a play:

> **Characters**
>
> **Sid,** *17, sporty possibly wearing a beenie. Blind in one eye.*
>
> **April,** *45, schoolteacher, prides herself on her youthfulness.*
>
> **Gordon,** *46, tendency to dishevel, big man about town.*

Now here is the first page of the script itself:

> **Scene One**
>
> *A country kitchen.*
>
> *The characters occupy the same space but are not aware of each other. It is as if they are in the same place but at different times. April irons and folds shirts, and does the washing up.* **Gordon** *is on hold on a mobile, going through insurance documents and eating.* **Sid** *is mainly concerned with his laptop, mobile and walking around.*

Active learning

Think of a room you have been in at some point in the last week. That is the setting of your play. Now think of three characters. They cannot all be the same sex. Also, there must be at least at 20-year age gap between two of the characters. Now do this:

1 Write a cast list and brief character description, as in the example above.

2 Write the stage direction that shows us how the play begins, as above.

Playscripts can be tricky. You can only put in what we can actually see on stage. In a story, you can tell the reader, 'Paul had never got on with his sister Clare.' In a play, you cannot do this. If you want those watching the play to know these characters do not get on, you either have to have Paul saying, 'I've never got on with Clare', or have her saying, 'I know you and I have never got on'. But, even that is a challenge. Why would Clare tell Paul something they both already know?

Write at least one page of script for your three characters. In that script, one of these things should happen:

- One of them should try to start a conversation about a subject that another one of the characters really does not want to talk about.
- One character should get annoyed with another, while the third tries to calm the situation down.
- One character should get annoyed with another, while the third just makes things worse.

Scripts are made up of more than speech. They also show how lighting and sound contribute to the play. A spotlight might be used to pick out a particular character. A change of lighting colour could create a certain mood. Dimming the lights could suggest night.

Go back to the pages of script you have just written. How could a lighting direction add to its power?

If your teacher wants you to write a script, this will probably arise from your other work in class. For example:

- If you have been reading a play in class, you might write an extra scene involving some of the characters.
  OR
- If you have been reading a novel or a story, you might take a section of that text and turn it into a script featuring the same characters.

If you want to create your own script from scratch, you could try one of the tasks below. They each focus on small numbers of characters – it is hard to have a large cast without also forcing yourself into writing a long script!

Write one of these scripts.

A scene of dialogue between two people. One is, or both of them are, packing. What they talk about will suggest their relationship, and how they feel about each other.

Hint: think about why the character(s) is/are packing. To go on holiday? To pay a family visit? To go on a work trip? To go to war? To leave home for university? To leave home because a relationship has broken down? Maybe the character is packing her bag for school, or packing his groceries at the supermarket checkout. Maybe the character is packing for someone else.

OR

Two characters are trying to have a serious discussion but they keep being interrupted, perhaps by a waiter, plumber, child, pet, etc.

Hint: decide what the two people are trying to talk about before you start writing. Do they even both want to have this conversation? How much do they agree, or disagree, about this subject? Who or what is going to interrupt them? Will they manage to complete the conversation?

Check over your script before you give it to your teacher.

- Does it have the right ideas and content?
- Does the script fulfil its purpose to entertain?
- Is it written to reach its target audience?
- Have you followed the guidelines for layout as well as those for content?
- If you are aiming for National 5, have you used detailed language?
- Is it technically accurate?
- Is the meaning clear at first reading?

Monologues

A monologue is a particular type of script. The word monologue has its roots in Greek. The *logue* part tells us that it is something to do with words and speech. The *mono* part means *one*. You might recognise this from words such as *monopoly*, which is when one company is in control of a business sector (or when one person in the game of the same name ends up with all the money), or *monotone*, which means just having the same one boring sound all the time.

A monologue is a script for only one character. If this script is being acted out, we will just hear and see one actor talking. In some monologues, you can tell that the character thinks he/she is talking to a particular person, though the audience does not see that person. In other monologues, the character is talking directly to the audience.

Because a monologue is a form of script, it should also use stage directions, lighting cues and other staging information.

Read the extract below, written by Alan Bennett. It is the opening of a monologue called *A Cream Cracker Under the Settee*.

As you read, think about:

- the kind of person Doris is
- who the other people in her life are
- the situation Doris is in.

Doris is in her seventies and the play is set in the living-room and hallway of her semi-detached house. She is sitting slightly awkwardly on a low chair and rubbing her leg. Morning.

It's such a silly thing to have done.

Pause

I should never have tried to dust. Zulema says to me every time she comes, 'Doris. Do not attempt to dust. The dusting is my department. That's what the council pay me for. You are now a lady of leisure. Your dusting days are over.' Which would be all right provided she did dust. But Zulema doesn't dust. She half-dusts. I know when a place isn't clean.

When she's going she says, 'Doris. I don't want to hear that you've been touching the Ewbank. The Ewbank is out of bounds.' I said, 'I could just run round with it now and again.' She said, 'You can't run anywhere. You're on trial here.' I said, 'What for?' She said, 'For being on your own. For not behaving sensibly. For not acting like a woman of seventy-five who has a pacemaker and dizzy spells and doesn't have the sense she was born with.' I said, 'Yes, Zulema.'

She says, 'What you don't understand, Doris, is that I am the only person that stands between you and Stafford House. I have to report on you. The Welfare say to me every time, "Well, Zulema, how is she coping? Wouldn't she be better off in Stafford House?"' I said, 'They don't put people in Stafford House just for running round with the Ewbank.' 'No,' she says. 'They bend over backwards to keep you in your own home. But, Doris, you've got to meet them half-way. You're seventy-five. Pull your horns in. You don't have to swill the flags. You don't have to clean the bath. Let the dirt wait. It won't kill you. I'm here every week.'

I was glad when she'd gone, dictating. I sat for a bit looking up at me and Wilfred on the wedding photo. And I thought, 'Well, Zulema, I bet you haven't dusted the top of that.' I used to be able to reach only I can't now. So I got the buffet and climbed up. And she hadn't. Thick with dust. Home help. Home hindrance. You're better off doing it yourself. And I was just wiping it over when, oh hell, the flaming buffet went over.

Pause

You feel such a fool. I can just hear Zulema. 'Well, Doris, I did tell you.' Only I think I'm all right. My leg's a bit numb but I've managed to get back on the chair. I'm just to sit and come round a bit. Shakes you up, a fall.

Pause

Shan't let on I was dusting.

She shoves the duster down the side of the chair.

Dusting is forbidden.

She looks down at the wedding photo on the floor.

Cracked the photo. We're cracked, Wilfred.

Active learning

Now answer these questions:

1 What sort of person is Doris? How do we know this?

2 What is Doris scared of?

3 What has happened to her? How did it happen?

4 How does she feel?

5 Who is Zulema? What is the relationship between Doris and Zulema like?

6 Who is Wilfred? What has happened to him? How do we know this?

If you think about it, Doris is the sort of person who is not much listened to in real life. Sadly, the world does not take much interest in the opinions of old ladies. The monologue is a brilliant form for letting overlooked characters speak. The characters we do not listen to might have fascinating stories to tell. These people may have been paying attention to us while we have been ignoring them. They might have noticed a lot.

Work with a group. **Make a list** of overlooked characters who might have a lot to say if we let them speak, e.g. the homeless person sitting outside a shop or the school lollipop lady.

Share your suggestions with the rest of the class to build up a bigger list of characters.

Choose one character who you are interested in. Using the Bennett monologue as an example, **write** the first page of a monologue for your character. Remember to start with a stage direction that helps the audience to picture the character and set the scene.

Swap your monologue opening with someone else who does not know what you were writing about. What can you **work out** about each other's characters?

If you would like to write a longer monologue, here are some suggestions of how you could come up with a character:

1 You could just completely invent a new character.
2 You could carry on writing about the character you have started with.
3 You could use one of the other characters from the list your class made.
4 You could pick a real person – a character from the news or from history – and write from his/her point of view. This would involve some research first, to find out what this person was like and some details of his/her life.
5 You could choose a character from a text your class has been studying and write from his/her point of view. This can work very well if you choose a minor character. You need to know your class text well in order to do this.

Active learning

If you have decided to write a full-length monologue, it is time to do it now. Thinking about these things will help you:

- **Point of view**
  - What would this character think and feel about events or other characters he/she observes?
  - How would this character think and feel about his/her own situation?
- **Voice**
  - How will you make the reader feel as if this character is speaking to us?
  - How will you bring the character to life through the monologue?
  - What kind of language would this character use? Think about vocabulary, and about the kinds of sentences the character would use.

Check over your monologue before you give it to your teacher.

- Does it have the right ideas and content?
- Does the monologue fulfil its purposes: to share the character's thoughts, feelings and observations?
- Is it written to reach its target audience?

- Have you used stage directions and lighting and sound cues?
- If you are aiming for National 5, have you used detailed language (so long as this is appropriate to the character who is speaking)?
- Is your writing technically accurate?
- Is the meaning clear at first reading?

Diaries

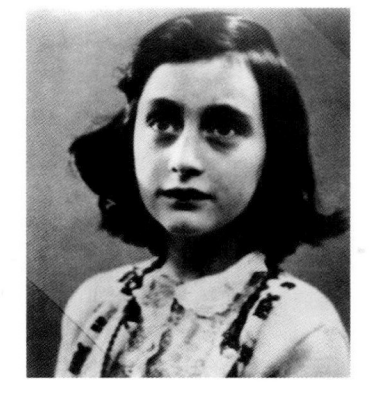

Diaries – sometimes called journals – are a way for people to keep a record of **what has been happening** to them, and of **how they think and feel** about this. Perhaps the most famous real diary ever published is the one written by a young Jewish girl called Anne Frank.

Anne lived with her family in Amsterdam during the Second World War. After the Nazis occupied the Netherlands they began to persecute Jewish people. Anne's father, Otto, took his family to live secretly in a set of rooms hidden behind a bookcase within the offices of his business. They moved in just after her 13th birthday and stayed there in hiding for 2 years, until they were betrayed and captured. Anne and most other members of her family died in concentration camps, but her father survived. After the war he found her diary, in which she had described their years in the secret annexe.

Active learning

Read the following extracts from Anne's diary. As you do so, look out for any times when Anne:

1 tells us about her thoughts

2 tells us about her feelings

3 uses details and description to bring an experience to life.

Tuesday, October 20, 1942

My hands are still shaking, though it's been two hours since we had the scare. I should explain that there are five extinguishers in the building. The office staff stupidly forgot to warn us that the carpenter, or whatever he's called, was coming to fill the extinguishers. As a result, we didn't bother to be quiet until I heard the sound of hammering on the landing (across from the bookcase). I immediately assumed it was the carpenter and went to warn Bep, who was eating lunch, that she couldn't go back downstairs. Father and I stationed ourselves at the door so we could hear when the man had left. After working for about fifteen minutes, he laid his hammer and some other tools on our bookcase (or so we thought!) and banged on our door. We turned white with fear. Had he heard something after all and did he now want to check out this mysterious-looking bookcase? It seemed so, since he kept knocking, pulling, pushing and jerking on it.

I was so scared I nearly fainted at the thought of this total stranger managing to discover our wonderful hiding place…

Saturday, 15 July, 1944

It's a wonder I haven't abandoned all my ideals, they seem so absurd and impractical. Yet I cling to them because I still believe, in spite of everything, that people are truly good at heart. It's utterly impossible for me to build my life on a foundation of chaos, suffering and death. I see the world being slowly transformed into a wilderness, I hear the approaching thunder that, one day, will destroy us too, I feel the suffering of millions. And yet, when I look up at the sky, I somehow feel that everything will change for the better, that this cruelty too shall end, that peace and tranquility will return once more.

Anne's diary is a real one. It tells us a true story, from her point of view. Some other well-known diaries are completely made up.

Active learning

Read the following extract from *The Secret Diary of Adrian Mole* books by Sue Townsend. As you do so, work out the answers to these questions:

1 What sort of person does the diary writer, Adrian Mole, seem to be?

2 How do we know this about him?

Thursday January 1st

My father got the dog drunk on cherry brandy at the party last night. If the RSPCA hear about it he could get done. Eight days have gone by since Christmas Day but my mother still hasn't worn the green lurex apron I bought her for Christmas! She will get bathcubes next year.

Just my luck, I've got a spot on my chin for the first day of the New Year!

Friday January 2nd

Bank Holiday in Scotland. Full Moon

I felt rotten today. It's my mother's fault for singing 'My Way' at two o'clock in the morning at the top of the stairs. Just my luck to have a mother like her. There is a chance my parents could be alcoholics. Next year I could be in a children's home.

The dog got its own back on my father. It jumped up and knocked down his model ship, then ran into the garden with the rigging tangled in its feet. My father kept saying, 'Three months' work down the drain', over and over again.

The spot on my chin is getting bigger. It's my mother's fault for not knowing about vitamins.

Saturday January 3rd

I shall go mad through lack of sleep! My father has banned the dog from the house so it barked outside my window all night. Just my luck! My father shouted a swear-word at it. If he's not careful he will get done by the police for obscene language.

I think the spot is a boil. Just my luck to have it where everybody can see it. I pointed out to my mother that I hadn't had any vitamin C today. She said, 'Go and buy an orange, then'. This is typical.

She still hasn't worn the lurex apron.

I will be glad to get back to school.

Active learning

It is time to write your own diary. It could be **true**, like Anne Frank's diary, or **fictional**, like *The Secret Diary of Adrian Mole*.

If your diary is going to be **true**, start by choosing which experience you are going to write about. You could keep a diary during a holiday or a school residential trip. You could write a diary in the run-up to some event you are preparing for: a big sports game, a performance, being bridesmaid at a wedding.

If your diary is going to be **fictional**, you could base it on a class text. Imagine that you are one of the characters in the novel, play or film you have been studying. Thinking about these things will help you:

- **Point of view**
  - What would this character think and feel about the events in the text?
  - How would this character view the situation?
- **Voice**
  - How will you make the reader feel as if this character is writing from the heart?
  - How will you bring the character to life through the diary?
  - What kind of language would this character use? Think about vocabulary, and about the kinds of sentences the character would write.

Whether your diary is true or fictional, you should aim to write between four and six diary entries from different days, so that we see events and feelings developing.

Check over your diary before you give it to your teacher.

- Does it have the right ideas and content?
- Does the diary fulfil its purposes: to share thoughts and feelings, and to show events developing?
- Is it written to reach its target audience?
- Have you followed the guidelines for layout by giving each entry a date?
- If you are aiming for National 5, have you used detailed language (so long as this is appropriate to the character writing the diary)?
- Is your writing technically accurate?
- Is the meaning clear at first reading?

Web-based texts

You will be very aware of web-based texts. You look at them every day. Some of these, such as Twitter, are not so relevant for us here because tweets are very short forms of writing. Likewise, a social network such as Facebook is probably not relevant to what we are working on in this chapter either.

If you want to display your writing skills in a web-based text, you should be thinking about **blogs, wiki pages**, and **websites**. However, there are some possible complications. Anything you use as evidence that you have passed a unit assessment should be done under what is called 'controlled conditions'. This means that your teacher needs to be able to oversee the process, so that he/she knows you have done the work yourself. You cannot just produce the material at home and then go on to the internet in school or at college to show it to your teacher.

So, if you think you would like to be assessed on the basis of a web text, check this with your teacher:

 Does your school or college have IT facilities you can use, so that your teacher can oversee you producing this text?

If you and your teacher are both sure that you could be assessed on a web-based text, and that you can produce the assessment under the right conditions, read on.

Blogs are sometimes described as online diaries, but this is not always the case. In diaries, as we have seen, the writer describes what has been happening to him/her and shows his/her thoughts and feelings about this. Blogs often have a theme — baking, a particular period of history, creative writing, a religion, a sport, films. Think of any subject, and somebody will be blogging about it.

Active learning

This might be a homework task. Alternatively, if your teacher can book your whole class into a computer suite, you might be able to work on it in school or college.

Think about a subject you are interested in. Find two different blogs about this subject. (The easiest way to do this is to type, for example, 'find food blog' or 'find movie blog', into Google.) Read a selection of pages from each blog. Be ready to report back on the following questions:

1 What were the strengths of each blog?

2 How could each blog have been improved?

3 What did you find most interesting in blog 1?

4 What did you find most interesting in blog 2?

5 What have you learned or observed that you could use in making your own blog?

You can use sites like www.blogger.com and www.wordpress.com to create your own blog. You might decide to present your findings from the Added Value Unit as a blog.

You might decide to create a **wiki page**. Anyone can put a page up on Wikipedia, and most of its pages can also be edited by anyone. For guidance on how to do this, you can go to: http://en.wikipedia.org/wiki/Wikipedia:Starting_an_article.

If you want to be assessed for writing, you will need to create your own page from scratch. Just editing a page that exists already would be plagiarism – using someone else's words and passing them off as your own.

If you want to make a **website** that will last just long enough for your teacher to see and assess it, go to www.simplesite.com. This site enables you to build your own website for free. The site lasts for 1 month after you set it up, though you can keep it for longer if you choose to pay a small subscription after that.

! Warning

If you do produce a web-based text for one of your unit assessments, remember it is the **writing** in that website, or blog, or wiki page, that your teacher is looking at and marking. Your teacher cannot mark you down for any weaknesses in things like design, layout and graphics, because they are not part of the writing. That is the good news. On the other hand, if there are weaknesses in your writing, all the whizzy graphics in the world will not make you more likely to pass.

Active learning

Decide if you would like to produce a web-based text for your writing assessment. Remember, to meet the assessment conditions, you have to be able to produce this in school or college.

You might choose to do any of the following:

- Create a blog about a subject in which you are interested.
- Present your final piece of work for the Added Value Unit as a blog, wiki page or website.
- Create a website or wiki page about a text, or author, or director you have been studying in class.

Remember, you are being assessed on what you write, not on how smart or stylish it looks!

Check over your work before you ask your teacher to assess it.

- Does it have the right ideas and content?
- Does the text fulfil its purpose? (This is probably the purpose of giving information.)
- Is it written to reach its target audience?
- Have you followed the conventions for the kind of text you have made?
- If you are aiming for National 5, have you used detailed language?
- Is your writing technically accurate?
- Is the meaning clear at first reading?

Talking

So far this chapter has dealt with one of the Creation and Production skills, *writing*. Now we are going to move onto the second of these skills, *talking*.

What you will be assessed on

In the end, whether you are sitting National 4 or National 5, you have to show all the appropriate talking skills by taking part in at least **one spoken interaction**. (You will discover what is meant by 'spoken interaction' soon.) This interaction should be clearly **understandable at first hearing** – in other words, your listeners should not have any difficulty working out what you say or what you mean. Your meaning will be this clear if you choose the right sort of **language** and vocabulary. Your meaning will also come across though your use of non-verbal communication – your eye contact, gestures, facial expression and body language.

There are some other choices you need to make too. You must choose the right **ideas and content** to use. You must also choose **a format and a structure** that suit the **audience** you are talking to and the **purpose** of this talk. If you are sitting National 4, this spoken interaction should show your command of **straightforward** language. If you are sitting National 5, it should be in **detailed** language. (Look back at the Introduction to this book to find out more about what 'straightforward' and 'detailed' mean here.)

Your spoken interactions should be of some length – you need to speak for long enough to let your teacher see you demonstrate all the skills.

Your teacher may use a number of different methods of assessing your work. He/she could:

- Make a video or audio recording.
- Assess your work against a checklist.
- Make notes of what he/she observes.

However your teacher assesses you, an accurate record should be kept.

Combined assessment

The work you do for the Creation and Production Unit may help you with some other part of the course.

- It might be possible to use this work as evidence of talking for the National 4 Literacy Unit (or the National 5 one, if your school or college teaches this).
- It might also be possible to pass the talking part of this unit by producing a spoken response at the end of your National 4 Added Value Unit.

Ask your teacher if he/she is hoping to combine assessments in this way. He/she must be sure that you have covered all the skills each unit asks for, remembering that literacy assessments should be based on non-fiction uses of language.

Spoken interactions

We saw above that you need to demonstrate your skills in talking by taking part in at least one spoken interaction. This might mean:

a presentation to an audience	a pair or group discussion
a debate	an interview
hot seating	a video or audio podcast

The key word here is *interaction*. Even if you are mainly just standing up at the front of the room giving an individual presentation, you should be *interacting with* the audience, not *talking at* them. You need to engage and involve the audience, and show that you are involved with them. We will cover how you can do this as we work through this part of the chapter.

As the most common types of spoken interaction are individual presentation and group discussion, we will begin by looking at them.

Individual presentations

First, some people feel extremely nervous about talking, especially about individual presentations to an audience. This is completely understandable. For every raging, egomaniac extrovert in your class who just loves being listened to, there is going to be someone who would wish the carpet would open up and swallow them.

But you need to learn to talk in school because this is such a valuable life skill. Unless you plan on working as a mime artist, you will need talking skills at work. Unless you intend to go and live in a cave in a desert, hunting wild animals, you will need communication skills to talk to family, friends and those you encounter each day. If you think you might be a parent in the future, you will need excellent skills of persuasion and negotiation.

This chapter will help you focus on the skills you will need. It will give advice about planning, preparing and practising for your talk. It will also give you hints for overcoming or hiding your nerves in order to make you more confident about this skill for learning, work and life.

Preparing your talk

You can avoid those nerves if your talk is well planned and properly prepared. The best way to use this section on individual presentations is to prepare one as you work through the next few pages. Check with your teacher that you understand what the task is, and what he/she will be looking for as he/she assesses you.

Now that you have your raw material, let us look at how to shape it into a successful presentation.

Good openings

Look at the two openings below. Which one do you think belongs to the National 4 presentation, and which one begins a presentation by a National 5 student?

> Doctors, nurses, patients …
> As you've probably guessed I spent my work experience week in a hospital.

> I'm going to talk about my week's work experience. I spent my time at a hospital.

You should have spotted that the first one is the National 5 one. The distinctive difference is that this speaker draws the audience in, intrigues them, and immediately starts painting pictures in the listeners' heads, while the National 4 speaker starts by saying something pretty basic.

Language and vocabulary

One of the things the assessor will be looking at is the language and vocabulary you choose to use. You will show your knowledge and understanding of how language works, and what makes it effective, by making good choices.

First of all, and especially if you are a National 5 candidate, you should **vary your vocabulary**. To do this, choose different words, rather than repeating the same ones. You should also choose interesting, less common, words rather than more ordinary and predictable ones.

> My favourite film is *Argo*. It is based on a true story. This film is about rescuing some American diplomats from Iran. The Americans are in the Canadian embassy after the Iranians took control of the American embassy. The film shows how the CIA rescued them. The CIA pretended to be making a film called *Argo*. They pretended that the American diplomats were part of the film crew who had come to find places to film.

> I adore the Oscar-winning movie *Argo*. It dramatises the true story of how six American diplomats were extracted from Iran, having taken refuge with the Canadian ambassador after the American embassy was captured. The movie depicts the CIA's clever invention of a sci-fi epic called *Argo*, and how they passed off the fugitives as members of the film crew, in Iran to scout for locations.

1 Where did the second student choose different words, rather than repeating?

2 Where did the second student choose interesting, less common words?

You should have noticed that this student, studying National 5, also used longer, more complicated, sentences.

As well as varying your vocabulary, there are other language techniques you can use to engage your audience and give impact to your talk.

Register

In this context, this does not mean the list of class names your teacher uses to check who is in the lesson. Register here is the choice of language you make to suit your purpose, your audience, and the situation in which you are speaking.

You are quite skilled already at choosing the right register. There are certain words you use when talking to your friends that you know you should not use to your teacher – or your granny if you want to stay out of trouble. You speak quite informally to your friends and family but a bit more formally to the teachers you see each day. If you had to go for a job interview, or if you suddenly got summoned to the Head Teacher's office, you would speak even more formally.

So, at its simplest level, register is often about choosing how formally to speak. As being assessed is one of the most formal parts of school life, you should be choosing a fairly formal register for your individual presentation and for group discussion – though what you say still has to work as an interesting and engaging speech.

Active learning

This speaker has been a little too informal in explaining his hobby of bread making. Can you formalise his words a little?

You need to chuck a load of flour all over the table. Then you get your dough in a massive great lump and wap it down on the table. Get your fists in there and knead it about a bit, really really squeeze it and pull it. Basically you just thump it around for a wee while until it feels all bouncy and elastic.

Did you let the student keep using 'you', which he says a lot? If you did, go over the paragraph again and try to replace that word. Using 'you' in speech, and in writing, can be a problem. It is rather vague, and too impersonal. The student is talking about his hobby. Why is he using 'you' as if it is the audience's hobby? If you are talking about yourself, use 'I'. If you are talking about people in general, use 'we' or 'us' to involve the listeners.

If you are aiming for National 4, knowing that a talk assessment is a formal situation and being able to speak formally is important. If you are aiming for National 5, take your understanding of register a little further. National 5 students should be able to use a little bit of slang, or dialect, or informality, to gain certain effects and to make their speech vivid. In this case, using slang, dialect, or informality is evidence of your ability to choose the best words at the best time.

Active learning

Read this extract from a presentation about the use of Scots. Where has the speaker used carefully chosen register to bring the talk to life?

I find myself becoming quite dejected, in fact right disjaskit, when the Government talks about using Scots. Any visitor to the Parliament at Holyrood will see signage up in English, Gaelic, and Scots. But the Scots on show is the language of Southern Scotland. It bears little resemblance to the language of Orkney or Shetland. It has little in common with the Doric of the northeast, where my grandparents live. What would happen if I greeted the Holyrood doorkeeper with a cheery, 'Aye, aye. Fit like?' He'd be affa dottled, that's fit'd happen.

Humour and anecdote

One of the easiest ways to win over your audience is to give them something to laugh at – especially if that something is you. Being funny to order may sound like a hard thing to do, but we all make our friends laugh all the time in real life by using **anecdotes**. An anecdote is an amusing story, often one we tell about or even against ourselves.

Let us imagine you have been asked to give a presentation about a hobby. You might start it like this:

> **I'm going to talk to you today about my hobby of dancing. I was just three when I appeared in my first show.**

Or you might start it like this:

> I've never forgotten my first dance show, even though I was only three. I was a chubby wee thing back then, but that didn't stop me from imagining I was some sort of prima ballerina. I loved my tiny pink tutu and my matching pastel pumps. Sadly, I didn't love following instructions. Long after the rest of my group had finished their 'pretty little mice' dance and scampered off to let the next class come on, I was still pirouetting across the stage, waving my long pink tail and squeaking. My mum still has the video. She says she'll show it to any boyfriend I ever bring into the house.

Which opening is more likely to capture your listeners?

Although anecdotes are especially useful in personal talks you do not have to personally star in each one that you use. An anecdote can just as easily be something you observed, or an experience that you know happened to someone else.

Exaggeration

You may have noticed that if you tell a particularly good anecdote more than once it tends to grow in the telling. Imagine you are at the park when a child loses control of his pet dog, which runs into the pond. If you told your friends about it straight away, it might sound like this:

> I felt sorry for the wee boy, so I stepped into the edge of the water, took hold of the dog's collar, and got it out.

By the time you tell another friend about it on the phone later it might sound like this:

> The wee boy was getting upset, so I waded into the water and rescued his pet.

If you meet someone else the next day, the anecdote might have grown into this:

> The wee boy was bawling his eyes out and yelling the dog's name. I can't swim, but what else could I do? I dragged my shoes off, threw them down on the bank, waded waist deep into the pond and picked the struggling puppy up in my arms.

The third version may bear a bit less relation to the truth, but it is a much better anecdote, and one that you can really liven up in the telling.

Rhetorical questions

Let us go back to the student on page 55 who was talking about her work experience in a hospital. Look at the following three sentences she could use:

> Most people would feel sick if they had to watch an operation.

> I'm sure some of you would feel sick if you had to watch an operation.

> How would you feel if you had to watch a surgeon doing an operation?

The first sentence is a bit dull. The second one is better, because it uses the word 'you' so the speaker is engaging more with her audience.

The third sentence is an example of a rhetorical question. The speaker does not expect anyone to answer, but the audience understands this. Nobody is going to stand up and interrupt her by saying, 'A bit sick actually, since you're asking'. What the question does is makes the audience feel involved. They go beyond just listening to your presentation and start to really think about your situation and sympathise with you.

Good use of rhetorical questions can be another detail that separates the National 5 students from the National 4 ones.

Go back to your notes. Try to find a couple of places in your presentation where you could change statements into rhetorical questions.

Emotive language

Of the particular techniques we have looked at so far, anecdote and exaggeration are especially useful in personal presentations, and in those where humour is appropriate. Rhetorical questions can be useful in all sorts of presentations. One technique that can be particularly helpful in serious or persuasive ones is to use **emotive language**.

Emotive words are strong ones that rouse the listeners' emotions. If you read tabloid newspapers, listen to politicians, or read the advertising sent out by charities, you will find a lot of emotive language.

Active learning

Some emotive language aims to cause negative emotions such as anger or disgust. Look at the words in the box. How many similar ones can you think of?

disgusting	terrible	appalling	shocking	vile	dreadful

Some emotive language aims to cause more positive emotions. Look at the words in the box. How many similar ones can you think of?

fantastic	wonderful	amazing	marvellous	fabulous	great

Active learning

Go back to your notes. Try to find a couple of places in your presentation where you could make suitable use of emotive language.

Good endings

Endings matter too. Lots of speakers just stop. They make their last point, and then come to a halt, leaving the audience wondering if this is just an awkward pause and whether there is more to come.

The very final words of your presentation should make it clear that you have finished. You could use phrases like:

> **Thank you for listening.**

> **Does anyone have any questions?**

> **I hope that you enjoyed hearing about …**

As well as these final sentences, you should use the whole of the last section of your presentation – the last card of your notes – to let the audience know that you are building up to a conclusion. If you are talking about a hobby, you could sum up what you enjoy most about it. If you are talking about a film or a book, again you could give an overall opinion. If your presentation is about a personal experience, you could sum up how you think this experience has affected you, or why you think you still remember it so clearly. In other words, you can use some of the reflective techniques covered in Chapter 5 on the National 5 Writing Portfolio.

Using notes

There is nothing wrong with using notes. However, you do have to use non-verbal communication, such as gesture and body language, and the way you handle your notes can affect these.

Your notes are there to support you if you need them. You should never just read your presentation out – this is not what you are being marked on. The best way to avoid this is to keep your notes as short as possible, so that you **cannot** just read them.

Let us imagine you are doing a talk about your work experience, and that you spent the week at a hospital. You might want to say something like this:

> **As soon as I arrived on the first day I was given a white coat and a hospital ID card. This made me feel as if I belonged. Once I put the coat on I thought I looked as if I could be a medical student. In fact, I began to worry that I looked too good. What if one of the consultants suddenly asked me to take blood or put in some stitches?**

If you get up to deliver your presentation with all these words written out, you may be tempted to just read them. You need to reduce them to key words. You can start by underlining or highlighting the most important words and phrases:

> As soon as I arrived on the <u>first day</u> I was given a <u>white coat</u> and a hospital <u>ID</u> card. This made me feel as if I <u>belonged</u>. Once I put the coat on I thought I looked as if I could be a <u>medical student</u>. In fact I began to <u>worry</u> that I looked too good. What if one of the consultants suddenly asked me to take <u>blood</u> or put in some <u>stitches</u>?

However, if you speak from notes like these, you will still have to do a fair bit of scanning to find your key words. The next step is to put the key words onto small cards or slips of paper using strong colours and large print. You can also use layout to show the connections between ideas. Your card might now look like this:

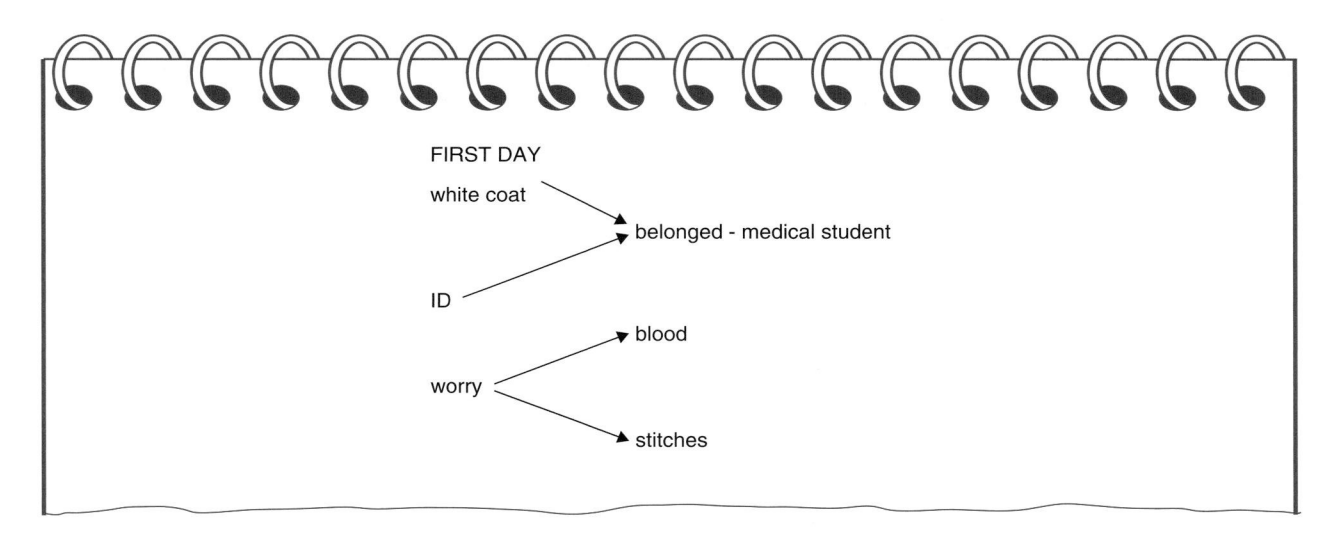

By the time you get to this stage, you will know your material so well that a quick glance down at these few words will bring up all you want to say.

Active learning

Go back to your notes. You should be able to set your whole talk out on cards, using colour, key words and simple symbols to bring everything quickly to mind.

Delivering your presentation

Using props

As we saw earlier, you are being assessed on your interaction with others: you are not just talking at them. The more ways you can find to interest your audience, and to engage with them, the more interactive you are being.

It can be a very good idea to use props in your presentation. For instance, if you are talking about a sport you play, you could bring some of the clothing or equipment. If you are talking about a personal experience, you could bring some object associated with that memory.

Holding a prop gives you something to do with your hands, which may help you control signs of nerves. Passing a prop around is interesting for the audience and connects you more strongly to them. If your presentation is well prepared, then using props may remind you of everything you want to say, and help you to speak without notes.

Active learning

Go back to your planned presentation. Is there a prop you could use in your delivery?

Using PowerPoint and other technology

You may decide to use a PowerPoint presentation to bring more interest and interactivity to your talk. A word of warning though – many PowerPoint users make a classic mistake. Instead of talking to the audience, they just read out what is on the screen.

This is just repetition, and it will bore your audience. Instead, use PowerPoint to support your words. The student talking about Scottish inventors could put up pictures of these men as each name is mentioned, or images of their inventions. If you are talking about a foreign country, use PowerPoint for maps, or photographs of places. If you are describing a personal experience, put suitable pictures in a PowerPoint or load them up as a slideshow.

The same goes for DVD clips, YouTube videos, and any other visual material. It is there because it is visual – it should be doing something you cannot do in words, not repeating in images something you have already said verbally.

You should not use PowerPoint, or any other technological prop, unless you are absolutely sure how it works, and how it works in your school or college. Even if you know how it would run on your computer at home or how to bring up a clip on your own DVD player, make sure you get a chance to set up and practise on the equipment you will be using at school.

Eye contact

Eye contact is one of the key aspects of non-verbal communication.

If you have produced good notes as discussed already, then you are on your way to good eye contact, because you should not **need** to keep looking down. If you feel that you might **want** to keep looking down, there is a section coming up on dealing with nerves that you will find helpful. If you want to look up but you are not sure how to, keep reading.

Your teacher will probably be sitting in the audience, making notes or following a checklist so that he/she can assess your presentation, or perhaps filming your talk. Lots of students make the mistake of staring at the teacher, or at the camera. Some others look at their best friend in the class, because they know that person will support them. Others just look straight ahead.

Try this instead. Imagine you are a lighthouse. Although you are standing still, your eyes – the lamp of the lighthouse – can move, sweeping across the class like the light sweeps across the sea. Whenever you are able to look up for a few seconds, sweep your eyes across the class, taking in most of the room. You might notice that this is what your teachers do when they talk to their classes. The reason this works so well is that it makes everyone in the audience feel they should pay attention to you all the time, because they know you could look at them at any second.

Active learning

This activity gives everyone in the class a quick chance to practise eye contact. One by one, each student should come up and talk for 30 seconds about the most interesting experience OR the most boring experience they have had this week. (You will all need a minute or two first to think about what you are going to say.)

As they talk, every student should try to keep their eyes on the audience at all times, moving their eye contact around the room like a lighthouse as they do so.

Body language

This is another aspect of non–verbal communication.

> **Active learning**
>
> Think of a television presenter who is good at his/her job. (It should be a presenter rather than a newsreader who reads from a prepared script.) Now try watching him/her with the television sound muted so you can focus on only what he/she does and not what he/she says. Make a list of the gestures he/she uses. Can you work out, from the gestures alone, what he/she is talking about, or how he/she feels about that subject?

You should find that the television presenter's body language helps him/her to put across the message. Unfortunately, bad body language can lower your mark, and there are a few things to avoid.

Some people fidget terribly. All sorts of 'head' fidgets, like earring twisting, ear rubbing, nose scratching and hair twiddling are really your subconscious mind trying to send your hands to cover your mouth and stop you talking. These fidgets muffle what you say, and they display your nerves to the whole audience.

Some people, both girls and boys, hide behind their hair. If yours is long, tie it back. If your fringe tickles your eyes, just for as long as you are up there talking, do not keep flicking your head to get it out of the way – you will look like a pony being annoyed by a fly!

Some people stand awkwardly, twisting their arms behind their backs or crossing their legs while standing up to talk. Try to plant your feet firmly, about shoulder-width apart — if not, the audience will not be able to concentrate on your presentation, they will just be waiting to see you tip over sideways.

If your classroom has a lectern or book stand, try putting your notes on that. You could even borrow a music stand. This way you can lightly place your hands on the stand, and move them when you want to make a gesture. If you have to hold on to your notes, keep them in one hand and use the other for gestures.

Gestures

These are any movements that you can make that support the meaning of your presentation. It can be a little bit hard to plan these – if they work, it is usually because they look like they have come naturally. Here are some examples:

- A student talking about a costume she had worn for a performance put her hand up to the opposite wrist when she was describing the bracelets and bangles that were part of her outfit.
- A student describing the atmosphere at a rugby game he had been to made the excited, air-punching hand gestures that spectators had made when their team scored.
- A student telling the audience about an owl flying right over her head made a whooshing gesture with her hand across her hair.

Any uses of good eye contact, suitable body language, or appropriate gesture will make your presentation more interactive. Gestures connect you to the audience and engage the attention of your listeners.

Voice

We have thought a lot about the visual elements of your presentation: props, PowerPoints, eye contact and body language. But your voice is a key tool. It needs to be varied and interesting. There are several ways you can do this:

- Vary the speed of what you say, speaking more slowly to create moments of emphasis and tension, or to highlight what is most important.
- Increase the volume of your voice at moments of excitement.
- Use intonation for emphasis, leaning more heavily on the most important words: this is the spoken equivalent of using bold in our writing.

If your audience were to sit there with their eyes shut, they should still find you fascinating.

Active learning

Find a partner. Ask this person to sit with their back to you. Practise your talk, or a section of it, so that your partner can hear you but cannot see you. Ask for feedback on how interesting and varied your voice is. Then swap roles and do this again.

Other ways of interacting with your audience

Remember the best way to engage your audience is by giving an interesting presentation that they feel they want to listen to. The advice so far about visual aids, body language, eye contact, and voice will all help you with that. However, there are a few other hints and tips to help you get the audience on your side:

- As mentioned above, one way to do this is by showing them something. This can be something electronic that you show on screen, or a real prop that you pass round.

- Try asking questions, not only rhetorical ones but perhaps also ones where you clearly expect one or two of the audience to answer.
- Use a quiz, perhaps at the start of your presentation to find out how much your listeners know about your subject, or at the end to see what they have picked up and learned from you.
- Get them to raise their hands to vote on something you have said, or to show that they have had a similar experience to the one you are describing, e.g. 'How many of you had a pet when you were young?'
- Give them the opportunity to ask you questions at the end.
- Get them to laugh, and show them you appreciate that laughter by not talking over it.
- Use language that includes them, e.g. 'I'm sure **we** have all at some point in **our** lives had to face something **we** were really frightened of.'

Dealing with nerves

Although we have left this to last, it is actually the first thing that comes to mind when many people find out they have to do a presentation. If you have prepared well, and taken on board all the advice already given, then that should help you to feel less nervous and better equipped. Another way to defuse nerves is to practise: on family, on friends, in the mirror or just alone in your room.

Another good way to look confident is to use the **six Ss** as you deliver your presentation:

- **STEP** forward.
- **STAND** there, nice and still.
- **SMILE** at your audience.

- **SPEAK** to them, giving the presentation you have prepared and practised.
- **SMILE** again at the end.
- **STAND** and wait for the applause.

You should be ready to do your presentation now. Remember everyone in your audience probably has to do one too and feels as nervous as you do. If there is someone in the class that you really do not want to talk in front of, you could ask the teacher if that person could be asked to wait somewhere else while you speak. You might also find that asking to be assessed first and getting it over with stops the nerves building up too much.

Remember: step – stand – smile – speak – smile – stand. Good luck!

Group discussion

If you have worked through the section on individual presentations, then you already know a lot of what you need to do in a group discussion. However, the group situation does introduce a few differences:

- You may have less choice about what you talk about. Your teacher will probably provide you with a discussion topic, a set of questions, or some other sort of group task.
- You probably will not get much of a chance to prepare your contribution, and might have to produce a good performance almost on the spot.
- You may or may not get to choose the people who are in the group with you.
- You may be given a particular role to play in the group during the discussion.
- You need to show that you know how to behave in a group situation, respecting and interacting with the others in your group.
- You must make sure you contribute enough to the discussion that your teacher can find evidence to assess you on. At the same time though, you must not take over the group. This is a tricky balancing act.

We will deal with particular group roles later. First, let us look at how body language and spoken language can be used to show that you are taking account of others in your group.

Active learning

Imagine you had these two people in your group. Which person's body language shows that they are taking an active part in the group? Which one seems to have opted out?

So we can easily see how your body language shows that you are actively taking part. However, you need to go beyond that. National 4 students will show that they are taking account of other group members by **supporting** and **challenging** what other people say.

During the discussion you should be doing more listening than talking. Listening does not mean staying quiet for as little time as possible until you can wedge in something that you have already decided to say. After all, you have two ears and just one mouth. What you say when you speak should build on and support what you hear when you are listening. If you disagree with what you have heard, there are ways to express this and to challenge the other speaker without giving offence or seeming arrogant.

Active learning

The comments in the speech bubbles below fit into two groups.

- Some phrases show that you support the previous speaker and agree with what he/she has said.
- Some of them will let you express disagreement, so that you can challenge the previous speaker.

Can you work out which comments belong in which groups?

I agree with you because …	On the other hand, …
I don't agree because …	I think you're wrong because …
But in my opinion …	I see your point but …
You're right to say that …	Actually I don't think …
Actually what happens is …	That's a good idea …
But don't you realise that …	I'm sorry but I think that …
That might be true but …	I'm afraid you're wrong because …

It is perfectly all right to disagree with other group members, as long as you can do it in a respectful way.

As well as being able to support and challenge other group members, National 5 students should be able to use some of these skills in responding to others:

developing   summarising   refuting   justifying

Active learning

Copy and complete the following table to show your understanding of these concepts.

Concept	What this concept means	What Student A might say	How Student B could respond
Developing			'That's not the only reason New York is interesting. It's also …'

Summarising			'You seem to be saying ...'
Refuting	Using evidence to prove that someone else is wrong.		
Justifying	Using evidence to prove that you are right.	'I'm afraid I don't agree. I think *The Hunger Games* films are over-rated.'	

You may also notice that someone in your group is not contributing much, or is having trouble getting a word in because of more confident speakers hogging the conversation. If you can find a way to involve that quiet person, you are displaying a maturity and skill that will be rewarded. Try using some of these phrases to help you:

I'd like to hear X's opinion about ...

What would you like to say?

What's your opinion?

Is there anything you'd like to add?

What do you think?

Possible roles in groups

In some group discussions you may be asked to take on a certain role. If so, your teacher will be looking for evidence of how well you carry out this role. If others in your group have been given roles to play, you need to know what they should be doing so you know how to react to them.

If you are given a role, your teacher should make clear what is expected of you. Here are some of the more common roles:

- **The chair** should lead the discussion and keep it moving along. The chair should also solve any conflicts or arguments and should try to encourage any shy group members, while trying to stop confident speakers from dominating.

- **The leader** has a similar role to the chair, but may also be responsible for reaching a decision or conclusion or having the casting vote if the group cannot agree.
- **The reader** may be asked to read out instructions, information or questions to the group.
- **The recorder** takes notes of what is said. Near the end of the discussion it is a good idea to read your notes back to the group so that they can agree the recorder has kept a fair record.
- **The reporter** may be asked to give a verbal report back to the whole class on what the group talked about.
- **The timekeeper** may be responsible for keeping the discussion moving, or for ensuring that you reach a conclusion or solution within a given time.

Your own teacher may use different titles for some of the roles, but these are the main responsibilities that people are generally asked to carry out in groups. Just make sure you know what is involved in any role you are given, and you will be fine.

Other spoken interactions

At the start of the talking section of this chapter, we mentioned four other sorts of spoken interactions.

a debate	an interview
hot seating	a video or audio podcast

We will take a brief look at each of these now.

Debates

Debates are ideal for tackling controversial topics. A debate takes some time and preparation, but can allow your teacher to assess a number of people during one event.

There is a set of classic rules that a debate usually follows.

1. You debate a controversial subject. This is called the **motion**, and is usually phrased as a statement. For example:
   - *This house believes all drugs should be legalised and sold from pharmacies.*
   - *This house would not fight for its country.*
2. There are two sides.
   - The **proposition** side supports the motion.
   - The **opposition** side speaks against the motion.
3. The two sides take turns to put their points.
   - The first proposer makes a short speech in favour of the motion.

- The first opposer makes a short speech against the motion.
- The second proposer makes a short speech adding more points and ideas in favour of the motion. This person may also pick up on points made by the first opposer.
- The second opposer makes a short speech adding more points and ideas against the motion. This person may also pick up on points made by the proposers.

4 This pattern can go on for as long as groups have been able to come up with new points to make. This relies on groups and speakers preparing very thoroughly **before** the debate takes place.

5 At the end of the debate:
- Someone from the proposition side sums up their position.
- Someone from the opposition side sums up their position.

6 The audience members who have been watching the debate now vote on the motion.

Active learning

Find a partner. Try to come up with at least three suitable topics for a debate. Make sure you word them as statements, using the 'This house believes …' style. Share your ideas with the rest of the class.

Interviews

An interview, if it works properly, should allow your teacher to assess both the **interviewer** who asks the questions, and the **interviewee** who answers them.

To help an interview go well, and to get enough assessment evidence out of it, you need to know about using **open questions** and **follow-up questions** rather than **closed questions**.

Closed questions can be answered in one word:

Have you been on any good holidays?

Yes.

What's your favourite place to go out for food?

Nando's

Open questions need longer answers:

What's the best holiday you've ever been on?

My parents took me to Disneyland Paris for my tenth birthday.

Where do you like to go out for food and why?

I love Nando's because it's a great place to go with a group of friends.

Follow-up questions give you a chance to find out more:

Where do you like to go out for food and why?

I love Nando's because it's a great place to go with a group of friends.

Why's it so good for groups?

Everybody pays for their own food when they order so there are no arguments about the bill.

Are there any other reasons why it suits groups?

There's something to suit everybody, whether you like your food really mild or ridiculously hot and spicy.

Follow-up questions can be especially useful if you think the interviewee is being a bit evasive:

Which member of your family are you most likely to argue with?

My sister.

Why is that?

Various reasons.

Can you tell me what some of those reasons are?

She's quite a difficult person.

In what way difficult?

She always has to have her own way.

Can you give me an example?

Whenever we go to the cinema she always has to choose the film. If she doesn't like the sound of something, there's no way she'll watch it, and she won't listen to what anyone else wants.

Active learning

Come up with a list of twelve interesting, open questions you could use to interview someone you do not know very well. The questions should be designed to help you learn as much as possible about that person.

Hot seating

Hot seating means putting one person on the spot, i.e. in the 'hot seat', to be questioned by others. It is often used as part of studying a novel or a play. The person in the hot seat takes on the role of one of the characters from the class text. Other members of the class ask this character questions. For example, if the speaker was taking on the role of Katniss in *The Hunger Games* you might ask, 'How did you feel when Prim was chosen to fight for District 12?' or 'How did you feel about Peeta at the end of the Games?'

Hot seating works best for confident people – not everybody likes to be the centre of attention. The person in the hot seat needs to be confident not only about the whole situation of being questioned, but also that he/she has enough knowledge and understanding to be able to come up with answers on the spot.

Hot seating will also probably only give you evidence of talk assessment for the person who is in that seat. It is not likely that anybody else in the room will have enough to say to demonstrate all the assessed skills, though a number of people might show some aspects of skill.

It can be fun though, if you have got people with the confidence to try it.

Videos and podcasts

We live in a technological world. The Curriculum for Excellence, of which National 4 and 5 are a part, recognises this. Videos and podcasts are recognised as being texts that you can produce using your language skills for an audience. So, in theory, you could have your talking skills assessed through a video or audio podcast you have produced.

However, there are some possible complications. Anything you use as evidence that you have passed a unit assessment should be done under what is called 'controlled conditions'. This means that your teacher needs to be able to oversee the process, so that he/she knows you have done the work yourself. You cannot just produce a video or podcast at home and bring it in to school or college to play to your teacher.

So, if you think you would like to be assessed on the basis of a video or podcast, check this with your teacher.

 Does your school or college have IT facilities you can use, so that your teacher can oversee you producing a video or podcast?

This brings us to the end of this chapter on Creation and Production. Writing and talking are essential skills for life and for work, which is why we focus on them so much in school. You should now feel more ready to be assessed on these skills, and more able to show how well you have mastered them.

CHAPTER 3 The Literacy Unit

If you are a National 4 student you **must** pass a unit on Literacy. There is also a National 5 Literacy Unit, but you **do not have** to pass this to pass the course. For this reason most schools do not ask their National 5 students to take the Literacy Unit.

This chapter is a short one. There is a reason for this. Literacy means the ability to use language. It requires the skills of *reading*, *writing*, *talking* and *listening*. Sound familiar? These skills have all been covered already in this book. *Reading* and *listening* are tested in the Analysis and Evaluation Unit. *Writing* and *talking* are tested in the Creation and Production Unit.

We do not need to go into these skills again in detail here, but the tables below show how the skills match up across the units. The language you will see is taken from the SQA documents teachers use for guidance.

Reading National 4

Analysis and Evaluation Unit	Literacy Unit
Identifying the purpose and audience, as appropriate to genre.	Explaining aspects including audience and purpose.
Identifying the main idea and supporting details.	Selecting and using relevant information.
Applying knowledge of language to explain meaning and effect.	Commenting on effectiveness.

Listening National 4

Analysis and Evaluation Unit	Literacy Unit
Identifying the purpose and audience.	Explaining aspects including audience and purpose.
Identifying the main idea and supporting details.	Selecting and using relevant information.
Applying knowledge of language to explain meaning and effect.	Commenting on effectiveness.

Writing National 4

Creation and Production Unit	Literacy Unit
Selecting ideas and content, using a format and structure appropriate to purpose and audience.	Organising writing appropriately.
Applying knowledge of language in terms of language choice and technical accuracy.	Selecting and using appropriate language.
Communicating meaning at first reading.	Using appropriate spelling, grammar and punctuation.

Talking National 4

Creation and Production Unit	Literacy Unit
Selecting ideas and content, using a format and structure appropriate to purpose and audience.	Organising spoken communication.
Applying knowledge of language in terms of language choice.	Selecting and using straightforward language.
Communicating meaning at first hearing.	
Using aspects of non-verbal communication.	Using non-verbal conventions.

Reading National 5

Analysis and Evaluation Unit	Literacy Unit
Identifying and explaining the purpose and audience, as appropriate to genre.	Explaining a range of aspects.
Identifying and explaining the main ideas and supporting details.	Selecting and using relevant information.
Applying knowledge and understanding of language to explain meaning and effect, using appropriate critical terminology.	Evaluating effectiveness.

Listening National 5

Analysis and Evaluation Unit	Literacy Unit
Identifying and explaining the purpose and audience.	Explaining a range of aspects.
Identifying and explaining the main ideas and supporting details.	Selecting and using relevant information.
Applying knowledge and understanding of language to explain meaning and effect.	Evaluating effectiveness.

Writing National 5

Creation and Production Unit	Literacy Unit
Selecting significant ideas and content, using a format and structure appropriate to purpose and audience.	Organising writing appropriately.
Applying knowledge and understanding of language in terms of language choice and technical accuracy.	Selecting and using appropriate language.
Communicating meaning at first reading.	Using appropriate spelling, grammar and punctuation.

Talking National 5

Creation and Production Unit	Literacy Unit
Selecting significant ideas and content, using a format and structure appropriate to purpose and audience.	Organising spoken communication.
Applying knowledge and understanding of language in terms of language choice.	Selecting and using detailed language.
Communicating meaning at first hearing.	
Using significant aspects of non-verbal communication.	Using a range of non-verbal conventions.

Do not worry if everything in these tables does not make sense – the wording was written for teachers rather than students. You should, though, be able to see that the Literacy Unit tests very much the same skills as are required in the Analysis and Evaluation Unit and the Creation and Production Unit, or a little less. So, it is fairly easy to tick this unit off your 'to do' list.

How you can be assessed for literacy

There are several different ways you can be assessed for literacy:

1   The 'Combined assessment' boxes in other chapters of this book show how you might pass parts of the Literacy Unit while working on other units.
2   Your teacher might also use a Unit Assessment Support Pack specially designed to test your literacy skills. These are often based on a theme, with reading, writing, talking and listening tasks all organised around the same subject.
3   Your teacher might create his/her own Literacy assessments in these four areas.

The guidelines

When your teacher is choosing how to assess your literacy, he/she must remember the following:

1   There are guidelines for **what** you should read, write, or listen to.
    –   The texts you work with, or create, should be what is called '**functional or transactional**'. This means they should be non-fiction texts, i.e. something based on facts and real life.

Active learning

Look at the list of texts. Decide which ones are 'functional or transactional'.

news story about a general election

letter from a character in a novel

recipe

ghost story

job application letter

website where fans of a television show put up stories they have written involving the characters

poem

government website with road safety advice

radio play

magazine article about make-up techniques

building instructions for flatpack wardrobe

television soap

web page listing cinema times

novel set in Italy

takeaway menu

travel guide to Italy

track listing on CD case

song lyrics

Now look at the list of transactional and functional texts. Some of them are probably not going to be much use in the Literacy Unit, even though they are the right sort of text.

●   Which ones probably will not be used? Why not?

2   There are guidelines for **how much** you should write.
    –   To show your literacy skill in Writing at **National 4** level you should write a piece of more than **300** words.
    –   To show your literacy skill in Writing at **National 5** level you should write a piece of more than **500** words.

If you are doing National 4, your teacher will make sure you are assessed for literacy.

CHAPTER 4 The National 4 Added Value Unit

This is one of the units that you must pass to complete the National 4 course. The unit is designed to challenge you, and to get you to apply your English skills to investigate a topic you have chosen for yourself. You can choose to study literature, language, media, or a mixture of these.

You will choose your topic, then explore it through at least TWO straightforward texts. **One of these MUST be a written text**. In the end, you will present your findings by writing or speaking, and then answer questions about your work.

What you will be assessed on

As you investigate your chosen topic, you will show that you can:

- understand and evaluate at least two straightforward texts
- select relevant information from these texts to use in your presentation
- present what you have found out
- respond to questions about your topic.

Your teacher will assess this unit in your school or college. You will know if you have **passed** or **failed**. If you do not pass, you will be given another opportunity to be assessed, and your teacher will advise you about what you still need to do to pass.

This unit gives you a fantastic opportunity to make your own choices about what to study, and how to present your findings. You will be given quite a lot of time to work on it, probably some of it in class and some working independently at home. Wherever the work takes place, you can still have guidance and support from your teacher.

Your teacher will discuss your topic with you and agree when you have chosen well. He/she can help you choose the texts you study. Your teacher will also give you overall guidelines for working on this assignment. These guidelines could include questions, short tasks, checklists, fill-in sheets or prompts. The guidelines will help you divide this big task into clear, manageable stages. Your teacher may also use this unit as an opportunity to teach you particular skills such as note-making or delivering a presentation.

The Added Value Unit (AVU) allows you to demonstrate many different skills:

investigating and researching	your knowledge of your topic	presentation skills
working with others	analysing and evaluating	drafting
answering questions	planning and organising	IT skills
independent working	taking notes	facts and ideas
editing	explaining your ideas	

If this all sounds a bit scary, do not worry. Remember: you will have teacher support, and you will complete the work in steps and stages. The best thing about this unit, and the thing that most students really enjoy, is that you can make your own choices about what to study.

Combined assessment

The work you do on this unit may help you to pass another unit as well.

- If you choose to do a spoken presentation at the end, it may also be used as evidence of talking for the Creation and Production Unit, or for the Literacy Unit.
- If you choose to do a written presentation at the end, it may also be used as evidence of writing for the Creation and Production Unit, or for the Literacy Unit.
- The research work you do as you study your texts may count as evidence of reading for the Literacy Unit, or for the Analysis and Evaluation Unit.

Ask your teacher if he/she is hoping to combine assessments in this way. Your teacher must be sure that you have covered all the skills each unit requires.

Your teacher might get you to do all your work on this unit at once, or might spread it out over several weeks or months by spending a bit of time on it each week. Altogether the work should take you about **40 hours**. Only about 4 of these hours should be spent on producing your final presentation. In the AVU, **how** you work – the process – is in many ways just as important as **what** you do in the end.

 Warning

The AVU gives you so much freedom that there are lots of potential ways to tackle it. The rest of this chapter explores one way to work through this unit. Your teacher may take a different approach at times. Your teacher will also decide (or help you decide) which parts of the work you do in class, and which at home.

Step 1: choosing topics and texts

Remember, you need to choose a topic, and you need to explore that topic through two (or more) texts. Remember also, one of your texts must be a written one.

Active learning

Work with a group. Make a list of all the different kinds of written text you can think of. Here are some to get you started:

novel   blog   recipe   magazine

Share your answers with the rest of the class.

Now work in your group again. This time make a list of all the non-written texts you can think of. Here are some to get you started:

film   television soap   podcast

Share your answers with the rest of the class.

You know already that 'text' can mean all sorts of different things. You may have produced all kinds of texts during the rest of your National 4 course. The reason you have been listing types of text now is to open your eyes to the very many different sources you could choose to investigate for your AVU.

For the next part of this task, you will need a paper copy of the sheets on the next two pages. Ask your teacher to make photocopies of the sheets for you to write on.

Active learning

Work in your group again. Each person in the group needs a copy of the sheets. You have 5 minutes to fill in as many ideas as you can in each large box. DON'T write in the spaces at the bottom of each column. The boxes have some suggestions to get you started.

When you have completed each box, share your answers with the class. If other groups have interesting ideas that you did not think of, add them to your own list.

You will end up with six lists of quite specific and interesting ideas.

Now read all the lists over on your own. In the smaller boxes at the bottom of each page note down your favourite ideas, i.e. the ones you find most interesting.

Topics	Written texts	Non-written texts
• friendship • meerkats • the 1960s • Canada • chocolate • current news stories (say which ones) • controversial topics (say which ones)	• Harry Potter books • Roald Dahl short stories • restaurant review blog • song lyrics (say which ones)	• James Bond films • *Horrible Histories* television show • Radio 5 Live film review programme • *Top Gear*

Now pick **your favourite** one or two ideas from each list above.

Topics	Written texts	Non-written texts

Authors	Directors	Hobbies and pastimes
• Stephanie Meyer • Anthony Horowitz	• Stephen Spielberg • Peter Jackson	• scouts/guides • playing an instrument • playing a sport

Now pick **your favourite** one or two ideas from each list above.

Authors	Directors	Hobbies and pastimes

You should have lots of ideas now. It is a good idea at this point to go away and do some more thinking on your own. Ask your teacher to give you a deadline for when he/she needs to know your topic and your texts.

As you decide, keep in mind that you are going to spend quite a long time working on these texts. Make sure you like them, or at least find them interesting. You also have to find a lot to say about them in your final presentation.

- If you choose to do a written presentation, it should be **700–800 words** long
- If you choose to do a spoken presentation, it should last for **4–6 minutes**.

Still a bit stuck? Here are some topics students have enjoyed doing.

- A student who was interested in cars watched an episode of *Top Gear* and read a car magazine.
- A student who loved dance watched the movie called *Step Up* and read a book about dance.
- Another student watched the documentary *Supersize Me* and read the McDonald's website.
- A student read a magazine article about a new film, then watched the film in the cinema.
- A student compared the novel and movie versions of *The Hunger Games*.
- A student read the lyrics of the Bob Dylan song *Hurricane* about a boxer accused of three murders, and then watched the Denzel Washington movie *Hurricane*, which tells the same story.

Still a bit stuck? Here are some possible approaches:

- You could look at two written texts (poems, stories, novels, plays) by the same author.
- You could compare a written text with its television or movie version.
- You could look at two novels from a series (e.g. *Hunger Games, His Dark Materials, Harry Potter*) and show how a character or some characters change and develop as the series goes on.
- You could study two texts about the same period of history, e.g. the film *War Horse* and a First World War poem; the film *Gladiator* and the *Horrible Histories: Rotten Romans* book.
- You could compare any factual television programme with a book, magazine or website about the same subject.
- You could compare a tourist brochure or travel guidebook with a television programme about the same place.
- You could look at how two different travel writers (e.g. Bill Bryson, Michael Palin, Simon Reeve) have written about the same country.

- You could study a television documentary and a piece of journalism on the same topic, e.g. climate change.
- You could look at the websites, or printed material, of two charities that work in the same area.
- You could look at the websites, or printed material, of two campaigning groups who have very different ideas about the same issue.
- If a company has been criticised in the press (e.g. for not paying its taxes, exploiting its workers, producing bad or dangerous products or causing pollution), you could compare newspaper or television coverage of the company with what it says on its own website.
- You could start by picking a topic you have strong views or opinions about.
- You could pick a particular year, or a decade, and research it: find out about world and UK news stories at that time; fashions; sports events; movie releases; music, etc.

And, you could speak to these people:

classmates	school or local librarian	teachers
friends	teammates	family members
anyone you can think of who might be an expert on your topic		

Active learning

You are going to meet your teacher soon to persuade him/her to agree with your chosen topic and texts.

To get ready for this, pair up with someone else from your class and explain your ideas to each other.

Alternatively, work with a group. Get the other group members to listen while you pitch your idea to them. Try to convince them it will help you produce really good work for your AVU.

It is time now for you and your teacher to agree on your topic and texts. Your teacher might ask you to submit this information in writing or to meet for a chat. He/she might then respond with written notes, or by talking with you.

However you do it, you and your teacher need to agree that you have made good choices about:

- your topic ✓
- text 1 ✓
- text 2 ✓

Just double check that at least one of your texts is a written one and you are ready to start studying them.

Step 2: getting a basic grasp of your texts

To help you feel that you are getting to grips with your texts, you are going to prepare a summary of each one. This task is best done as homework because the people in your class will all need different lengths of time to do this in, depending on which texts they have chosen.

Active learning

Read or watch your first text again. As you read or watch, prepare a basic one-page summary of your text to give to your teacher.

You should choose a format for your summary that it clear and easy for you to make, and for your teacher to understand. It could be in sentences and paragraphs, in bullet points, or presented as a mind map.

You can photocopy the next page of this book to give you a format for your summary page.

Basic summary sheet: text 1/text 2

Student's name: _____

Deadline for handing in summary: _____

Text title: _____

My summary

Teacher's response

As we said, your summary might be in sentences, bullets, or a mind map. For example, here is a summary in sentences of *Toy Story 3*.

> **Andy is about to go to college. His toys fear he has forgotten them and that they will never get played with again. After a mix-up when they think they are being thrown out, the toys choose to go to Sunnyside Day Care. Woody escapes to go to college with Andy. Sunnyside seems very nice, until the toys realise that the children play very roughly, and that Lotso the bear runs the place like a dictator. Woody comes back to rescue them. After nearly being crushed and then burnt at the rubbish dump, the toys, Woody included, start a new life with an imaginative little girl called Bonnie.**

Sentence summaries can be good for something that tells a story in some way. If you are working on something more factual, a bullet point summary might be more helpful. Below is a summary by a student who was looking at a tourist guide to Edinburgh.

• Getting to Edinburgh	• National Gallery
• Hotels and other places to stay	• Princes Street
• Castle	• National Portrait Gallery
• Holyrood Palace	• Zoo
• Parliament	• Botanic Gardens
• Holyrood Park	• Royal Yacht Britannia

A spider plan is a good way to show how ideas connect together.

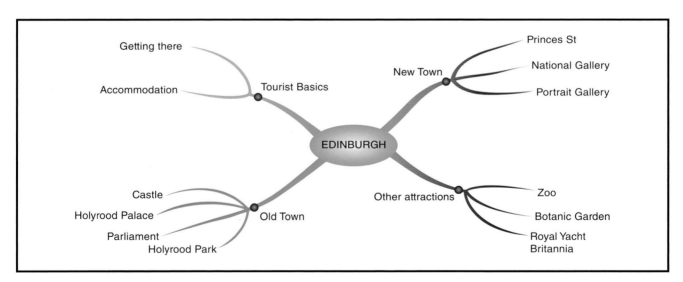

When you have completed the summary of your first text, give it to your teacher and wait for his/her written or spoken response. This will let you know if you have summarised well, and will give you some guidance about summarising your second text.

Now read or watch your second text again. As you read or watch, prepare a basic one-page summary of your text to give to your teacher.

You should choose a format for your summary that is clear and easy for you to make, and for your teacher to understand. It could be in sentences and paragraphs, in bullet points, or presented as a mind map. Because you are now working on a different text, you might use a different sort of summary.

You can make another photocopy of the summary page from this book on page 89 to give you a format for to use.

When you have completed the summary of your second text, give it to your teacher and wait for his/her written or spoken response.

You should know by now if you have chosen useful texts, and if your teacher thinks you have got a basic understanding of both of them. Your teacher might suggest that you should use one more text as well as these, or might say you need to think of a new text instead of one of those you have read already. If that happens, remember it is so that you can come up with really good material to talk or write about in the end.

Step 3: choosing a structure for your presentation

The SQA guidance for teachers about this part of our National 4 course only says that you need to 'investigate and report on' your chosen topic and then present your findings and respond to questions. The guidance does not say exactly *how* you should investigate your topic. It is a good idea for you to decide now, roughly how you are going to do it. This will make the rest of your working process much clearer.

Below are two routes you could take.

Route 1	Route 2
Take this route if you began by being most interested in your TOPIC.	Take this route if you began by being most interested in your TEXTS, WRITER OR DIRECTOR.
Your final presentation can be spoken or written. In it, you will give your readers, or your audience, interesting information about the topic.	Your final presentation can be spoken or written. In it, you will give your readers, or your audience, interesting information about the texts and how they are written.

Route 1	Route 2
You will explain, in speech or writing, what you have learned. You will use your texts as sources of **information** about that subject or topic.	You could **compare** the two texts, looking at how they are similar. You could also **contrast** them, showing how they are different. You could look at some of the techniques the writers use.
If you do this kind of presentation, you probably do not need to summarise the texts for your audience. Decide whether you should, or not. The summary sheets you made already are still useful to clarify your own understanding of the texts.	If you do this kind of presentation, you probably need to start by summarising the texts for your audience. The summary sheets you made already will help you here.

Active learning

Find a partner. Explain to him/her:

- what your topic is and why you chose it
- what your texts are and why you chose them
- what kind of presentation structure you think you are going to use: information, or compare and contrast
- why you have chosen this presentation structure.

Ask your partner to check if your explanations and reasons are clear.

Once you can explain and defend your choices, let your teacher know what you have decided. You could do this in writing, or by having a conversation.

Make sure your teacher agrees that you have chosen the right approach.

Step 4: studying your texts in detail

You already have a basic understanding of your texts. You have read them at least once already, and summarised them.

Now you are going to read them in much more detail, making notes as you go. This stage of the AVU will get you to gather all the details and information that you will use in preparing your final presentation.

You will gather the information in different ways, depending on which structure you have chosen for your presentation. There are some pages in this book that you can photocopy to help you here.

But first, we need to look at **bibliographies** and **plagiarism**. These matter for both structures.

Bibliographies

A bibliography is a list of texts you have studied. You should make a bibliography to keep track of what you have been reading or watching.

- If you read a **book**, make a note of the title, the author, the publisher, and the year it was published. You should also keep a record of which pages or chapters you have made notes from.
- If you watch a **film**, make a note of the title, the director, and the year it was released.
- If you watch a **television programme** or listen to a **radio programme**, make a note of the title, the channel, and the date of broadcast.
- If you read a **newspaper or magazine article** note down the title of the publication, the headline or title of the article, the name of the journalist, and the date of publication.
- If you read a **website**, make a note of the page address. Something like 'BBC News' is not detailed enough. You need to note down 'BBC News/science/climate-change/glaciers'.

For other types of text, ask your teacher what you should record in your bibliography.

As you make your detailed notes, keep recording in your bibliography exactly what you have been studying.

Plagiarism

Plagiarism is using someone else's words as if they were your own. You are not allowed to do this. First, it is a kind of stealing. Second, if you want to show you understand something, the best way to do this is by explaining it in your own words. This is called **paraphrasing**.

Look at this paragraph a student found in a website about snakes:

> **Snakes are elongated, legless, carnivorous reptiles that can be distinguished from legless lizards by their lack of eyelids and external ears.**

Now look at how the student put the same information into her own words to prove she understood it.

Snakes have long, stretched-out bodies, and no legs. You can tell them apart from legless lizards because snakes do not have eyelids, and they do not have ears that show on the outside of their heads. They eat living things.

Active learning

Work with a partner. Make a list of all the things the student did to translate the paragraph into her own words.

Share your answers with the class.

Did you notice what the student did NOT change? Why were these words left as they were?

Active learning

You are going to see some words students found while reading their research texts. These students needed to put what they found into their own words.

Translate the original sources into your own words. The first paraphrase has been done for you as an example.

1   Daniel Jacob Radcliffe (born 23 July 1989) is an English actor who rose to prominence playing the title character in the Harry Potter film series. Radcliffe made his acting debut at age ten in BBC One's 1999 *David Copperfield*, followed by his film debut in 2001's *The Tailor of Panama*. At age eleven he was cast as the title character in the first Harry Potter film, and starred in the series for a decade until the release of the eighth and final film in July 2011.

> Daniel Radcliffe is English. This actor was born in July 1989. He became known for playing the main part in the Harry Potter movies. He started acting when he was ten in 'David Copperfield' on BBC 1. He was in his first film 'The Tailor of Panama', in 2001. He got the part of Harry Potter when he was eleven and played Harry for ten years. The last film came out in July 2011.

2   Meerkats work together in numbers. A few will typically serve as lookouts, watching the skies for birds of prey, such as hawks and eagles, that can snatch them from the ground. A sharp, shrill call is the signal for all to take cover. While a few individuals guard the group, the rest busy themselves foraging for the foods that make up their varied diet. Meerkats will eat insects, lizards, birds, and fruit. When hunting small game, they work together and communicate with purring sounds.

3   Ferrari is a multinational Italian sports car manufacturer based in Maranello, Italy. Founded by Enzo Ferrari in 1929, the company sponsored drivers and manufactured race cars before moving into production of street-legal vehicles in 1947. Throughout its history, the company has been noted for its continued participation in racing, especially in Formula One, where it has had great success. Ferrari road cars are generally seen as a symbol of luxury and wealth.

4   Steven Spielberg's films often deal with several recurring themes. Most of his films deal with ordinary characters searching for, or coming in contact with, extraordinary beings, or finding themselves in extraordinary circumstances.

5 Situated on the continent of Antarctica, The South Pole is the southernmost point on the surface of the Earth and lies on the opposite side of the Earth from the North Pole. The first humans to reach the South Pole were Norwegian Roald Amundsen and his party on 14 December 1911.

Although you should paraphrase, and use your own words, as much as you can, sometimes you will want to quote, i.e. to use someone else's words. It might be because they said something especially clever, or interesting, or because you want to give a sense of what that person is like by quoting what he/she said. It is all right to do this, as long as you show you are quoting. In a written presentation, this means using quotation marks around the words. In written or spoken presentations you should also explain who you are quoting from, and show why you have chosen to quote instead of using you own words.

So, now that we have covered bibliographies and plagiarism, it is time for you to study your two chosen texts in detail. There are ways to do this, depending on whether you are mostly interested in finding out **information** about a topic, or whether you are mostly interested in **comparing and contrasting** your two texts. Remember this will be a decision you have already made, and have agreed with your teacher.

Studying your texts to find information on a topic

Your focus here is on finding information. You need to understand the ideas in your texts, and to be able to pick out useful and interesting details.

On the next few pages there are a number of different formats you can use to make your notes and record your information. Read them over to decide which sheet(s) would be most helpful for you to use. Discuss this with your teacher if you are not sure. The first one, the three key findings sheet, is the simplest to use, and they get a little more complex after that.

- The **three key findings sheet** gives you a clear and straightforward way to record simple, important information.
- The **KWL (What I Know, What I Want to know, What I Learned) chart** gets you to think and plan before you start reading and note-making. It helps you to use any knowledge you have already and to give yourself goals for your research.
- The **QADS (Question, Answer, Detail and Source) grid** works quite a lot like the KWL chart, but also helps you to keep track of the information that should go in your bibliography.

- The **main ideas and supporting details sheet** is the most complex one to use. It will be useful for you if you have a significant amount of quite detailed information, and you want to keep track of how it all fits together.

You will need to fill in at least one sheet for each of your texts. You can make extra photocopies if you have a lot of information. You might not use the same sheet for each text – different sorts or lengths of text might work better with different sheets.

Remember, you should make your notes by **paraphrasing** the sources into your own words, and you should keep your **bibliography** up to date as you go.

Three key findings sheet

Text	
Topic	

My three key findings about this topic:

1
2
3

KWL chart

Topic _____   Text _____

What I Know	What I Want to know	What I Learned

QADS grid

QUESTION – what do I want to know?	ANSWER – what have I found out?	DETAIL – what interesting facts and details have I learned?	SOURCE – what should I record in my bibliography?

Ideas and details sheet

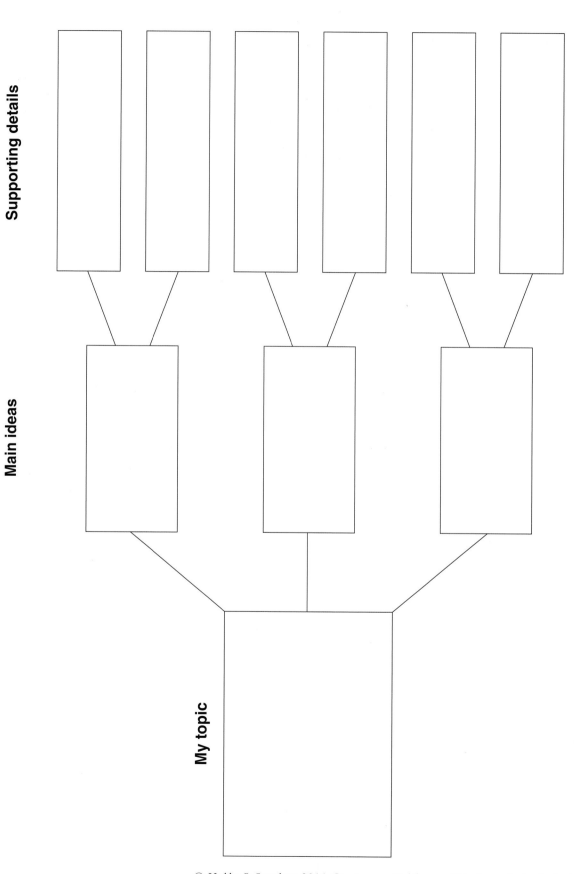

Supporting details

Main ideas

My topic

Your teacher should give you a deadline when you have to hand in the notes from your first text. He/she will respond to or comment on these notes in some way. Your teacher will then give a deadline for making notes on your second text, and will respond to these notes too.

Studying your texts to compare and contrast them

Your focus here is on understanding how your texts have been written. You will be making this clear to your audience, and also showing how the texts are similar to, and different from, each other.

The next few pages give you formats to use as you make your notes and record your information. First of all, choose which **examining your text** sheet is most suitable for you to use. You will need two copies of this, so that you can use one page for each text. You will need just one copy of the **text comparison** sheet.

Remember, you should make your notes by **paraphrasing** the sources into your own words, and you should keep your **bibliography** up to date as you go.

Your teacher should give you a deadline when you have to hand in the notes from your first text. He/she will respond to or comment on these notes in some way. He/she will then give a deadline for making notes on your second text, and will respond to these notes too.

Once your teacher has seen the notes about your individual texts, you can go ahead and fill in the comparison sheet.

Examining your text: fiction

Main or first important character
Details and evidence to describe that character

Second main or important character
Details and evidence to describe that character

Setting
Details and evidence about that setting

Technique used by the writer
Details and evidence to show the use of that technique

Examining your text: non-fiction

Key information given	How is the information given?
1	1
2	2
3	3

Is any key information missing? What?

Does the writer show an opinion about this topic? What? How?
Do I agree with the writer's opinion? Why/Why not?

Techniques used by the writer (e.g. graphs, diagrams, maps, quotations)
Why the author uses these techniques

How useful is this book? Why?

Examining your text: media

Main or first important character
Details and evidence to describe that character

Second main or important character
Details and evidence to describe that character

Setting
How the director/maker created that setting

Important media techniques (e.g. sound, lighting, editing, music)
Details and evidence to show the use of these techniques

Text comparison

Use this page to keep a note of the similarities between your texts, as well as the differences. These can include:

- characters
- themes
- setting
- techniques
- events
- anything else you notice.

Similarities

Differences

Text 1	Text 2

Step 5: evaluating your texts

If you have worked through this chapter so far you should understand your chosen texts: you know **what** they say. Now you need to think about **how** they say it, and **how well** they say it.

Different types of texts try to do different things. That means we have to evaluate them in different ways. For example, we might evaluate a novel or a film by looking at whether the characters are well developed. We might evaluate a piece of journalism by commenting on how well it puts across the point being made. We might evaluate a web page by looking at whether the format, the style, and the layout are effective.

Active learning

Make notes to record your evaluation of your two texts. You could:

- Evaluate the format or language used.
- Evaluate how characters are portrayed.
- Comment on how effectively your text explores a theme.
- Comment on how well information or ideas are presented.

For each text, try to record two positive comments, and one that shows a way in which you think the text could have been more effective.

Step 6: reviewing your progress

Congratulations! You have done lots of independent work. It is nearly time to prepare your final presentation.

The following questions will help you self-evaluate. You can write down the answers, or discuss them with a classmate, or with your teacher.

- How well am I doing?
- How do I know this?
- What am I most satisfied with so far?
- What has been most difficult so far?
- Do I know where all my notes and materials are?
- Have I kept my bibliography up to date?
- Do I need any other information? If so, what?
- Do I need any particular help? If so, what?
- What do I need to do next?

Step 7: preparing your final presentation

You can present your work by speaking or by writing. If you choose to give a spoken presentation, the talk should be **4–6 minutes**, including questions. You should be able to answer questions as part of your presentation. If you choose to create a written presentation, its length should be appropriate to purpose but is likely to be **700–800 words**. You should be able to answer questions about what you write.

Now that you have all your research material, you should choose whether you want to present your findings in speech or in writing. Here are some ideas to help you think about this.

So long as it takes 4–6 minutes, including questions, a **spoken presentation** can include:

- talking
- PowerPoint slides
- film clips shown from DVDs, YouTube, iPlayer, programme websites, BBC Class Clips
- music and other sounds
- asking questions to the audience, or getting them to do something.

A **written presentation** could be:

- an informative essay or report
- a critical essay
- an argumentative essay
- a poster
- a leaflet
- a set of museum exhibit boards
- a blog
- a website
- a Wikipedia page.

and it can include:

- pictures
- maps
- diagrams
- headings and sub-headings.

Decide what kind of presentation you will create. Explain to your teacher whether you will be writing or speaking. Tell your teacher why you have chosen this style. Make sure he/she understands and agrees that this is the best option for you.

> ### *Active learning*
>
> Now prepare your presentation. This chapter is NOT going to tell you how to do this. Go back to Chapter 2 on the Creation and Production Unit if you need more advice.
>
> You should not spend too long preparing your presentation. Remember that in the Added Value Unit, the way you work – the process – is just as important as what you produce at the end.
>
> Your presentation should include:
>
> - what you learned and understood about your topic
> - what you learned and understood about your two texts
> - your evaluation of these texts.

Step 8: your final presentation

When you are ready, give your written work to your teacher, or deliver your spoken presentation to an audience. (This might be your whole class, or it might be a smaller group.)

Then you must answer questions on your work. Even if you presented your work in writing, you must still answer questions about it. Some of these questions might be about the content of what you said or wrote. For example:

- Why did you choose this topic?
- Why did you choose these texts?
- What is the most interesting thing you learned about …?
- Could you explain more about …?

Some of the questions must get you to critically evaluate. For example:

- Which source was most useful in your research? Why?
- Which source was least useful? Why?
- If you were going to do this task again, what would you do differently? Why?
- What advice would you give to someone else who wanted to research this topic?

Once you have done this, use the sheet on the next page. Fill in the self-evaluation sections first. Then give it to you teacher to complete the other sections.

Step 9: what happens next

Your teacher will let you know if you have passed this unit. If you have not passed, your teacher will explain why and will give advice about what you still need to do to pass.

Your teacher will also be able to tell you if your work in this unit will count as a pass for any outcomes in one of the other National 4 units.

Evaluating the added value unit

The process of work throughout the unit

	My response	Teacher's response
What went well		
Even better if . . .		

The final presentation

	My response	Teacher's response
What went well		
Even better if . . .		

CHAPTER 5 The National 5 Writing Portfolio

To pass National 5, you need to pass the Analysis and Evaluation and the Creation and Production Units. These are covered in the first two chapters of this book. You also need to pass the course assessment. One part of this is the question paper – an exam that you will sit. This is covered in Chapters 6 and 7. The other part of the course assessment is the Writing Portfolio, which you will learn about in this chapter.

Your Portfolio is worth 30 marks. It is designed to challenge you to use a greater level of skill. You will apply these skills by producing **two** pieces of writing, each marked out of 15. These pieces will come from different genres. You will write these pieces at school, under some supervision and control. The Portfolio will then be sent away to the SQA to be marked.

You will complete your Portfolio by building on skills you have already developed in the Creation and Production Unit. This time though, you will use these skills more independently.

Although this chapter comes near the end of the book, it may take you most of your National 5 year to get your Portfolio together. You may wish to try the different sorts of writing taught here at different times, and produce a number of different first drafts before you decide, with help from your teacher, which two are best and should be redrafted for the Portfolio. You are not allowed to redraft any piece more than twice.

What you will be assessed on

In both of your pieces, the discursive and the creative, the markers will be looking at three particular areas of your writing skill: **content, style** and **technical accuracy**.

- Your piece should have the right **content**. This means that you will stick to your chosen purpose and write something that fits your chosen audience.
- **Style** includes being able to use the conventions of your chosen genre effectively. Your word choice should be varied and effective. The structure of your piece will help it to achieve its purpose.
- **Technical accuracy** is how well you use the English language. This includes your paragraphing, spelling, grammar and punctuation, which should all be consistently accurate, with few errors. You should also aim for variety by, for example, using different sorts of sentence structure, or being able to use confidently some of the less common punctuation marks.

There are also particular assessment guidelines for each genre of writing. You will find these in the sections of this chapter that deal with those genres.

Combined assessment

The work you do on your Portfolio may help you to pass one of the units as well.

- It might be possible to use this work as evidence of writing for the Creation and Production Unit.
  or
- It might be possible to use this work as evidence of Writing for the National 5 Literacy Unit if your school or college teaches this.

Ask your teacher if he/she is hoping to combine assessments in this way. Your teacher must be sure that you have covered all the skills each unit asks for.

 Warning

The next few pages contain lots of information about the course requirements for writing. Do not panic. You do not have to try to memorise all of this. As you read it over, just make sure you understand everything. You can look back at these pages at any time to make sure that you are following the rules and guidelines properly.

What you can write

Your Portfolio should contain two pieces in two different genres. One piece should be what the SQA calls '**creative**', which means that you can produce any one of the following types of writing to fulfill the requirements for the creative genre:

- a personal or reflective essay
- a piece of prose, e.g. a short story or an extract from a novel
- a poem or a set of linked poems
- a drama script.

Later in this chapter you will learn about how to write in the first two of these styles, the personal or reflective essay and prose fiction.

The second portfolio piece should be what the SQA calls '**discursive**', which means that you can produce any one of the following types of writing to fulfil the requirements for this genre:

- a piece of transactional writing
- a persuasive essay
- an argumentative essay
- a report.

Later in this chapter you will learn about how to write in two of these styles, persuasive and argumentative. (Although this chapter does not focus on it, you may be wondering what *transactional* writing is. This term means a piece of writing that aims to give information on a subject to a specific audience. Film reviews and biographies are two types of transactional writing.)

Length

Your portfolio pieces should not be more than 1000 words long. If your pieces (except for poems) are much shorter than this they are unlikely to get high marks because they probably will not demonstrate the sort of developed skills that the markers want to see. If your piece is too long, marks may well be deducted.

Your title, any footnotes, and any bibliography or list of sources are not counted. If your piece contains quotations these are regarded as part of the word count.

Authenticity

Because your portfolio is worth 30% of your marks, a sizeable chunk of the entire National 5 Course Assessment, it is vital that the SQA can be sure that every student is working in the same way and under the same conditions, so that marking is fair. Your portfolio has to be your own work, and at National 5 level you are not allowed to have too much support or detailed input from your teacher.

What you can do	What you cannot do
Be given teaching that extends your knowledge, understanding and appreciation of a range of genres.	Rely heavily on ideas or wording that you found in a printed or electronic source.
Use printed or electronic sources to find background information or ideas.	**What your teacher cannot do**
Use a dictionary, spell-checker or thesaurus.	Give you detailed advice about how to restructure or reword your first draft.
Discuss your ideas with your teacher as part of your planning.	Pick out and correct specific mistakes in your expression or your technical accuracy.
Be given written comments on your first draft, and discuss that draft with your teacher.	Tell you that you must write about a certain genre or topic that he/she has chosen.
Be given broad suggestions for how to improve your first draft.	Give you notes, or a specific plan or a model so detailed that you do not come up with your own structure.

This might all sound very detailed and strict. Remember you can check back at these rules at any point in your work. Remember too that their purpose is to get you to do what you should want to do anyway – to use your own ideas to write your own piece that shows your own abilities.

Sources

You will probably need to refer to outside sources as your write your discursive piece. These must be acknowledged. You **absolutely cannot, ever**, copy and paste, or retype, exact wording from a website or from anywhere else and pass it off as your own work.

- If you use a newspaper or magazine article you must name the writer and give the title of the publication and the publication date.
- If you use information from the internet you must give the name of the site and the specific page address.
- If you quote from a book you must give the title and publication date.
- Any quotations should be inside quotation marks.

Drafting and redrafting

All real writing is drafted and redrafted. However, because your National 5 Portfolio is a test of how well you can write, and to make sure that everyone is being tested fairly, you are not allowed to keep endlessly polishing your work.

Your teacher should keep a note of your title and ideas, your plan, your first draft and a copy of your final version safely at school. The SQA might ask to see these.

Your teacher can write comments and suggestions on your first draft, and can discuss these with you, but cannot mark mistakes in detail. (For more on how your teacher might correct your writing, see Chapter 2 on the Creation and Production Unit.) It is up to you to be able to correct your first draft. You should not normally have more than two goes at writing any particular piece.

You will need to sign a declaration to say that your portfolio is your own work. The two pieces that go into that portfolio should be produced under conditions that help to ensure that the work is your own. In practice, the easiest way to do this is to write your first draft of each piece in class. Your teacher will compare that draft to any later versions to make sure that the work, while it improves and develops, is without a doubt still your own.

Presentation

The marker may have several hundred portfolio pieces to assess: following the guidelines below will help the marker by making your work clear and easy to read.

Your portfolio pieces should be typed, and printed in black ink on just one side of the paper. Use a clear standard font in 12 point. Your text should be justified – it should have a straight margin on the left. Margins should be 2 centimetres wide all round the page and you should use double line spacing, with a double return for new paragraphs.

Well done! You have made it through pages of rules and guidelines. Did you understand it all as you read it? Remember that you can refer back to these pages at any time. In fact, you should keep coming back to these pages and double-checking that you are following the rules.

Now let us move on to the enjoyable part, the writing itself.

At the start of the chapter we saw that the SQA wants you to write in two different main genres, **creative** and **discursive**, and that these break down into eight types of writing altogether. We will look here at the four that students are most likely to want to write: **prose fiction** and **personal reflective writing** from the creative genre; and **argumentative** and **persuasive** writing from the discursive genre. You will find information about other sorts of writing in Chapter 2.

Prose fiction

What you will be assessed on

We have already seen that all your portfolio work is assessed for its **content, style** and **technical accuracy**. Your prose fiction work will also be assessed for its **creativity**. The markers want to see you making good use of the **genre conventions** of fiction.

The genre of prose fiction includes all short stories and novels. We are going to concentrate on short story writing.

Active learning

Work with a group. Make a list of all the rules and guidelines that you think would help you recognise a short story. It may help you to think about length, number of characters, number of settings and time covered.

Share your answers with the rest of the class.

Now read this story.

> ### Absolute
>
> 'Daddy, what's wrong?' Four-year-old Hannah was tugging at Michael's hands, trying to pull them away from his ears. 'Daddy are you all right?'
>
> He was not. He was crouching on the platform at Haymarket Station, his forehead against his knees and his arms wrapped around his head. Everything around him was clattering. The trains screeched in like someone scraping a canteen of knives against the rails. Everyone was on their phones, baying at listeners who would not hear them and would have to be texted later from blue tartan seats. Suitcase wheels trundled like coal trucks. Worst of all was the tannoy, too loud to ignore but too quiet to make any sense of. Would they ever get out of here?
>
> 'Daddy, let's go. I'm scared.'
>
> He must control himself. He unfurled, stretched, hearing the popcorn crackle of his knees as they straightened. 'I'm scared too Hannah. Let's go.'
>
> ★ ★ ★ ★ ★
>
> She seemed to have forgotten his panic already. In the coffee shop she sat carefully colouring in each letter O in that day's *Scotsman* and drinking a glass of milk. He felt battered by the squinking of her pen against the newsprint, the scratch of the milk as it climbed the straw.
>
>
>
> In the kitchen, someone was torturing the washing up. It was a warm day and the café door was pegged open. Splinters of other lives forced their way towards him.
>
> '– don't judge me because I'm not who you thought I was –'
>
> '– and then I'll finally be able to tell her to go and –'

Michael stood up with elaborate care, lifting all four feet of his stool and placing them down again eighteen inches further back. He lifted his bag, vertically, not allowing it to drag across the flag-stoned floor. 'Let's go Hannah. Daddy's tired. We'll go to Glasgow another day. Daddy needs to go home now.'

★ ★ ★ ★ ★

The first place he tried was at least in Scotland. 'Welcome to Pluscarden Abbey,' boomed a monk.

Michael took a notebook from his pocket, wrote a few words and tore the page out. Each tiny rip against the metal rings of the spine went off like a bomb inside his head. He handed it over.

'Yes, it is a silent retreat,' said the monk, 'but only after supper on the first night. It's important to share what has brought us all here. Then we can be quiet together without feeling alone.'

Michael wrote another note, handed it over and walked away.

★ ★ ★ ★ ★

He read about a Canadian nickel mine, two kilometres underground. He paid for a $200,000 life insurance bond. He let them search him for cameras, handed over his phone, agreed to wear only the boiler suit and rigger boots they gave him, all so that they would plummet him into the blissful dark.

At the bottom of the lift shaft he turned left as they had told him, and strode out for as long as he could bear the earthquake of loose stones under his ridged soles.

He dropped his sleeping bag on the tunnel floor and lay down on top of it. His breathing slowed. This would be the place. It would be quiet, and he would rest now.

It would not, and he would not. The emergency lighting buzzed like a wasps' nest. Every drip of water from the roof was a belly-flopping fat boy in a council swimming pool.

He rolled up his sleeping bag and turned right, back to the lift shaft.

★ ★ ★ ★ ★

At last, he heard about – for everything is noise and all of life is hearing – the anechoic chamber. He flew to Minnesota.

'Welcome to the Orfield Laboratories Mr. Wright. I understand you have some very specific requirements?'

'Yes, but very simple. I just need to be somewhere totally quiet for as long as possible.'

'I'm sure we can help you with that,' said the scientist. 'If a soft whisper is measured at twenty decibels, then our anechoic chamber is just one sixteenth of that. We're proud to be listed as the Guinness World Records' quietest place on earth. NASA astronauts do part of their training here, so they can learn to cope with the silence of space.'

'Can you guarantee it? I know you've seen the reference from my doctor.'

'Certainly Mr. Wright. We fully appreciate how much it matters to you and your family that you should find somewhere quiet. Our chamber is massively insulated with layers of concrete and steel to block out exterior noise. Even the floor is a suspended mesh to stop any sound of footfalls.'

'That sounds wonderful.' Michael tried to put warmth in his voice, but he had forgotten how after all these months of whispering. 'I'd like to try forty-five minutes.'

The scientist looked up from his clipboard. 'Sir, many people find perfect quiet upsetting. Being cut off can induce fear. Some nations use this as a form of torture.'

'I understand.' His voice was a leaf in a tornado.

'Being in an anechoic chamber for longer than fifteen minutes can cause claustrophobia, nausea, panic attacks and aural hallucinations.'

'I understand.' His voice was a dragonfly's wingbeat in a hurricane.

'Mr. Wright, we had a violinist here last week. He wanted silence so he could run through a score in his head. He was crying after four minutes.'

'I understand.' His voice was a mackerel fin against a North Sea storm.

When the heavy door shut behind him, he was plunged into darkness – no lights humming this time. He strained. He heard nothing.

Then, after a minute or two, he became aware of the sound of his own breathing. He held his breath.

His heart thumped, like a derrick in an oil field. Next, he started to hear the blood swooping in his veins, a racket of purpose. He frowned and heard his scalp shuffle over his skull.

He'd have to be dead for absolute silence.

Michael screamed.

Work with your group again to add to your list of rules and guidelines for a short story.

Share your answers with the rest of the class.

Have you ever thought about there being rules for a short story? Maybe the idea is quite new to you. By now, you should have come up with some of these. A short story:

- focuses on few characters
- has few settings
- has clear, simple action.

This particular story cheats a little on one other story guideline. It is a good idea to keep your stories within a short time frame, maybe covering even just one event. This story covers quite a long period in Michael's life: the writer gets away with this because the action stays clear and simple.

The rising action story structure

We are going to look now at one classic structure for writing short stories. This is not the only way to tell a story, but it is a good one.

Using this structure will help you plan clear and effective stories without flabby, padded sections in them. We are going to think of this structure in five steps. To help you understand these, each step will be compared to something in the story *Absolute* (above), which you have just read.

Step in the structure	How we see this in *Absolute*
1 Exposition This is what is revealed or told at the start of the story. It sets the scene and establishes character(s). Not too much, or you will bore your reader, not too little or you will confuse.	We are introduced to Michael, the father, and his daughter Hannah. They are at a railway station waiting to catch a train.
2 Initiating incident Something happens at the start of the story. This kicks off the action by creating a problem, or challenge, or new situation for the main character(s).	Michael has a panic attack created by the noise in the station.
3 Development This is where the characters try to solve their problems. Any action has to fit the character – a gentle person will not try to solve his problems with a shotgun. The story	Michael tries to deal with his problem in a number of different ways. He goes to the café. He goes to an abbey. He goes underground in a mine.

tests the character: how is this person going to deal with this problem? You cannot sort out the problem too easily or you end up having no story. The character will probably make several unsuccessful attempts to solve the problem, and some of these may even lead to little turning points within the story. This is how your story develops. It is where we see the action of the story rising.	
4 Climax This is the point the story has been leading up to. Afterwards the story may change mood or direction.	Michael visits the anechoic chamber and is shut in there alone.
5 Resolution After the climax, there will be consequences that affect the fates of all those involved. The story should feel properly brought to a close.	Even the chamber is not silent. Michael screams, and the reader realises there is no way to solve his noise phobia.

If you are a more visual sort of person, it might help you to think of the story as having a shape like this:

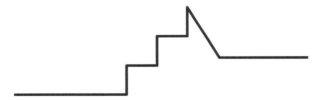

If you want to read another story that follows this structure, try 'On the Roundabout' by Bernard MacLaverty from the collection *Matters of Life and Death*. Be warned, it includes some strong language but it does tell, in just four pages, a powerful story of rising action. It also has a small cast of characters and a clearly drawn main character, a very restricted setting, and a short timescale – so it sticks to all the rules we have discussed in this chapter. If you read it, try to work out which part of the story corresponds to each of the five steps in the table above.

Show, don't tell

We are going to leave the idea of structure on one side for now, and look at some more general writing skills that will help to bring your chapter to life.

First, we are going to look at a skill that is often summed up in the words: **show, don't tell.** To make that clear, have a look at the following sentences.

> I opened the envelope. I took the letter out and read it. I put it down.

Now look at these sentences.

> I tore open the envelope. I pulled the letter out and scanned it. I flung it on the floor.

How does the speaker feel about the letter? Angry, of course. But notice, he does not actually say, 'I felt angry about what was in the letter.' Instead, by changing the simple verbs like *opened, took, read* and *put* into more expressive ones like *tore, pulled, scanned* and *flung*, the narrator shows us the emotion.

Active learning

Go back to the first basic set of three sentences beginning, 'I opened the envelope …'. Rewrite them to show the following emotions:

- The narrator is afraid of what the letter says.
- The narrator is very attracted to the writer of the letter.
- The narrator is surprised or shocked by something in the letter.

As you can see, the difference between showing and telling often comes from choosing interesting vocabulary. By using the right words to put across how characters move, act, appear, or speak, we can show what they are like, or how they are feeling.

Active learning

Now try writing these paragraphs, which all require you to show rather than tell:

- Show that a character is angry just by describing the way he/she buys three items at the supermarket.
- Show that a character is afraid just by describing the way he/she starts a car and drives off.
- Show that a character is worried just by describing the way he/she answers a ringing phone.
- Show that a character is exhausted just by describing the way he/she arrives home.
- Show that a character is shy just by describing the way he/she comes into a crowded room.

The best writing always leaves at least a little for the reader to do. This makes the reader feel clever, and shows that you are a skilful writer.

Active learning

One more task on showing, not telling. This one will take us towards ideas about creating characters.

Write a paragraph to describe, in as much detail as possible, a room. This room should be one that 'belongs' to a character. If your character is a child or teenager, you probably want to describe his/her bedroom; if it is an adult you might want to describe his/her sitting room, or office at work. The most revealing room for some characters might be their kitchen, or what their garden shed is like. The way you describe the room, the objects you put in it, and how everything has been set out, should start to show the life and personality of the character. For example, lots of dirty coffee cups sitting on the floor suggest one kind of person, a nearly empty desk with a ticked 'to do' list on it suggests quite another.

Do not use any characters, action or speech in your writing, just description. When you have written your piece, swap with a partner and see what you can work out about each other's characters.

We will return to ideas about characters later as you plan the main character for your story.

Style

You know already that the markers want your writing to be stylish. But what does that mean? It means that the language you choose, and the techniques you use, are under your control and help to make the story distinctive.

Active learning

Go back again to read the story *Absolute* on page 115. You are going to look for three particular features of the writer's style:

1 The word choice the author uses to describe sounds; look especially in the station, café and anechoic chamber sections of the story.

2 The metaphors and similes she creates: look especially in the anechoic chamber section of the story.

3 Her use of repetition – this might be repetition of words and phrases, but also repeats that create the wider structure of the story.

Make notes of what you find as you read the story. Share your answers with the class.

Looking at a real example

Below is a short story written by a student.

> ### Active learning
>
> First, read through the piece of writing. You may wish to do this aloud around the class, or you might want to read it on your own.

Dark encounter

Green eyes full of pain stared deep into my own. I reached my hand up to my face and felt the normality of my skin under my fingertips. The mirror told a different story. A sunset cascaded down from the left side of my face and onto my neck. Blues, purples, and a light stain of orange formed a masterpiece of bruises, and they seemed a mere gift next to my broken ribs and arm. Mackenzie Robertson was inside me, but my outside was that of a broken man. Fragile, I felt humiliated. After one dark encounter I'd lost my self worth. What I'd lost in pride, I'd gained in suffering.

'Mr Robertson? Mackenzie?'

The light stung my eyes as I drew back from the darkness that had been luring me in for days.

'I'm sorry, I know you'd rather be somewhere else, but we need to finish these questions.' The policewoman's warm smile fitted with the homely surroundings of my living room, quite unlike her harsh black and white uniform.

'Sorry,' escaped from my lips as I sat up and winced at the stab of pain from my rib. 'I was at a party, got stupidly drunk, and was attacked on the way home.'

The policewoman snapped back to business mode as she turned to face my parents. 'And you found him on your doorstep during the night, Mr and Mrs Robertson?'

'Yes, that's right,' said my mum. 'But he doesn't usually do this. He's a rugby star! Why did you get drunk Mackenzie? Why did you do it?' Anger and frustration: that's how she felt. I shrugged my shoulders as if I was five years old, not seventeen.

'What do you remember from the attack Mackenzie?'

'A black hoodie. Kicking, punching, and that black hoodie.' My eyes fogged over as the darkness tried to pull me back in.

The interview was finished. I set off on the newly discovered hike to the top of our stairs.

The darkness. The laughter. The pain. The hoodie. I lay on my bed every night terrified of my own recent past. Who was it? Why did they do it? My thoughts were fogged and wouldn't let me sleep freely. I closed my eyes and prayed my brain would register the plea for sleep. Thankfully it did.

* * * * *

The car door slammed, pulled by my dad, not pushed by me. I slowly walked up to the building I'd been gone from for two weeks. The surroundings lay still. Apparently I couldn't handle walking in with the other 1700 students. My capacity for even such an everyday task was in question. Humiliation didn't cut it. Reaching for the double doors and dragging them open I welcomed myself back to the normality of school life, to a sense of structure. I was back to being Mackenzie.

* * * * *

'So all you remember is her, I mean his or her, jacket?'
'Yeah, their hoodie. Well, and their laugh.'

My best friend Natasha stared intently at my bruises. Her hand shakily reached out to touch them. 'Oh Mackenzie you really are in a bad way. I mean, if you can't protect yourself, who can?' She flailed her arms in exasperation and at last made eye contact.

'Well I wasn't in the best of states, was I?' I murmured quietly as our chemistry teacher Mrs Robinson entered.

'Morning class! Nice to see you back Mackenzie! Natasha, will you please take the hoodie off!'

I suddenly didn't feel right. My brain was trying to decipher something. Uneasy. Unsafe. If it was trying to sift memories of Natasha, of course it was having a hard time – that's a lot of sifting. I made myself focus on the chemistry task in front of me, never so glad to have been in a classroom.

Throughout the day my uncertainty about my safety grew. Alarm bells kept going off. Sirens. Warnings. My head was trying to tell me something, but I couldn't pick out what. Aching. Pain. Nausea. Sorting through years of information. Something was being picked out, I just couldn't see what. The dark encounter circled my brain and slipped down every nerve. The darkness was dragging me deeper.

I pulled myself back into the light. For now.

* * * * *

'Mackenzie. It's safe. It's just my room.' Natasha smiled and ushered me in. My head pounded. This didn't feel right. My palms sweated as I sat on the edge of her bed. Resting my head in my hands I pushed my fingers against my skull in an attempt to make this all stop.

'Mackenzie what is it? I won't hurt you!' Her shrill laughter filled the room. Recognition. Her hoodie. Her laugh. The perfect match.

'It … it … it was you, Natasha. I have to leave.' My head reeled as I stood. I felt my pulse quicken. My temperature rose.

Natasha pushed down on my broken arm. 'Took you a while, didn't it, golden boy?'

'Why did you do it?' I asked, sick to my stomach.

'I know you've always liked me, Mackenzie. When you pushed me off you at that party I got angry. I wanted control.'

'I … I never liked you Natasha, not that way. I have to go.' Standing up, I towered over her. I felt nauseous, lost. Humiliated.

* * * * *

'Wait, so you're saying a five foot, size eight, girl did this to you, a six foot two sports star? Mr Robertson, I hope you understand my disbelief.' The policewoman looked at me as if I had completely lost it.

'It's fine,' I murmured. 'I didn't expect you to believe me anyway.' My parents didn't believe me. The police didn't believe me. My friends didn't believe me. This dark encounter had left me completely alone.

Active learning

Now that you have read the story once, you are going to analyse it in more detail. Consider these questions.

1 Did the writer use the short story rules we have been learning about?

2 Did the writer do anything that surprised you?

3 What features of this writer's style did you notice?

4 Write a couple of sentences to show what made it a good piece of writing.

5 Suggest two things the writer could have done that would have made the story work **even better**.

Choosing a narrative style

Some stories, such as *Absolute*, are told in the third person, using 'he' or 'she'. Some stories, such as *Dark Encounter*, are told in the first person, using 'I', as if the storyteller was also in the story.

Active learning

Copy and complete the following table to help you think about these two different ways of telling a story. Fill in as many ideas as you can think of in the empty boxes. See if you can add other ideas to the ones that are already there in some of the boxes.

Person	Advantages	Disadvantages
First	Feels like the character is speaking to the reader.	
Third		The reader might not feel so involved or care so much.

Starting in the middle

That might seem like an odd heading. Stories start at the beginning. If you have been following this chapter, you know there should be a little (sometimes a very little) bit of exposition and scene setting at the start.

But you do not need to go too far back. *Absolute* starts in the middle of the scene at Haymarket Station, when Michael is already on the ground, curled up and panicking. It does not tell us how he got there, or why, or exactly what made him collapse. *Dark Encounter* starts in the middle of the conversation between Mackenzie and the police officer.

We are not told directly why the conversation is taking place or what has happened to Mackenzie; we work it out from the small fragment of that conversation that we see.

That is what we mean by staring in the middle. It makes your story more interesting; it saves you words when you only have 1000 to use; it also (like the 'show, don't tell' technique we covered earlier) flatters your readers by getting them to do a little thinking.

Planning your own story

People often ask writers where they get their ideas from. The writer of *Absolute* got the idea from a newspaper article about the man who had broken the Guinness World Record for the longest stay in an anechoic chamber. The writer of *Dark Encounter* started with only that title. Ideas can come from anywhere.

Active learning

You need to do a little preparation for this. Get everyone in your class to bring in a newspaper – preferably a quality one like the *Guardian, Scotsman, Herald, Independent* or *The Times,* though there can be some quite intriguing articles in the *Metro* that might just work for this task.

Swap papers with someone else. Flip through the paper you have got and try to find an idea that inspires you to write a story.

For example, a news item about how the government wants all pet dogs to be electronically 'tagged' made me wonder what would happen if parents started asking vets to tag their children. A feature article about working in a pawnbroker's shop made me want to write about why a character has brought in one particular item as a way of raising money. A piece about a newly built block of flats standing unsold and empty made me want to write a spooky story about what happens to some teenagers who break into an empty block as a dare.

Tell someone your idea. Listen to theirs.

If you still do not have any ideas, ask your teacher if the school keeps copies of the writing papers from the old Standard Grade exam. Get hold of a selection and pick out a story stimulus that appeals to you.

Now it is time for you to plan your story.

You need to plan, in quite a lot of detail, two main aspects of your story. If you have planned stories in the past, what you probably did was plan the **plot** of your story, i.e. the events that would take place in it. We will get round to that later. First you need to plan, and get to know, your main **character**.

Active learning

Using the following list of questions and prompts, make a list of details that show that you know, and have carefully thought about, your main character.

- male or female?
- age?
- appearance?
- home/family situation?
- main personality traits?
- any unusual quirks, habits, hobbies?
- what is this person's background?
- what motivates him/her in life?
- how would this character's friends describe him/her?
- what makes your character happy?
- what makes your character angry?
- plus anything else you know about your character.

Once you know the answers to these questions, pair up with another student. Introduce and explain your characters to each other.

Once you have answered all these questions you should know your character well, and be able to write about him/her. **Be careful!** That does not mean that you will actually use all these details in your writing. You should never end up writing something like:

> **Mackenzie thought of himself as a supreme physical specimen. He was proud of his height and his sporting achievements.**

That would be a horrible example of telling when you should be showing. Instead, the author of *Dark Encounter* writes:

> **Standing up, I towered over her. I felt nauseous, lost. Humiliated.**

We can tell from this that Mackenzie is tall and strong; his pride in this is shown through his humiliation that such a petite girl could hurt him.

Once you know your **character**, it is time to start thinking about your **plot**. Remember you want to try to use the rising structure we looked at earlier in this chapter. You can make a copy of the next page and fill it in to help you here.

Step in the structure	How I will do this
1 Exposition This is what is revealed or told at the start of the story. It sets the scene and establishes character(s).	
2 Initiating incident Something happens at the start of the story. This kicks off the action by either creating a problem, or challenge, or new situation for the main character(s).	
3 Development This is where the characters try to solve their problems. The story tests the character: how is this person going to deal with this problem? You cannot sort out the problem too easily or you end up having no story. The character will probably make several unsuccessful attempts at solving the problem, and some of these may even lead to little turning points within the story. This is how we see the action of the story rising.	1 2 3
4 Climax This is the point the story has been leading up to. Afterwards the story may change mood or direction.	
5 Resolution After the climax, there will be consequences that affect the fates of all those involved. The story should feel properly brought to a close.	

You should now have an outline for your story and you should know your main character really well.

Active learning

When your plan is finished, pair up with another student and explain your plans to each other. Do not be afraid to ask each other questions or to help your partner fix things that do not quite work yet.

Using speech

Just before you write your story, one final thing to think about — using speech.

Human beings basically never shut up, so you must make sure you use dialogue in your story. If your characters do not speak to each other, they will never seem as if they are alive, and your story will feel completely flat and dull. Not only does speech give your story life, but the way characters speak and the words they use reveal lots about them.

If you are writing dialogue, you need to know how to punctuate it. Poor use of speech marks can make writing almost impossible to follow. There are three, basic rules to remember when you are using speech marks.

1   Put the speech marks round the actual words the person says.

    'I need a doctor.'

2   Use a new paragraph when you are about to change who is speaking.

    'I need a doctor!'

    'I'm a doctor.'

3   The words that tell the reader who is speaking go in the same paragraph as the words that speaker says.

    'I need a doctor!' screamed the woman as she rushed into Casualty.

    Dr Brown ran to her side. 'I'm a doctor.'

There are other, more complex rules too, about the placing of commas and other punctuation marks inside the speech marks.

4   Any exclamation marks or question marks that belong to the speech stay inside the speech marks.

    'I need a doctor!' screamed the woman.

5   If the speaker's sentence should end with a full stop, but the sentence you are writing will carry on, finish the speech with a comma before the speech marks.

'I'm a doctor,' said Dr Brown.

6   If the sentence begins with words that introduce the speech, put a comma after these words and before the opening of the speech marks.

Dr Brown said, 'I'm a doctor.'

Active learning

Using all the speech rules, the three simpler ones and the three more complex ones, punctuate the following story. You will need to put in the questions and exclamation marks as well.

When you have done this, check your work against the answers on page 258.

I need a doctor screamed the woman as she rushed into Casualty. I'm a doctor yelled Dr Brown, hurtling down the hospital corridor. What seems to be the problem. I've gone deaf said the woman. I woke up this morning and I wasn't able to hear anything out of my right ear. And she went on it tickles. Oh dear said Dr Brown. That does sound nasty. Let me take a look at it. He led her into a consulting room and shone a bright light in her ear. Hmm, yes he muttered. Do you have any children madam. I have a little boy, Liam. He's only four. But what has that got to do with my ears? Did you make him have peas for dinner last night. The woman nodded. I did, but I still don't see what this has got to do with me going deaf. And does he hate peas. Yes but I still don't understand the connection. Keep quite still said Dr Brown. You may feel an odd sensation but it shouldn't hurt. Ow yelled the woman, who certainly appeared to think that it had hurt. Aha exclaimed Dr Brown. He showed her the point of a pen lid, on which perched a slightly waxy-looking pea. I think your son got his revenge while you were asleep.

Active learning

It is now time to write your piece.

When you have written it, read your work over before you hand it in to your teacher. Ask yourself the following questions:

Content

- Have I used the rising action structure to shape my overall story?
- Have I used structural devices such as starting in the middle, flashbacks and cuts to give my work impact throughout?

Style

- Have I used good vocabulary and different sorts of sentences?
- Have I used techniques such as simile and metaphor?
- Have I written believable dialogue and punctuated it accurately?
- Have I used the genre conventions of the short story?

Technical accuracy

- Are my spelling, grammar and punctuation all accurate?
- Does my story make sense on first reading?
- Is my work well paragraphed?

Once you have checked over your work, hand it in to your teacher. He/she will mark it and give you feedback and suggestions about ways to improve it.

Personal reflective writing

This is a genre of writing that many students do very well in. It is also one that you have probably worked on earlier in your school career.

What you will be assessed on

We have already seen that all your portfolio work is assessed for its **content**, **style** and **technical accuracy**. In your reflective writing the markers also want to see that you can express and explore your **feelings**, **experiences** and **reactions** with **insight** and **sensitivity**. This means that they expect you to show yourself to be mature, wise and thoughtful.

Active learning

Divide the class into two halves, and then divide each half into small groups of three people. Work in these groups for 5 minutes.

All the groups in one half of the class should list all the reasons why they think people do well at personal reflective writing. All the groups in the other half of the class should list the particular features that we look for in a piece of personal reflective writing.

Each group should share their answers with the rest of the class.

Genuine reflection

Remember the markers want to see that you can express and explore your feelings, experiences and reactions with insight and sensitivity. You need to come across as mature, wise and thoughtful.

It might help if you think of the piece of writing like this:

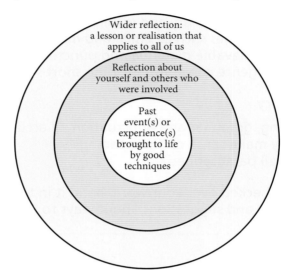

The best way to show you an example of what we mean by this is to look at a piece written by a student.

Active learning

Read this piece called *Blood, Scars and Tears.* As you do so, pay close attention to the ideas in the section that starts, 'The scars on my arms and legs aren't completely gone, …' and ends '… would be a lot worse.' where the writer questions our attitude to self-harm and other emotional difficulties.

Blood, Scars and Tears

I can't remember why it started. All I remember is having my dad complain that I wasn't working hard enough for my exams and my dance teacher complaining that we weren't putting enough effort into our show pieces. That's when I snapped.

I still don't know why I had a razor in my room. I think I must have recently bought them and not put them away yet. I remember walking into my room, full of anger and the thought that I wasn't good enough. Then the glint caught my eye. Before I knew it, I had picked up the blade and run it across my arm.

I barely felt any pain. In fact, I felt relief. As I watched the scarlet blood trickle down, I felt as though all the anger and self-loathing was flowing out of me too. It was only after, when I finally felt the pain, that I realised how stupid I was to have done that. I promised myself that I would never do anything that ridiculous again. I didn't count on the fact it would become an addiction.

You don't realise the impact of an addiction on a life until it affects yours. Every time I got angry or upset, all I could think about was razor blades and blood. I wish I had found a different method of coping like the ones I use now: singing loudly and badly to my favourite songs; doing some form of exercise. That would have saved me a lot of problems.

The scars on my arms became red and raised after only a day. They hurt every time I moved my arm and were extremely obvious. I began covering them up with stark white bandages and long sleeved tops.

I only got away with this for a short time though.

It was the day of my dance show. As our outfit consisted of a tank top and shorts, I needed to find some way of covering the scars. I thought that fake tan might work. I was standing in a vest top, with my arms out like a scarecrow, letting them dry, when my mum walked in to ask me what card I wanted her to buy my dad for Father's Day. I didn't notice her looking.

'What's on your arm?' she asked, pointing to it.

I quickly hid it behind my back and came up with a lie. 'Erm, I scratched myself.'

'Over and over again?' she replied, the disbelief evident on her face. She moved closer. 'Show me your arm.'

'No.' I replied, hiding my arm more fully behind my back.

'Show me your arm!' she commanded this time, moving even closer.

She looked so angry, upset and scared, that I couldn't hide it any more. I held out my arm. She looked at it, before asking me one question: 'Why?'

I hesitated. Did I really want to tell her that it was her and my dad's fault? So I lied again. I told her one of my friends was being mean to me. I wasn't lying too much about the friend. She had been mocking me slightly, but had never driven me to cutting myself. After a long hug, and a promise to never cut myself again, my mum left.

While my mum had looked and acted calmly, thinking about it now makes me realise how scared and shocked she must have been. On the other hand I know I must have looked and felt extremely nervous, but realise now that I shouldn't have been. I know now that she would support me, and not think I was insane or send me away to a psychiatric hospital.

The scars on my arm and legs aren't completely gone, but no one has noticed. This shows how unobservant we all are. If one of your close friends started wearing a lot of long-sleeved tops, and refusing to roll up the sleeves, would you think something was wrong? Probably not. Even if you did, would you say anything?

We are just too scared or nervous to talk about 'taboo' subjects, such as self-harm, suicide, depression and eating disorders. Even if we notice signs of these things, we rarely speak out. We fear for the negative impact it will have on us, rather than the possible positive impact it will have on the other person.

I'm just as bad. About a year ago, my friend Niamh and I were washing dishes together in Hospitality. As she pushed her sleeve up to avoid it becoming wet, I noticed red scars lying horizontally across her wrist. Yet I didn't say anything, I was too scared too.

Everyone needs a close friend or friends to go to in their time of need. I do believe that without my friends' support, even though they didn't know exactly what was happening, my situation right now would be a lot worse.

Quitting an addiction is one of the hardest things to do. It left me frustrated, upset and more often than not, crying into my pillow. But, apart from a few relapses, it worked. While I won't consider myself free from self-harm until I am clean for a year, I am on my way there. Now instead of looking to pain for an answer, I look to joy and fun, in the form of singing, reading or acting. I also found hope in the Butterfly Project. The project encourages self-harmers to draw a butterfly on their wrists, and letting it fade without being cut or scrubbed off, so that it has lived a long happy life. If you cut however, you have killed the butterfly.

I think of my journey like a mountaineer's. It takes a lot of courage to start, the journey is hard and if you slip you can tumble down; but, with the right support system, you can make it to the summit, your goal.

We will return to this piece, and the idea of wide and genuine reflection, as we work through this chapter. For the moment, just keep in mind that this is the kind of piece you are aiming to write.

Choosing what to write about

It should not be too hard for you to choose a topic. After all you know yourself better than anyone else does. You are unique, interesting and well worth writing about.

And you have to choose your own topic. Not only is your teacher not allowed to give you an exact subject to write about, in this case your teacher just cannot. Only you have lived your life and you are the only person in the world who has had your particular set of experiences. You are the only person in history who ever had the exact set of family and friends that you have. Your brain is the only one in the entire universe to hold your set of memories, thoughts and feelings.

Stop and think. Is there an experience you have had that matters to you very much, one that you would like to write about in your personal reflective essay? Remember that you must be able to get that wider reflection out of it, the kind that applies to us all. If you can think of such an experience, make a note of it now. If not, read the next section and follow the prompts.

Narrowing down your ideas
If you do not already have a subject in mind, then it may help you to think very quickly about a lot of different experiences you may have had, and see if any of them are suitable for a longer piece.

Active learning

Take the question 'What is the … thing that has ever happened to you?' and insert the seven words below in turn. Can you write one paragraph for each option?

1 worst

2 hardest

3 happiest

4 saddest

5 most frightening

6 strangest

7 most confusing

Active learning

Can you write just one paragraph for each of these eleven options below?

Which event or time in your life …

1   … has most shaped you?

2   … made you grow up or mature?

3   … most changed your family?

4   … was the biggest challenge for you?

5   … was when you experienced great loss?

6   … was when you experienced great success?

7   … was when you experienced failure?

8   … was when you had to take responsibility?

9   … made you feel most isolated?

10   … showed you the best of people/someone?

11   … showed you the worst of people/someone?

Active learning

Now you are going to think about the eight ways below that a person could make an impact on your life. Again, can you write just one paragraph for each option below.

Which person …

1 … has most influenced you?

2 … has most helped you?

3 … has most hurt you?

4 … do you miss most?

5 … have you been in most conflict with?

6 … have you had the most complicated relationship with?

7 … have you had a very changeable relationship with?

8 … are you most glad to be rid of?

You should now have as many as 26 short paragraphs in front of you. Read them over. Which one could you write about in depth in your personal reflective essay? Remember, you need an idea that will lead you on into the wider kind of reflection we already saw in *Blood, Scars and Tears*.

Although you will not be writing your essay for a while, it is a good idea to choose your topic now, so that as you work through the rest of this chapter you are doing it with your subject in mind.

If you still do not have any ideas, ask your teacher if the school still keeps copies of the writing papers from the old Standard Grade exam. Get hold of a selection and pick out a personal writing stimulus that appeals to you. If you are still really stumped, go home and look through some photographs to see if that sparks anything off.

To give you time to think about your overall idea, we are going to concentrate now on some aspects of style.

Good writing techniques

Thoughts and feelings

Your personal reflective writing will really come to life when you include your thoughts and feelings. No one else knows these. Only you can tell the reader about them.

To show you what I mean, let us look at an example from a book called *Toast*. The writer, Nigel Slater, was at school in the early 1970s. Obsessed with food, he has finally managed to get into the Home Economics class, an unusual place for a boy to at that time. His home life is difficult – his mother died when he was nine, and he does not get on with his stepmother Joan, as he feels she dislikes him.

'It isn't just about making scones for tea,' said Miss Adams, straight-backed, cold and rather old for her years, as she introduced the cookery syllabus to the Wednesday class. Beverly Brown, kind, round and pumpkin-faced, deflated instantly like a burst balloon. The lovely Dee Hanratty whispered 'Good' behind her hand, 'I hate sultanas.' I suddenly got nervous, wondering just how difficult my first cookery lessons were going to be. Did Miss Adams mean we were going to be boning whole lambs and making soufflés then? 'We will be doing everything from cooking rice to costing entire meals,' she warned, her voice getting higher with every word. The word rice put the fear of God into me. I'd never even eaten the stuff, let alone cooked it.

The first lesson, a week later, couldn't have been easier. My Victoria sandwich rose like a dream and had, according to Miss Adams, a perfect 'crumb' and a fine flavour. Even Beverly, who was obviously born both to bake and eat the results, was impressed. I lowered my sugar-topped success into a Peak Frean's biscuit tin and squeezed it into my duffel bag for the journey home.

I couldn't wait to show my father, who for all his disinterest couldn't fail to congratulate me. He was late as people always are on occasions like this. I kept looking at the clock, desperate for him to come home. To see and smell my cake. To eat it. The cake had been sitting on the kitchen table, Joan sitting next to it smoking Embassy after Embassy, occasionally glancing in the direction of my cake.

'Look at that!' said my father, obviously as proud as punch despite everything. 'Isn't that a beauty?'

'Hmm,' said Joan abruptly, swishing her head to the left and blowing out a last cloud of smoke. She then tightened her lips into a straight line and stubbed out her cigarette in the Royal Worcester ashtray like she was trying to squash a cockroach.

Active learning

The different characters in this extract show a mixture of emotions, some positive, some negative. Copy and complete the following table to help you explore these emotions. You should be able to find a wide range.

Emotion	Felt by	Evidence
disappointment	Beverly Brown	'deflated instantly like a burst balloon'

Interestingly, people often write extremely well about hard experiences. If we go through sad, difficult or tragic events we are strongly aware of how we feel at the time. Sad events affect and shape us. We have to keep working with and processing the memories, thoughts and feelings that go with these events.

Here is another extract from *Toast*. This one is from earlier in the book. Nigel Slater is younger, only nine, and his mother is still alive, but much more ill than he can understand at the time. He is out for a walk with his parents.

I am dawdling twenty feet behind them, catching the odd word here and there. 'Not in hospital, at home…' 'Please, please let me be at home…' '…be able to cope…', 'If only he was tougher…'

My father bends his head. 'If the worst comes to the worst…', '…taken into care, it's not like it used to be.'

I guess my mother is pregnant, that she doesn't want to have the baby in hospital and that for some reason it may have to go into care. I rather fancy the idea of a little brother or perhaps a sister.

We walk on, my face getting so cold and numb I can barely feel my tongue. We keep walking, and now both of them have their heads bent down against the stinging rain. My father puts his arm around my mother. He has never done this before. Perhaps she's cold. I think they are crying. Not once do they look back at me.

Active learning

Go back to the piece of reflective writing by the student on page 132. Pick out that writer's thoughts and feelings.

Details and description

Because your memories are important to you, when you bring them to mind they will be full of minute details that you noticed at the time. Many of these details might not be very important in themselves, but they are important in your writing because they bring that memory to life.

To let you see what I mean, here is another extract from *Toast* in which Slater describes eating a bowl of ice cream.

> The meal cannot move on quick enough. I sit there, urging everyone to eat up so that we can get to the ice cream. Why would anyone take their time over a ham salad when there is ice cream to follow? There's the wafer, of course, a thick, smooth fan if we're lucky, two thin regular wafers if not. I eat them not because they taste good – they are about as flavoursome as a postcard – but because of the way they stick to your bottom lip.
>
>
>
> There is a moment, shortly after the waitress puts down the battered silver coupe of ice cream, when life is pretty much perfect. I am not sure it is possible to be happier than I am at this moment. I eat all three flavours separately, trying not to let them merge on the spoon. The vanilla and chocolate are OK together, but the strawberry and chocolate don't marry well. As the cold, milky balls of ice cream disappear I scrape up every last drop, the edge of the spoon tinkling on the dented silver dish. I try not to scrape too loudly. When every last pool of melted ice has gone I use my finger to catch the drips of vanilla ice and the pearls of condensation that have run down the outside of the dish. The cold ice cream in the hot sun is too much for my mother and she turns discreetly away to use her inhaler.

This short passage is packed with detail. Slater manages to use nearly all of his senses to bring the description to life.

Active learning

First **list** your five senses. Then **reread** the Nigel Slater passage above. Next, **note down** the details that fit each sense. Which sense has the writer not used in this extract?

It is easy to use your sense of sight as you describe what you remember in detail, but Slater's example is a good reminder to bring in as many of our other senses as is appropriate.

Active learning

Go back to the piece called *Blood, Scars and Tears*. Pick out the details that bring it to life.

Using dialogue

Something else you can do to bring this genre of writing to life is to put speech into it. Just as it makes stories vivid, dialogue does the same for personal reflective writing. Do not worry if you cannot remember the exact words you and other people said, you can make up something that seems close enough.

The following extract comes from a book called *The Life and Times of the Thunderbolt Kid* in which the travel writer Bill Bryson describes his childhood in 1950s America. Having often heard that children who visit the Tea Room at Younkers department store get to choose a treat, he is very excited to be taken there at last.

I cared nothing for the food of course. I was waiting only for the moment when I was invited to step up to the toy box to make a selection.

When that moment came, it took me for ever to decide. Every little package looked so perfect and white, so ready to be enjoyed. Eventually I chose an item of middling size and weight, which I dared to shake lightly. Something inside rattled and sounded as if it might be die cast. I took it to my seat and carefully unwrapped it. It was a miniature doll – an Indian baby in a papoose, beautifully made but patently for a girl.

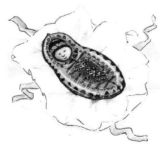

I returned with it and its disturbed packaging to the fellow who was in charge of the toy box. 'I seem to have got a doll,' I said, with something approaching an ironic chuckle.

He looked at it carefully. 'That's surely a shame because you only git one try at the gift box.'

> 'Yes, but it's a doll,' I said. 'For a girl.'
>
> 'Then you'll just have to git yourself a little girl friend to give it to, won'tcha?' he answered, and gave me a toothy grin and an unfortunate wink.

Active learning

Just to show why the version with dialogue is better, try to rewrite this piece so that we get all the same information, but without either of the characters speaking.

Now think about the piece that you are planning to write. Where could you use speech to bring it to life?

Using storytelling techniques

Earlier in this chapter, when you were preparing to write your piece of prose fiction, we looked at the technique of showing, not telling. This is just one of many storytelling techniques (and the dialogue that you just worked on above is another) that will help make your personal reflective writing better.

Active learning

First, go round the class and give everybody a letter A or B. All letter-A students should reread the piece of writing called *Blood, Scars and Tears* on page 132. All letter-B students should reread the three extracts by Nigel Slater and the one by Bill Bryson above.

As you reread your piece(s), look for and note down evidence of the writer using any of the following techniques:

- dialogue
- imagery
- flashback
- minor sentence
- repetition
- showing not telling
- starting at a moment of action
- short sentence or paragraph for impact
- jump cut to a different scene or action
- use of incident or anecdote.

Now think of one technique you think your writer could have used but did not. When could he/she have used that technique? How would this have improved the piece of writing?

Now find someone with the other letter, who has read the other piece(s) – not someone who sits near you in class. Share what you found with each other.

Being personally reflective

It is significant that this task is called personal **reflective** writing. To be able to pass, you need to write **reflectively**. This is something that only mature and insightful writers are able to do. You should be trying to reflect in a personal sense, but also more widely.

Reflecting in a personal sense means two things.

First, it means examining yourself. If you stand in front of a mirror you can examine yourself pretty thoroughly by looking at your reflection. Every spot and blemish will be visible, but you will also be able to see all your good features and everything that you like about yourself.

If you apply this idea to your writing it means that you might question and criticise yourself. On the other hand, you might realise that you handled the situation well. You may realise that certain experiences have shaped you and made you into the person you are, just as growing up changes the way your face looks in the mirror.

The second meaning of reflection is looking back. Think of the rear view mirror in a car. The driver can keep his/her eyes on the road ahead, while using the mirror to see what is happening behind.

Often events in our lives make much more sense once they are over and we are older and wiser. Perhaps when something happened to you it was a really terrible experience, but now you realise that you benefited from it in some way. Events may be confusing when they happen, but when you look back on them they may make more sense.

As well as reflecting on yourself you can reflect on others. You may also be aware of how events and experiences have affected other people as well as you. It may be that you disagreed with someone at the time, but you now realise he/she did the right thing. On the other hand, when we are young we sometimes accept the things adults do without question, but as we grow up we are not so sure about their motives.

Below is a list of reflective phrases. Any of these phrases can be used to begin a reflective sentence or a reflective paragraph.

Looking back …	On reflection …	With hindsight …
In retrospect …	Nowadays I feel/ think/believe …	If I could do this again …
If this happened now …	I learned …	I realise …
I understand …	I should have …	I could have …
I wish I had …	Because of this I am …	Since this happened I …
When I think back on this …	Thinking about it now I feel …	
At the time I … but now I …	If I could change things …	
It was a … thing to do because …		
I wish this had never happened because …		
Now that I have been through this …		
I grew through this experience because …		
This made me think about …	This experience shaped me by …	
I am glad this happened because …	That is when I realised …	

Although it says above that these phrases will help you to start reflective sentences and paragraphs, your writing will be more subtle, and therefore better, if you do not use them at the very start, so that you are not being too blatant.

> **Despite the difficulties we all faced during that time, I grew through this experience because…**

is better than:

> **I grew through this experience because, despite the difficulties.**

and

> **I was totally unwilling to admit it at the time, but on reflection I can see how selfish I was being**

is better than:

> **On reflection, I can see how …**

Active learning

Go back to the topic you have chosen to write about. Spend some time making notes on how you could use this experience for personal reflection. What lessons have your experiences taught you about yourself and those around you? How have these experiences shaped and changed you?

Being more widely reflective

Bringing personal reflection into your writing is important, but the best National 5 students will be able to take their reflection wider still. If you can do this, you will be showing that experiences have taught you something about life, about society, or about people in general.

Look at this extract from the piece you saw earlier. Most of the writer's wider reflection comes near the end of her writing.

The scars on my arm and legs aren't completely gone, but no one has noticed. This shows how unobservant we all are. If one of your close friends started wearing a lot of long-sleeved tops, and refusing to roll up the sleeves, would you think something was wrong? Probably not. Even if you did, would you say anything?

We are just too scared or nervous to talk about 'taboo' subjects, such as self-harm, suicide, depression and eating disorders. Even if we notice signs of these things, we rarely speak out. We fear for the negative impact it will have on us, rather than the possible positive impact it will have on the other person.

I'm just as bad. About a year ago, my friend Niamh and I were washing dishes together in Hospitality. As she pushed her sleeve up to avoid it becoming wet, I noticed red scars lying horizontally across her wrist. Yet I didn't say anything, I was too scared too.

Everyone needs a close friend or friends to go to in their time of need. I do believe that without my friends' support, even though they didn't know exactly what was happening, my situation right now would be a lot worse.

The writer considers how uncomfortable we are about certain topics, and challenges our values and actions.

Active learning

In your own words, sum up this writer's wider reflection. What did the writer learn?

Active learning

Here's an extract from Caitlin Moran's *How To Be a Woman*. Like Nigel Slater, Moran writes in the present tense while looking back on her past.

As you read, look for and note down any times when Moran:

- is being personally reflective and examining herself or those around her
- reflects in a way that lets her take a wider look at human nature and behaviour.

I am 16 and 16 stone. All I do is sit around eating bread and cheese, and reading. I'm fat. We're all fat. The entire family is obese.

The idea of suggesting we don't have to be fat – that things could change – is the most distant and alien prospect of all. We're fat now and we'll be fat forever and we must never, ever, mention it, and that's the end of it. It's like Harry Potter's Sorting Hat. We were pulled from the hat marked 'Fat' and that is what we must now remain.

But why did I get fat? Why was I eating until I hurt, and regarding my own body as something distant and unsympathetic?

Because people overeat for exactly the same reason that they drink, smoke, or take drugs. I must be clear that I am not talking about the kind of overeating that's just plain, cheerful greed. No, I'm talking about those for whom the whole idea of food is not one of pleasure, but one of compulsion. For whom thoughts of food, and the idea of food, are the constant, dreary, background static to normal thought. Those who think about lunch as they are eating breakfast, and pudding as they are eating crisps, who walk into the kitchen in a state bordering on panic and breathlessly eat slice after slice of bread and butter, until the panic can be drowned in an almost meditative routine of spooning and swallowing, spooning and swallowing.

In this trance-like state, you can find a welcome, temporary relief from thinking for ten, twenty minutes at a time until, finally, a new set of sensations – physical discomfort and immense regret make you stop. Overeating, or comfort eating, is the cheap, meek option for self-satisfaction and self-obliteration.

Active learning

Now go back to the topic you have chosen to write about. Spend some time making notes on how you could use this experience for wider reflection. What lessons have your experiences taught you about life, about society, or about people in general?

A real example

Below is another piece of personal reflective writing produced by a student. First of all just read through the piece of writing. You may wish to do this aloud around the class, or you might want to read it on your own.

Families are meant to be together.

They should support each other, and sustain one another, when life takes hold. The loss of a grandparent? The prime example of a moment during which family support is vital. The loss of a ball over the next-door neighbour's hedge? The ideal family will replace the ball, and the outdoor fun continues. However, I come from a different family, a broken family.

It began when I was at the innocent age of six.

'Come in, take a seat.' My mother's voice ushered me into the living room and, nervously, I sat on the nearest chair. There, staring back at me, were the two most familiar faces in the world – Mum and Dad. Yet on that day, as I vividly remember, there was an emptiness in their expression, a fading of emotion that terrified me.

The room, usually so vibrant, had dulled to a sombre grey. The TV was switched off, and the grass and branches of the trees outside were eerily still, entirely devoid of motion. There was the same intense silence that holds a television audience as they wait in anticipation for the results of the final, when the host is holding on to the news for what seems like an eternity, purely for atmosphere's sake. When I look back, I can't help but hear dreary music playing endlessly in my mind.

What truly scared me though was my parents' faces, right before they delivered their news. My dad, who was the sort of man who could entertain a room by opening a packet of crisps, was sullen. It was petrifying.

'Right …' Mum laid her hand on my knee. 'You're a bit young, but you're not a daft kid, right? Your dad and I have been having some problems.' I nodded my head. I might have been just six, but even the goldfish knew that Mum and Dad's nightly standoffs were a problem. In fact, I was growing up thinking that shouting was a good way to get the police round if you couldn't find your phone.

'Well …' Mum gazed reflectively at the far wall for quite some time, then dabbed her eyes with a tissue before facing me. She never took her eyes off me for the rest of the time we spent in the room that day.

'Your dad and I are getting a divorce.'

A waterfall of emotion came cascading over me. I sat there on the armcahir feeling perplexed, thrown, baffled, alarmed and afraid. An explosion of questions hurtled through my mind: Who was I going to be staying with? Did this mean I was getting a new set of parents? Why couldn't they just work it out? Would I start getting two sets of Christmas presents?

The more I was left to digest the situation, the more I hated the future. I couldn't help it. I liked things how they were: I liked my room, all my trucks and trains and the army of garden slugs I'd imprisoned in jars of leaves; I liked my school and my friends and the Crayola crayons I used to draw pictures in my school jotters.

Most of all, I liked my family. Mummy and Daddy did argue a lot, but they'd work it out. They'd grow old together, and they'd have old people stuff like tattered cookbooks and oil paintings and grey hair, and they'd have a house in the country, and a garden full of potatoes, and I'd bring my own kids over for Sunday lunch. Everything would be just bliss.

Now I didn't know what the future held. My security had been shattered. That was what I hated.

But, as it turns out, I can't claim the divorce affected me negatively. In fact, I emerged from it a steadier, deeper person. The same, sadly, cannot be said about countless other children of divorce. This, I believe, can be attributed to two major deciding factors.

The first is the individual's capacity to defend him or herself against hardship. One infant, during a violent storm, will collapse and cry; another, watching the same storm, will gaze up at the sky with excitement and awe. It's something we are born with, it's unchangeable, and it differs for every human being. Everyone deals with stress, fear, pain and difficulty in their own unique way.

The second factor is the uncountable tweaks to a person's course in life that follow from something as momentous as a divorce, and whether these have a positive or a negative effect. One divorce might see the mother and father agree to split custody fifty-fifty, remain on good terms, and each find someone new, someone liked by the child. In this case, that child will not be so badly affected. By the same token, another divorce might see the dad disappear never to be seen again, and the mother fall into lonely despair. Here, the child inevitably suffers. These examples are extreme, and in practice the situation is a million times more complex, but I hope I have made my point clear. Divorce is a game of Russian roulette that children are forced to play. I was just lucky.

Every now and again I look back on that day and startle myself with how much it decided who I am as a person. I could write a 4000-word essay on the reasons behind my parents' divorce, but that is a door I prefer to keep locked. I can say, however, that I have no reason now to fear the future. I am comfortable with who I turned out to be, someone who believes that what does not kill you can only make you stronger. Embracing that one difficult situation has prepared me to face all possible others. Bring them on.

Active learning

Now that you have read this personal reflective essay once, you are going to analyse it in more detail. The easiest way to do this is to have a photocopy of it in front of you. You will also need pens and pencils. If you have a variety of colours, that is even better. You may wish to work with a partner.

You will need to use the following symbols:

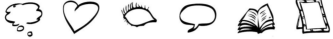

1 Every time you find the writer sharing thoughts, draw a think cloud beside this in the margin.

2 Every time you find the writer sharing feelings, draw a heart beside this in the margin.

3 Every time you find the writer using detail or description, draw an eye beside this in the margin.

4 Every time you find the writer using dialogue, draw a speech bubble beside this in the margin.

5 Every time you find the writer using a storytelling technique, draw an open book beside this in the margin. Write the name of the technique on the pages of the book.

6 Every time you find the writer being reflective, draw a mirror in the margin. If you think the writer is reflecting more widely, put a capital W on the centre of the mirror.

7 Write a couple of sentences to explain what made it a good piece of writing.

8 Suggest two things the writer could have done that would have made the work even better.

Planning your personal reflective piece

You have had a chance now to look at two long pieces of personal reflective writing produced by students, and at a number of shorter extracts from published books. Reading and examining all these pieces has shown you that you need to use all these genre features:

thoughts	feelings	detail and description
dialogue	storytelling techniques as appropriate	
personal and immediate reflection	wider reflection	

You will need a photocopy of the blank plan on the following page. You should have lots of ideas by now, so ask your teacher if you can a have a copy in A3 size.

Use the prompts and shapes to help you plan your piece of personal reflective writing. The shapes are those you used to annotate the piece about divorce, but they are bigger this time so that you can write your ideas on them.

What event or experience are you going to write about?

Which storytelling techniques will you use, and at which points in your writing?

PERSONAL REFLECTION

WIDER REFLECTION

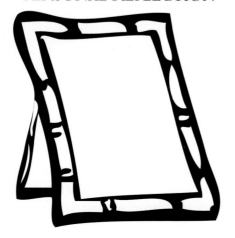

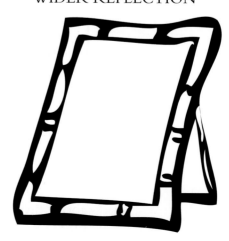

Active learning

Using your plan to help you, explain your ideas to another student. Your teacher may also want to see and discuss your plan. Remember that he/she also has to keep a copy of that plan in case the SQA asks to see it at any point.

Active learning

It is now time to write your piece.

When you have written it, read your work over before you hand it in to your teacher. Think about the areas you will be assessed on and ask yourself the following questions:

Content

- Have I included an experience, personal reflection and wider reflection?
- Did I use storytelling techniques to bring my writing to life?
- Have I shown myself to be mature, wise and thoughtful?
- Have I remembered to include some wider refection, considering the lesson or message for us all?

Style

- Have I followed the conventions and techniques of the reflective genre?
- Have I used good vocabulary and different sorts of sentences?

Technical accuracy

- Are my spelling, grammar and punctuation all accurate?
- Is my work well paragraphed?
- Does my essay make sense on first reading?

Your teacher will read your work and add comments so that you can discuss the piece and improve it.

What we have done so far

So far in this chapter we have found out about the rules and guidelines for National 5 Writing. We found out about the genre that the SQA calls **creative writing**. This covers four sorts of writing:

- a personal reflective essay
- a piece of prose: story or novel extract
- a poem or set of linked poems
- a drama script.

We learned in detail about the first two.

Discursive writing

Now it is time to go on to the other major genre, which the SQA calls **discursive writing**. Remember that in your Portfolio, you need one piece from the creative genre, and one from the discursive.

For this second Portfolio piece you can produce any one of the following types of writing to fulfil the requirements for this genre:

- a persuasive essay
- an argumentative essay
- a report
- a piece of transactional writing.

We are going to work on the first two of these in detail.

In **argumentative** writing you explore an issue or question by looking at both sides of the subject, and you will usually come to a conclusion at the end, while still allowing the reader to decide for him/herself.

In **persuasive** writing you start with a clear belief or strongly held point of view. In this kind of piece, you will try to use evidence and language to make the reader agree with you.

What you will be assessed on

We have already seen that all your Portfolio work is assessed for its **content**, **style** and **technical accuracy**. Your discursive writing work will also be assessed to see how well you can deploy your ideas and your chosen techniques. These ideas should have some **depth** and **complexity**, and in persuasive writing should have some **force**. In two-sided argumentative writing the markers should be able to see that you are being **objective**, and keeping both sides in balance. They should be able to see a clear **line of thought** or point of view.

You cannot really decide whether your piece will be argumentative or persuasive until you have chosen a subject, so let us deal with that issue first.

Subjects to avoid

Some topics come up again and again. Your teacher, and the SQA marker, have probably read all the arguments about **euthanasia**, **abortion** and **capital punishment** many times before, and will quickly notice if you miss out anything they expect to find, or if there is any important aspect of the argument which you do not explore carefully enough. Your teacher, and the marker, are probably also quite fed up of essays about **size zero models**, **Scottish independence**, **animal testing** and **why TV talent competitions are rubbish**.

Unless you are truly an expert, or really feel that you have something striking and original to say, steer clear of writing about these subjects. If you really do want to tackle one of these issues however, it is best to do it in a two-sided, argumentative way. Otherwise you will sound like an extremist.

Choosing a topic

Whether your writing ends up being argumentative or persuasive, you need to pick a topic about which people have strong opinions. It should also be a topic in which you have a genuine interest. You will only be able to give your essay depth, complexity and force if you care about the ideas in it.

So how do you choose a subject? You could:

- Ask yourself which subjects you are interested in or care about – these will often be tied in to the things you choose to spend your time on.
- Visit your school library – some publishers produce special series of books where each book contains articles on one controversial subject. Without actually reading the books at this stage, just finding out which subjects they deal with might help you think of a topic.
- Watch television news programmes, read newspapers and use news websites.
- Ask your teacher which topics his or her students have written successfully about in the past.

You should not go any further, or spend any time on research, until you know that your teacher thinks your topic is a good one. Once you have chosen a topic, write it down and give a note of it to your teacher.

If you know already which approach you want to take – two-sided argumentative or one-sided persuasive – write this down along with your subject. If you are not sure which approach to take yet, do not worry. It will become much clearer after you have done your detailed research.

As that research will take you quite some time, you need to start now.

Researching

Whether your piece of writing is one-sided or two-sided, and no matter how much you think you already know about the subject, you need to do some research. Everything you eventually write will be based on this and it is time well spent.

Your first port of call will probably be the internet. You could visit the websites of charities and pressure groups that have an interest in your topic. If, for example, you are writing about environmental issues you could visit the sites of organisations such as Friends of the Earth or Greenpeace. If your essay is about violence in films, you will probably be looking up the website of the British Board of Film Classification to see why it gives certain films certain age ratings.

Many newspapers have excellent websites. These can be very useful if your topic has been in the headlines recently, and often give real–life examples you can use. Two very good sites are **www.guardian.co.uk** and **www.bbc.co.uk/news**, both of which make no charge and are easy to search.

You need to take far greater care with Wikipedia because it is written by the people who use it. This means that although the contributors are genuinely interested in their subjects, some of what they write can be quite biased. You should not use Wikipedia as your only source, and you should check anything you find there against other sources to make sure it is accurate.

If you do not know which sites you want to use you will need to begin by using a search engine such as Google. Try to use only one or two keywords for your search. The computer does not know what you are thinking, or why you are looking these words up, so be as precise as you can about what you want.

If you are using a phrase, put double quotation marks round it. Let us suppose you are writing an argumentative essay on whether there should be a minimum price for alcohol. Looking for "alcohol pricing" will find web pages using that complete phrase. This might be just what you want to know:

> Strategic use of **alcohol pricing** can discourage underage drinking. As teenage drinkers tend to have little money, they purchase the cheapest drinks. Raising the price per unit of alcohol would therefore put it beyond the reach of this group.

If you type the same two words without quotation marks you will get all the pages that have the word *alcohol* and the word *pricing* anywhere on the same page. This is not as helpful:

> Working nightshifts in the supermarket was so boring that I took to consuming vast amounts of **alcohol** as I stood there with my sticker gun, **pricing** the unwanted items that ended up on the bargain shelf.

This is a good time to go back to your school or local library and ask the staff for advice about the most suitable sources of information on your topic. Your library will also have encyclopedias. These can be very good on established factual information, but as huge books like this take many years to write and put together, they are not great sources for material on current controversial topics. For that, you may be better going back to the internet, particularly news sites.

Depending on your topic, you might also speak to people about their own experiences. If you are writing about the rights and wrongs of how pigs are treated on British farms and you know a farmer, speak to him. If you are arguing that young people nowadays are put under far too much pressure to go to university, ask a teacher what he/she thinks.

By the way, and just in case you think you will not have to, or in case you think your topic does not call for it, *everyone* needs to do research. Even the most personal persuasive essay will only persuade and convince the reader if what you write is supported by facts, statistics, experiences and anecdotes.

Using your own words

There was one very important note of advice in the guidelines at the start of this chapter: you **absolutely cannot**, **ever**, copy and paste from a website or from anywhere else.

You are allowed to get ideas and information from sources, but you cannot use someone else's words and pass them off as your own. This is called **plagiarism** and if the examiners think that you have cheated in this way the consequences can be serious. You could fail English. You could also have all your other exam papers and coursework pulled out and re-marked as the examiners look for further rule-breaking.

To help you avoid accidentally falling into plagiarism, here is a useful piece of advice to follow during the research stage:

 Warning

It is fine to read, underline or highlight someone else's words, but **WHENEVER YOU MAKE A NOTE, DO THAT IN YOUR OWN WORDS.** It does not matter if you type the words, or hand write them — **WHENEVER YOU PUT WORDS ON A PAGE, THEY SHOULD BE YOUR OWN.**

I hope all those bold and shouty capitals gets the point across. The advice is only useful, of course, if you know how to put something into your own words. This skill is called **paraphrasing**. It is worth practising because you also need to be able to do this as you answer the question paper for Reading for Understanding, Analysis and Evaluation. In all your reading and writing, the best way to prove that you really grasp something is to be able to explain it yourself in a different way.

Look at this sentence found by a student who decided to research recycling:

> **The overwhelming consensus among local authorities is that reducing the frequency of domestic waste collections encourages an increase in the use of recycling facilities.**

The student needed to put this in his own words, which he did like this:

> **When councils collect rubbish less often from outside people's houses, these people recycle more. Almost all councils agree that this is the case.**

This student used a lot of different tactics as he paraphrased.

First, he changed some important words or expressions.

Active learning

You will see a list of expressions from the original sentence. What did he change each one into?

- overwhelming consensus
- local authorities
- domestic waste collections
- increase
- reducing the frequency of
- use of recycling facilities.

Second, he changed the number of sentences from one to two. Third, he put the two ideas in the original sentence the other way round. All of this shows that he has understood and can process the information.

What he did not change was the word *recycling* itself. Because that is his subject, and that is what his whole essay is about, he can keep using that word.

Active learning

Here are five more extracts students found while researching different topics. Remembering the techniques above, paraphrase each extract. The subject of each extract is given for you at the start.

1 [*Video game violence*] A burst of new research has begun to clarify what can and cannot be said about the effects of violent gaming. Playing these games can and does stir hostile urges and mildly aggressive behaviour in the short term. Moreover, youngsters who develop a gaming habit can become slightly more aggressive — as measured by clashes with peers, for instance — at least over a period of a year or two.

2 [*The Oscars*] The only thing wrong with the Academy Awards is they make people hate perfectly decent movies. How many times has it happened in the last five years that you have seen a film and liked it and not given it a second thought until it walks off with seven Academy Awards, at which point you have no option but to resent it for its pretensions to greatness, disown it when it comes up in conversation and frown over its flattening of far worthier competition.

3 [*The Olympic effect*] Britain hosted massively successful Olympic and Paralympic Games in 2012, winning the honour of doing so by promising to inspire a generation of young people to take up sport and adopt generally healthier lifestyles.

4 [*The pros and cons of private schooling*] Those who oppose private education say it widens social divisions, keeping children of different social classes apart and creating a gap that is never subsequently bridged.

5 [*Big businesses paying small taxes*] Despite soaring profits, tax payments by some of the best-known names in business have fallen by more than a fifth in the last decade. In the same period, the amount contributed by smaller businesses has almost trebled. Huge concerns like Amazon and Starbucks have become expert in moving profits around the world, avoiding tax as they do so.

Citing your sources

Another of the authenticity guidelines we saw at the start of the chapter was about being able to show where your information came from. As you research, take a note of all these things. You will need to list them in a **bibliography** at the end of your essay as follows:

- the writer and publication date of newspaper or magazine articles
- the website name and specific page address for any information found on the internet
- the title and publication date of any books referred to.

Two-sided argumentative or one-sided persuasive

If you have not already told your teacher whether your essay will be two-sided argumentative or one-sided persuasive, now is the time to do so. Read over your notes, and consider what approach you are going to take. These prompts should help you decide:

- If you find your topic interesting, but you are genuinely not sure what your stance on it is, or if you think it is a highly complex issue without an easy answer, you should go for the two-sided, argumentative approach.
- If you have developed a genuine opinion on the subject, and if you think you can put it across in a way that makes you sound engaged and committed without seeming to be a raving zealot, go for the persuasive approach.
- If the best writing style for you is to be measured and formal, then you should probably go for argumentative writing.
- If you know that you can write in a lively and witty way, you could try persuasive writing.
- Finally, more weighty subjects suit the argumentative genre better, while odder, less serious or more quirky subjects can benefit from a persuasive approach.

Using your research to support opinions

Once you have collected your information, you should try to find a way to make each fact or idea you have found support an opinion. **Facts** can be proved. They are true and nobody can argue against them. For example:

> **Haggis is made by stuffing the lining of a sheep's stomach with diced sheep's liver, lungs and heart. This is flavoured with onion and held together with a mix of oatmeal and suet.**

Opinions are more personal. They are what people think, and different people can have different opinions about the same thing. For example:

> **Haggis is a disgusting foodstuff. It was invented by starving, desperate peasants and has no place on the plates of a modern, educated nation.**

> **Haggis is delicious, and uniquely Scottish, making it something we should be proud to eat, not only on Burns' Night but throughout the year.**

In **persuasive** writing, organise the facts to support what you believe. In **argumentative** writing, organise them to support the two different sides of the argument.

Here is an example from a student who is writing persuasively about her belief that young people should be able to vote from the age of 16.

FACT/EXAMPLE FROM RESEARCH
Young people are expected to pay tax and National Insurance as soon as they turn 16.

HOW DOES THIS SUPPORT MY OPINION?
The fact that 16-year-olds pay taxes means they should be able to elect the government that spends and uses their hard-earned money.

Active learning

Look through the notes you gathered during your research. Remember, these should be in your own words by now. Organise your material as shown above, picking out the useful facts and working out how each one could be used to support an opinion.

A good writer will be able to 'spin' facts to support their opinion. Two newspapers could have two very different opening sentences at the start of their front-page stories.

Disgraced television presenter Gerald Carpenter will appear in court today charged with inventing quotes and falsifying stories to boost the popularity of his weekly news programme.

Gerald Carpenter, the host of *What a Week!*, goes to court today to clear his name and defend the reputation of his hugely popular show.

Both clippings are reporting the same story, but they have spun the facts to suit their opinion.

Being able to bend facts towards the direction you want to go is especially useful in persuasive writing when you are trying to make your readers agree with you.

Have a look at this example from the journalist Caitlin Moran. She is writing to persuade people not to spend so much money on weddings. Look how she builds a powerful paragraph round one fact, that the average cost of a wedding in the UK at the time she was writing was £21,000:

> The money is the key issue here – because of what it is spent on. Aside from getting together the deposit for a house, the average couple will probably never again spend that amount of money on a single thing in their lives. And what is it that that £21,000 buys? Very little that lasts. There are the overpriced photographs in the insanely expensive album, and then all the presents of course – but spending £21,000 to get £2000's worth of kitchen equipment from John Lewis is poor economics, whichever way you slice it. The dress is never worn again, you never get round to 'dying the shoes red, and wearing them to a party!' no matter how often you convince yourself you might, and as for the rings, I can hardly be the only married woman on her fifth wedding band, after losing various others in swimming pools, down cracks in worktops, and once in a loaf of bread. (It's a long story.)

Active learning

To sharpen your persuasive skills, you are going to write one paragraph on each of the following subjects. Your aim with each paragraph is to come up with the best possible reason you can think of to persuade your classmates to do each of following:

- to stage a pitch invasion at the Scottish Cup Final
- to spend the night in a haunted house
- to all come to school one day in their pyjamas
- to give up drinking anything except tap water
- to spend all their holidays in Scotland.

Planning two-sided, argumentative pieces

In these essays you should show that you understand the arguments on both sides. At the end you can give your opinion, and your readers can decide on theirs.

There are two ways you can structure these essays. We will look quickly first at the simple structure. It would be better though if you used the complex structure, and we will go in to that in more detail.

The simple structure

The simple structure works like this:

Step 1 A one-paragraph introduction to the topic:

> **Although it is illegal for doctors in Britain to assist patients to end their lives, there are many who would love to see this situation changed. These are often the terminally ill, or their friends and families, who seek an end to pain and suffering. Others however, see such a form of death, often called euthanasia, as completely unacceptable, even dangerous.**

Step 2 A link sentence, explaining which side of the argument you will begin with.

> **Those who support euthanasia have many firmly held beliefs.**

Step 3 Now take all of the points on one side of the argument. Each point should be in a separate paragraph, and these points should be backed up with facts, observations or personal experiences. Use **topic sentences** and the **PEE structure**. (You will find out more about these on page 165.) Start with the strongest, most convincing arguments and work your way down to the weaker ones. You should aim to have at least three or four paragraphs on the first side of the argument.

Step 4 Write a link sentence showing that you are about to switch to the other side of the argument.

> **Those on the other side of the argument are just as passionate in their belief that Britain should never legalise euthanasia.**

Step 5 Now do the same on this side of the argument as you did at Step 3 above, working again from the stronger points down to weaker ones.

Step 6 Finally, in your conclusion, briefly sum up what you have written. Now say which side you agree with and why. Show which arguments convinced you, or refer to an experience in your life, or the life of someone you know, that has convinced you that a particular side is right. You may wish to leave the reader with something to think about.

> **It is clear that both sides have strong arguments. Having examined them I feel that if we want to call ourselves a compassionate nation, we must offer a dignified release from pain. Any system that says euthanasia is cruel, but then forces people to endure suffering, is misguided and wrong.**

By the way, we have used the example of an essay on euthanasia deliberately because you should not be writing about it. It was on our short list of overworked topics earlier in the chapter.

The more complex structure

The more complex structure for two-sided pieces makes you look more skilled at handling your material. It works like this:

The introduction and conclusion are the same as they are in a simply structured essay. However, in the main body of the essay, you begin with the strongest argument from one side of the argument. Then, in the next paragraph, you work through a point on the opposite side that contradicts what you have just written about. Each of these paragraphs will use **topic sentences** and the **PEE structure** which will be explained on page 165.

To illustrate this, let us imagine an essay on another of those overworked and therefore banned topics, Scottish independence. Here is a point from the pro-independence side of the argument:

> **Perhaps the strongest argument for an independent Scotland is the example of other small nations. Norway, slightly smaller than Scotland with just over five million inhabitants, enjoys one of the highest standards of living in the world. If they can do it, surely Scotland can too?**

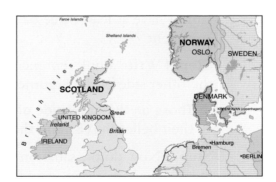

Now here is the answering point from the anti-independence side:

> **However, this assumes that Scotland is in a position to aim for Norwegian levels of success. This is not true. Yes, Scotland has North Sea oil just as Norway has reserves of oil and gas. But Norway decided decades ago to sell these resources, and to use the money to invest in roads, civil engineering projects and a huge state pension fund, all of which have benefited the country. Scotland cannot do this. Our oil reserves are already well-worked. Even if we gained independence, we would not own, or be able to sell, enough fossil fuels to create a Norwegian level of progress.**

Then take the second strongest point from the first side of the argument. Explain it, and then challenge it by making another point from the opposite side to contradict it. Keep going, following this pattern.

You may find that some of your points cannot be paired up in this way. You can deal with them just before you start your conclusion. All the remaining points can be rolled into two short paragraphs, one for the ideas that support one side of the argument, for example:

> **There are other valid reasons why many people think that we should be a sovereign nation …**

and the other for the evidence that concludes the other side of the argument, for example:

> **Those who are against this also have further important points to make …**

If you know that you are going to write an argumentative essay, decide now which of the two structures above would be best for you to use.

Structuring persuasive writing

Organising this kind of piece is similar, but simpler. In persuasive writing you do not have to switch from one part of the argument to the other, because you are always trying to defend your own point of view. The structure works like this:

Step 1 A one-paragraph introduction to the topic. Make clear straight away what you believe about the subject. Use your wit and passion to grab the reader's attention from the start.

> **Our supermarkets are full of cupcakes, the shelves of our corner shops are weighed down with cookery magazines, even our television screens are filling with bake-offs and chef-wars. We have become obsessed with the production of food. However, I firmly believe Britain would be a better place if we gathered up every macaroon, Victoria sponge and whoopee pie and put all that sugar to good use by building a massive bonfire.**

Step 2 Using the points you have planned, set out your argument. Each point should be in a separate paragraph, and these points should be backed up with facts, observations or personal experiences. Use **topic sentences** and the **PEE structure** whenever you can. (You will find out more about these on page 165.) Start with the strongest, most convincing arguments and work your way down to the weaker ones.

> What's most striking about foodie TV programmes is their failure to inspire. They inspire us to eat all right, but not to eat what they allegedly promote. A Masterchef contestant spends an hour (edited into highlights of course) making a fantastically complex, beautiful dish using the finest, seasonal ingredients; we watch from our sofas, grease dribbling down our chins from the bowl of meat slurry we bought in the supermarket, threw in the freezer last week, and dragged from the microwave five minutes ago.

You should aim to write about four paragraphs like this.

Although you are always defending your own position in this kind of writing, your argument will be stronger if you can show that you understood the other side's position and can disprove it.

> Some readers will defend these programmes by saying that they promote social values, and the importance of cooking for and eating with family and friends. Even if this is true, it is nothing but a new form of sexism. Feeding others in the home has always been women's work, and these programmes merely aim to drive women back into a kitchen some wish they had never escaped.

You should aim to include one or two paragraphs like this.

Step 3 You may find that some of your points are not strong enough to be dealt with in their own separate paragraph. If you still feel they are valuable and want to use them, then you can deal with them just before you start your conclusion. All the remaining points can be rolled into one short paragraph:

> As if all of this is not enough, we also have to remember …

Step 4 Finally, in your conclusion, briefly sum up what you have written. End with a strong, clear statement that shows again why you believe you are right. You may also want to challenge the reader to think or respond.

> It's time we put down our copies of BBC *GoodFood* magazine and turned off the *Great British Bake Off*. Eat when you're hungry, eat with someone else if you like them, cook for someone else if you love them, but don't pretend life is food. Food is just for mealtimes, life is for life.

Structuring your paragraphs

As well as structuring and ordering your whole essay, you need to have a clear structure in each paragraph. The best way to do this is to use **topic sentences** and **PEE**. You will have met these before when writing critical essays about the literature you have read, but they apply just as much here.

Topic sentences

A topic sentence is called this for two reasons.

1 It refers to the topic of the essay.
2 It introduces the topic of its paragraph.

The topic sentence is usually the first in the paragraph. Look at the following paragraph from our writer on the Scottish independence. The topic sentence has been underlined. The words that tie that sentence in to the topic of the whole essay are in italic.

> <u>Some wish to see *Scotland become independent* to put right a historical wrong</u>. In 1603, they argue, when Queen Elizabeth the First of England died without an heir, Scotland's King James the Sixth became James the First of Britain. Why, if we Scots took over ruling England, have we ended up ruled by it?

Using PEE

If you are writing an argumentative essay, then within each paragraph of your essay, apart from the introduction and conclusion, you should try to use the **PEE** structure. You may not be able to use this structure quite as often in persuasive writing, but you should still do so whenever you can. It goes like this:

- **P** – make a **POINT** that is relevant to the topic of your essay. This point is the topic sentence at the start of the paragraph.
  One reason why we should kick out the cupcakes is because they are making us fat.

- **E** – give **EVIDENCE** to back up the point you are making. This should be either a fact you found out during your research, something you have noticed, or something you have experienced yourself.

  Not that all our cups of tea should be downed without accompaniment, but we need to apply moderation. One lemon and poppyseed cupcake with cream cheese frosting contains 529 calories. You'd need to eat seven and a half digestive biscuits to consume that much energy – but I don't think you would.

- **E** – **EXPLAIN** this. If you are writing to persuade, show how it adds to your argument. If you are doing a piece of discursive writing, show how the point and evidence contribute to this side of the topic. **All this fancy, artistic baking is simply encouraging us to eat food we don't need, and our waistlines and health are suffering for it.**

Paragraphs that change direction

In the advice about planning persuasive writing we saw that it was a good idea to have some paragraphs in your essay that show you understand the opposition point of view, but that you have an answer for it.

To help you understand, here is the film critic Mark Kermode defending his right to have opinions about mainstream, blockbuster movies.

> Every time I complain that a blockbuster movie is dumb, or insultingly scripted, or crappily acted, I get a torrent of emails complaining that I am applying highbrow criteria that cannot and should not be applied to good old undemanding blockbuster entertainment. Critics are just too clever for their own good, have seen too many movies to know what the average punter wants, and are therefore sorely unqualified to pass judgement on the popcorn fodder that 'real' cinema goers demand from the movies. This is baloney, peddled by people who are only interested in money and don't give a damn about cinema. The problem with movies today is not that 'real' cinema-goers love garbage while critics only like poncy foreign language arthouse fare. The problem is that we've all learned to tolerate a level of overpaid dreadfulness that no one actually likes but everyone meekly accepts because we've all been told that blockbuster movies have to be stupid to survive.

Direction markers

Certain words and phrases signal the direction of the argument in a piece of argumentative writing, or emphasise the writer's point of view in persuasive writing. Most of these words and phrases appear at the start of a paragraph or sentence.

Active learning

You may wish to work with a partner or small group. Look at these four headings:

- Expressions that move the argument forwards
- Expressions that let the argument change direction
- Expressions that allow the writer to sum up
- Expressions that show the writer is sure he is right

Now look at the expressions below. Each one fits best under one of those headings. Get a piece of A4 paper and divide it into four large boxes. Put each heading at the top of a different box. Underneath the heading, list the expressions that fit there. Check any new words with a dictionary as you go.

nonetheless	rather	in contrast	instead
without a doubt	undeniably	surely	definitely
thus	otherwise	moreover	yet
nevertheless	finally	on the contrary	obviously
likewise	conversely	on the other hand	whereas
unquestionably	therefore	however	next
despite	similarly	in spite of	absolutely
at the same time	without question	and alternatively	
in retrospect	without doubt	significantly	in conclusion
first(ly)	accordingly	but	also
in brief	second(ly)	although	in addition
furthermore	as a result	indubitably	consequently
third(ly)	because	equally	on the whole
to sum up	to balance this	what is more	in other words
certainly			

Some other useful words

If you want to refer to another argument so you can knock it down, two useful words are **claim** and **allege**. They hint that you do not believe something the other side says. For example:

> The manager **claims** he passed the player over because of the need to rest him up before Saturday's cup match, and denies any bad feeling between them.

> Her enemies **allege** that she stole many of her ideas from a much less well-known series of novels about a forest full of talking animals. The author **claims** never to have read these books and says that it does not matter who has an idea, only who writes it best.

What is the writer suggesting about the manager and the author mentioned above?

Some words are useful if you cannot prove something for sure. These words are also usual for suggestions and rumours. These words include **reported, rumoured, believed, could, likely, would, reported,** and **may point to**. For example, here is a piece of gossip that may have very few provable facts behind it:

> It is **believed** that troubled TV presenter Warren Way **could** again be struggling with the marriage problems originally **reported** last year. It is **rumoured** that his rows with his former glamour model wife Syria **could have** risen to as many as four a day. It is **likely** that the Wonder Wedding Dating Agency, who pay him £1million a year to be the face of their 'Happy Hearts Make Happy Homes' campaign **would be** very unhappy to have a spokesman whose marriage was on the skids. The TV star's close friends are **reported** to be very concerned. Way's non-appearance on last night's edition of *How Mean Is Your Spouse?* **may point** to continuing problems in his stormy relationship with the curvaceous Syria.

Techniques for persuasive writing

Persuasive writing tends to use certain techniques. Some of the most common are:

- **repetition** of words or phrases
- dramatic-sounding **short sentences**
- including the reader by using **'we' and related words**
- asking **rhetorical questions** – which do not need an answer but make the reader think
- using **'the rule of three'**, i.e. doing something three times over. This might be three examples, three rhetorical questions, three uses of the same word or phrase, and so on.
- using an anecdote or personal experience to justify why the writer holds a certain opinion
- an **appeal to the reader's emotions**, or **emotive language** that stirs up the readers' feelings
- offering the reader a **vision** of success or achievement.

Active learning

Read the following text. It is part of a famous speech given by the American civil rights leader Dr Martin Luther King in 1963, shortly before he was assassinated.

As you read the piece, look for examples of each technique being used.

Go back to Mississippi, go back to Alabama, go back to South Carolina, go back to Georgia, go back to Louisiana, go back to the slums and ghettos of our northern cities, knowing that somehow this situation can and will be changed.

Let us not wallow in the valley of despair. I say to you today, my friends, even though we face the difficulties of today and tomorrow. I still have a dream. It is a dream deeply rooted in the American dream.

I have a dream that one day this nation will rise up and live out the true meaning of its creed: 'We hold these truths to be self-evident that all men are created equal.'

I have a dream that one day, on the red hills of Georgia, the sons of former slaves and the sons of former slave owners will be able to sit down together at the table of brotherhood.

I have a dream that one day even the state of Mississippi, a state sweltering with the heat of injustice, sweltering with the heat of oppression, will be transformed into an oasis of freedom and justice.

I have a dream that my four little children will one day live in a nation where they will not be judged by the colour of their skin but by the content of their character.

I have a dream today.

I have a dream that one day down in Alabama, with its vicious racists, with its governor having his lips dripping with the words of interposition and nullification, one day right down in Alabama, little black boys and black girls will be able to join hands with little white boys and white girls as sisters and brothers.

I have a dream today.

I have a dream that one day every valley shall be exalted, every hill and mountain shall be made low, the rough places will be made plain and the crooked places will be made straight, and the glory of the Lord shall be revealed and all flesh shall see it together.

This is our hope. This is the faith that I go back to the south with. With this faith we will be able to hew out of the mountain of despair a stone of hope. With this faith we will be able to transform the jangling discords of our nation into a beautiful symphony of brotherhood. With this faith we will be able to work together, to pray together, to struggle together, to go to jail together, to stand up for freedom together, knowing that we will be free one day.

Active learning

First, share your answers with the rest of the class. Next, give examples of any other techniques you found King using to make his argument effective.

Active learning

It is time to **plan your piece**. (You may already have done quite a lot of planning after the research phase if you organised your material into what the facts were, and how each fact could be used to support an argument.) Look back at all the material you gathered from your research. Double check that you put everything you found into your own words. Following all the advice this chapter has given you, prepare a paragraph plan for your piece. Remember you have a choice of simpler or more complex structures if you are writing an argumentative essay.

Active learning

It is now time to **write your piece**. Do not forget the bibliography of your sources at the end.

When you have written it, read your work over before you hand it in to your teacher. Think about the areas you will be assessed on, which were explained at the start of this chapter, and ask yourself if you have met all the criteria.

Content

- Have I used one of the suggested structures to help me organise the ideas in my writing?

Style

- Have I followed the conventions and techniques of the discursive genre?
- Have I used good vocabulary and different sorts of sentences?
- Have I used some direction language to shape my writing?
- Have I used some of the key persuasive or argumentative techniques?

Technical accuracy

- Are my spelling, grammar and punctuation all accurate?
- Is my work well paragraphed?
- Does my essay make sense on first reading?

Your teacher will read your work and add comments so that you can discuss the piece and improve it.

CHAPTER 6 The National 5 Reading for Understanding, Analysis and Evaluation Exam

Reading for Understanding, Analysis and Evaluation is a longer name for the skill your teacher probably calls 'close reading'.

You will be tested on this by sitting an exam (sometimes called 'the question paper') in May of your National 5 year.

If you are really serious about passing, you need to expand your experience of language and ideas now.

- Try to read regularly a quality newspaper such as the *Guardian, Scotsman, Herald, Independent* or *The Times*. Do not just read the news stories near the front, but also the feature articles and opinion pieces in the later pages.
- Expand your knowledge of language, and of how people debate and argue about their ideas, by watching television programmes such as *Question Time* and *Newsnight*.
- Fill your head with ideas by listening to *Today*, the morning news programme on BBC Radio 4, and by listening to other programmes on that station. Radio Scotland's morning news programme, *Scotland Today*, is also worth listening to.

If you encounter unfamiliar words, see if you can work them out from the context, or look them up. You will not be able to take a dictionary into the exam, so it is important to work on building up your vocabulary, and your command of ideas.

What you will be assessed on

You will be given a non-fiction passage, perhaps a piece of journalism or an extract from a book. It will be written in the 'detailed' language you have come to expect at National 5. You will have **1 hour** to read the passage and answer **30 marks'** worth of questions about it. Each question will probably be worth 2, 3 or 4 marks.

The exam tests your ability to **understand** the writer's ideas, and to **analyse** and **evaluate** the language he/she uses to put those ideas across. You will earn marks for everything you get right.

This chapter will introduce you to the skills you need to pass this exam, and to some of the types of questions you may be asked. You will see explanations and worked examples and then have a chance to try questions for yourself.

Using your own words

Many of the exam questions will ask you to **use your own words**. It is the most key and basic skill in all of close reading. If you can put something in your own words, you have understood it; if you do not understand something, you will not be able to express it in your own words. This skill is so important that it is emphasised on the front page of the exam paper where you will be told to:

> … **attempt all the questions, using your own words as far as possible.**

and is also mentioned in the questions themselves where you will often see **in your own words** or **using your own words** written in bold.

Using your own words means you may have to:

- Explain what a word or expression in the passage means.
- Explain the main point the writer is making.
- Give the reason for something that happens in the passage.
- Show that you understand a piece of information the passage gives.

Read the following article about job opportunities for people with autism:

'Autism doesn't hold me back. I'm moving up the career ladder'

1   Jonathan Young has big plans for his career. The business analyst at Goldman Sachs is on the autistic spectrum. But this, he says, is not something he allows to hold him back.

2   'I'm the company's global go-to guy for all the information used in every single one of our presentations,' he says. 'I'm moving up the ladder every year in terms of responsibility or promotion. <u>My ambition is to maintain this momentum</u>. In 10 years, I want to be someone fairly big.'

3   He is part of the most visible generation of young people with autism our society has ever known. Diagnosed early, this generation have been educated to expect not just a job when they leave school but a career on a par with their 'neuro-typical' contemporaries.

4   The confidence and determination of these graduates are forcing the pace of change in organisations previously inaccessible to those with autism. Businesses, from City law firms and banks to global healthcare companies, have begun to open their doors to young people once thought able only to do lowly jobs.

5   Young first went to Goldman Sachs as an intern in the National Autistic Society's specialist employment programme, Prospects. His time at the investment bank was such a success that the two-month internship swiftly became a full-time, permanent post.

6   'When I arrived, this role was a part-time job but I built it up into a key, full-time post and made it my own,' he said. 'Autism doesn't hold me back because I have had the correct support from a young age. It's key to have that support, both in education and in the workplace, but I don't require anything complicated: people just have to understand that I'm different.'

7   For all his confidence, Young admits that he considers himself fortunate. 'I never lose sight of the fact that I'm lucky to have a job that allows me to use all my intelligence and stretch my potential,' he said.

8   Penny Andrews got her job as a library graduate trainee at Leeds Metropolitan University in August without any help from a charity or specialist employment agency.

9   Having beaten 200 applicants to the job, she believes she has proved herself to be the best candidate. 'Sometimes I feel people think I should be grateful that I have a job but I'm performing a useful task and doing it well, so they should be grateful to me,' she said. 'After all, they wanted me badly enough to employ me a month before I had finished my degree.'

10   Far from feeling that her diagnosis of Asperger's is something to be 'got over', Andrews maintains it gave her a lead over the other candidates. 'I'm more focused, intense and honest than a neuro-typical person,' she said. 'I do things thoroughly and pay proper attention to detail. I'm always switched on: even when I'm not at work, I'll go to events that are relevant. Libraries are one of my autistic specialities and I harness that at work.'

11   Employers' attitudes might be changing but there is a lot of ground to make up. Just 15% of those with autism have full-time jobs, according to research by the National Autistic

Society (NAS), while 9% work part-time. More than a quarter of graduates with autism are unemployed, the highest rate of any disability group. Nevertheless, employers are increasingly coming round to the arguments that employing those on the spectrum is not about charity or social responsibility but about the empirical benefit of taking on people with unique skills.

12 Tom Madders is head of campaigns at NAS and responsible for its Undiscovered Workforce campaign to get young people with autism into employment. He talks of a 'vast pool of untapped talent' among those with autism.

13 'When someone has the intellectual ability and ends up doing a job like working in a supermarket, it's heartbreaking. It's such a waste because although everyone with autism is different, the things they bring that are additional to the rest of us include a very high concentration level, very good attention to detail and analytical skills,' he said. 'Why would employers want to miss out on those skills? In addition, those with autism have very specialist areas of exhaustive interest which, if these can coincide with the job in hand, can be extremely useful. They're much more reliable in terms of timeliness and absenteeism and very loyal. Often, they're very happy in jobs other people find boring.'

14 William Thanh has such severe autism that he can only communicate through his iPad. But his work at the Paul bakery in London is of such high quality that the manager, Salina Gani, is keen to increase his hours.

15 'When we decided to take on three young people with autism last year, we thought there would be limits to what they could achieve,' said Gani. 'But these young men have shown us that we shouldn't assume anything on the basis of their autism alone. Yes, they need work that's repetitive and structured, but

<u>much of the service industry is like that anyway.</u> We would gladly take them on full-time and increase the numbers of people with autism working for us across all our outlets.'

Adapted from an article by Amelia Hill, *Guardian* website, 9 March 2013, © Guardian News and Media

This underlined sentence from the second paragraph of the article:

My ambition is to maintain this momentum.

could also be expressed as:

My goal is to keep going on like this.

Active learning

Several other sentences in the article have also been underlined. Rewrite each one in your own words. You do not have to change every single word, and you may find that some long sentences can be reworded better as two or even three shorter ones.

Showing your understanding

It is unlikely that you will meet a question that just asks you to put part of the passage in your own words. The reason you need to use your own words, as we have seen in previous chapters, is to prove your understanding. The exam questions will usually want you to demonstrate your grasp of the writer's ideas and of what the passage is saying.

Active learning

Answer the following questions, using your own words as far as possible, to show your **understanding**. The number of marks available for each question suggests how many details or ideas you need in each answer.

1 Penny Andrews 'believes she has proved herself to be the best candidate'. **In your own words**, explain how paragraph 9 illustrates this idea.   2

2 What are some of the advantages for companies who hire members of staff with autism? Refer to paragraph 10 in your answer, **using your own words**.   4

3 **In your own words**, explain in what ways 'there is a lot of ground to make up' for people with autism in the workplace. Give evidence from paragraph 11 to support your answer.   3

The following question is a little different. You are asked to 'give evidence' and not told to use your own words. This means that your evidence could be in your own words, or could involve some use of short and well-chosen quotations.

4 Read paragraph 15. Identify Salina Gani's attitude to employing young people with autism and give evidence to support your answer.   2

For answers see page 259.

Context questions

You may be asked to work out from the **context** what a word or expression means. In these cases, the examiners think that you may not know the given word, but that you should be able to work it out from what surrounds it in the passage.

Context questions might be worded like this:

- Explain in your own words what is meant by '_____' in this context.
- How does the context of lines xx–xx help you to work out what is meant by '_____'?
- Work out from the context what is meant by '_____' in line xx.

You can learn a **formula** to help you answer these questions. Look at this extract from later in the same news article above about employees with autism:

> At Guy's and St Thomas' hospitals in London, an initiative was set up two years ago to help people aged 18 to 30 with autism gain work experience.
>
> Staynton Brown, associate director of equality and diversity at the hospital, dismisses any suggestion of the initiative being a philanthropic one. 'This is not a charitable gesture,' he said. 'We want to make sure we have the most talented workforce possible. It's in our interests in multiple ways. We've all benefited from the changes we've incorporated to accommodate those with autism. By clarifying the way we give information to and help introduce the interns into the hospital, we've made communication clearer for everyone, which leads to better patient care.'

Now here's a possible question:

How does the context of the second paragraph help you to work out what is meant by 'philanthropic'?

As you can see, the word 'philanthropic' in the passage is followed by Staynton Brown dismissing the idea that giving jobs to people with autism is a 'charitable' act. This suggests the writer is using 'philanthropic' to mean something that is done purely for the good of others. Here is a possible answer to the question:

> The word 'philanthropic' as used here means done out of feelings of charity or solely for the good of others. I can work this out from the context because the expression is followed with the idea that employing people with autism is not 'charitable'.

Context questions are usually worth 2 marks. You earn 1 mark for showing what the word means, and the second for showing how you could work this out from the context. Your answer should therefore be in two sentences, with the second including some short quotations from the context.

Use this pattern to structure your answers.

> The word/expression '_____' as used here means _____. I can work this from the context because . . .

Active learning

Answer these **context questions:**

5 Look back at the two-paragraph extract again. Using the formula given above, show how the context helps you to understand the meaning of the word 'accommodate' as it is used here.   2

6 Look back at the two-paragraph extract again. How does the context of these paragraphs help you to understand the word 'intern' as it is used there?   2

For answers see page 260.

Summarising questions

One key skill the examiners want you to have is the ability to follow, and summarise, a key idea or line of thought running throughout an article or passage. You can expect that the final question in the exam paper will test your ability to do this.

Active learning

Answer this question:

7 Referring to the whole article, both the main section and the later, short extract, list **in your own words** the key advantages for employers in hiring staff who have autism.   4

HINT: None of the details in your answer should be specific to just one employer or one employee. All the given details should be general advantages that any employers might find in hiring a person who has autism. As the question asks you to list the advantages, it is a good idea to present your answer as a series of bullet points. This will help you to keep track of ideas and to make sure you have given four answers.

For answers see page 261.

We have now looked at questions that ask you to show your understanding of the passage, at questions about meanings in context, and at summary questions. More examples of these will come up as you try other passages. For the moment, it is time to meet another type of question.

Word-choice questions

Of course, all words that a writer uses are chosen in some way, but when we talk about **word choice** as a technique, we mean that certain words are deliberately chosen to obtain particular effects or to suggest particular meanings.

Most words have two levels of meaning, a **denotation** and a more complex **connotation**. The denotation is the basic, simple, straightforward meaning. The connotations of a word are the ideas that a word suggests to us.

For example 'ate', 'gobbled' and 'nibbled' all have the same denotation. They all tell us that someone consumed food by putting it in his mouth. However, they all have different connotations – 'ate' is merely factual; 'gobbled' suggests either desperate hunger, selfish greed or some very poor-quality table manners; 'nibbled' implies that person ate delicately or nervously. (The context in which these words are used will help you to know more about which exact connotation to go for.)

Active learning

Below are pairs or trios of words. In each group, the words have the same basic denotation, but different connotations. For each group, work out the denotation they share, and the different connotations of the individual words.

bright	clever	genius
walk	stroll	hike
form	questionnaire	survey
naughty	bad	evil
bolted	ran	sprinted
baby	infant	
unusual	weird	
decorative	fussy	
old	senile	

Now pick one of the pairs or trios of words that you examined. Draw two or three cartoons to illustrate the different connotations, just as the ones you saw above to illustrate 'ate', 'gobbled' and 'nibbled'.

Active learning

When you answer word-choice questions you will usually need to identify and quote the carefully chosen words the writer uses, then explain and examine their connotations.

Read the following news article about an unlikely orchestra.

Paraguayan landfill orchestra makes sweet music from rubbish

1   They race towards a rubbish truck as it empties its load at a vast landfill on the edge of the city, hauling away bin liners that overflow with household waste. Their hands are black with dirt and their faces are hidden by headscarves that protect them from the high sun.

2   An estimated 500 *gancheros* work at Cateura on the outskirts of Asunción, where 1.5 tonnes of rubbish are deposited daily, separating plastic and aluminium that they sell on for as little as 15p a bag.

3   Among the mounds of refuse, however, are used oven trays and paint pots. Cast aside by the 2 million residents of the capital of Paraguay, they are nonetheless highly valued by Nicolás Gómez, who picks them out to make violins, guitars and cellos. Gómez, 48, was a carpenter and *ganchero* but now works for Favio Chávez, the conductor of Paraguay's one and only landfill orchestra.

4   The Cateura Orchestra of Recycled Instruments is made up of 30 schoolchildren – the sons and daughters of recyclers – whose instruments are forged from the city's rubbish. And while its members learned to play amid the flies and stench of Cateura, they are now receiving worldwide acclaim, culminating earlier this month with a concert in Amsterdam.

5   The project was born in 2006 when Chávez, 37, began work at the landfill as a technician, helping recyclers to classify refuse. But his passion for music took him home each weekend to the small town of Carapeguá, 50 miles from Asunción, to conduct a youth orchestra. After he brought the group to Cateura to perform, the *gancheros* asked Chávez if he

could teach music to their children, many of whom would spend afternoons playing in the rubbish as they waited for their parents to finish work.

6   But as the months passed, Chávez realised the ever-growing number of children under his tutelage needed to practise at home if they were to progress.

7   'A violin is worth more than a recycler's house,' says Chávez. 'We couldn't give a child a formal instrument as it would have put him in a difficult position. The family may have looked to sell or trade it. So we experimented with making them from the rubbish. We discovered which materials were most comfortable, which projected the right sound and which withstood the tension of the strings. It was fine to hand these out as they had no monetary value.'

8   Gómez travels three times a week to Cateura to dig out material. He shapes the metal oven trays with an electric saw to form the body of a violin and engineers cellos from oil barrels. The necks of his string instruments are sculpted from old strips of wood, called palé.

9   Now with the aid of colleagues, Chávez – who has been teaching music since he was 13 – uses the instruments to give classes to around 70 children and also directs weekly orchestra practice.

10   But he has a goal that goes beyond music. Chávez believes the mentality required to learn an instrument can be applied more widely to lift his students out of poverty. Paraguay is the fastest-growing country in the Americas, but nearly a third of its population lives below the poverty line. The *gancheros* and their children live in slums, called *bañados*, which occupy the swamps between Asunción and the River Paraguay.

11   Chávez says families can improve their lives by considering the long term. 'Poor people need to eat today,' he says. 'They don't think about tomorrow's problems. But learning music means you have to plan. It's very challenging to explain to a child who lives in adverse conditions that if his dream is to play the piano he needs to sit on a stool for five hours a day.'

12   Many parents also struggle to see the advantages of such an attitude. 'Most tell their kids that a violin can't feed you; that they need to work to eat,' says Jorge Ríos, 35, a recycler whose two daughters play in the orchestra. 'But thanks to that violin my kids have seen new countries. They have an opportunity for a better future.'

13 Ada and Noélia Ríos started attending Chávez's classes two years ago. They enjoy Chávez's strict regime, practising for two hours a day at their home – a shack with earth floors in the San Cayetano slum – and have travelled around Latin America with the orchestra.

14 'My dream is to be a musician,' says Noélia, 13, clutching her guitar, made by Gómez from two large tins that once contained a Paraguayan sweet potato dessert. 'Going to other countries has opened my mind so much,' says Ada, 14, a violinist. Following the trip to Amsterdam – its first outside of South America – the orchestra will play this year in Argentina, the US, Canada, Palestine, Norway and Japan.

15 Like her sister, Ada hopes to become a musician and also dreams of owning a Stradivarius violin, worth millions of pounds. But for now she is more than content to play her current instrument, whose face was taken from an old paint tin. 'I don't care that my violin is made out of recycled parts,' she says. 'To me, it's a treasure.'

Adapted from an article by Jonathan Gilbert, *Guardian* website, 26 April 2013, © Guardian News and Media

Active learning

Now look at this worked example of a word-choice question:

Q Explain how the writer's word choice in paragraph 1 helps to show that the *gancheros'* job is tiring. 2

A The writer uses the word 'hauling' to describe them moving the bags of rubbish. This suggests the bags are heavy or awkward to move, which would make this job exhausting.

Active learning

Now answer the following **word-choice questions** about this passage.

1 How does the word choice in paragraph 3 suggest that there is a lot of rubbish? 2

2 What does the word choice of paragraph 4 imply about the environment of the rubbish dump? 2

3 How does the word choice in paragraph 8 give the impression that Gómez is a skilled maker of musical instruments? 2

4 Show how the word choice in paragraph 10 creates an unpleasant picture of the *gancheros'* living conditions.   2

5 What does the word choice in paragraph 12 show about parents' attitudes to their children learning to play music?   2

6 Explain how the word choice of paragraphs 14 and 15 conveys the sisters' feelings about their instruments.   3

For answers see page 261.

Active learning

Earlier in this chapter you learned about how to answer questions on meanings in context. Each question is worth 2 marks. Using the formula you learned, show how the surrounding context helps you to understand the meaning of the following words:

7 *'gancheros'* in paragraph 2

8 'landfill' in paragraph 3

9 'tutelage' in paragraph 6

10 'monetary' in paragraph 7

11 'adverse' in paragraph 11

For answers see page 262.

Active learning

Earlier in this chapter you learned about how to answer questions that show your understanding of the ideas and information in the passage. Now answer these:

12 **In your own words**, explain why Chávez decided to make instruments from rubbish. Refer to paragraph 7 in your answer.   2

13 Referring to the whole article, **in your own words** explain the advantages for the *gancheros'* children of learning music.   3

For answers see page 263.

Imagery questions

Writers use images to strengthen what they say by putting all sorts of pictures in the reader's mind. Imagery is not the same thing as description. A description tells us **what something is like**. An image shows that **one thing is somehow like another**. The comparison tells us more about the thing that is being compared. Similes, metaphors and personification are all different sorts of image,

though most of the images you will be asked about will be metaphors.

To get us thinking about images, and how they add to our understanding, let us think about animal images. I could describe myself as:

Ms Cooper, that educational hamster

How am I like a hamster? I am small, with chestnut hair. I move around the classroom constantly, and I hardly ever stop talking. So, if you were to analyse the image of me as a hamster, you could do it like this.

Just as a hamster is small and brown, and scampers around squeaking, so Ms Cooper is a tiny woman with chestnut hair, who constantly scurries around her classroom talking all the time.

Active learning

Decide on an animal image that suits you. Try to think of one that applies to at least two aspects of your looks, behaviour or personality.

Then, get together with a partner who knows you quite well. Tell each other which animal images you have chosen for yourselves. Find all the ways in which your partner is like the image animal he/she chose.

Of course, there are ways in which I am not like a hamster. I do not have a tail. I chew my food and swallow it rather than tucking it into my cheeks. I weigh a lot more than 200 grammes. When you answer imagery questions, you are looking for the **similarities**.

There is a method for analysing images. You begin with what the image **literally** is like, or **literally** means. Then you go on to the **metaphorical** meaning, showing how that image applies to and adds meaning to the subject under discussion.

Use this structure for your analysis:

Just as … (explain the literal meaning), so … (explain the metaphorical meaning).

You already saw this structure used to examine the image of me as a hamster. Let us look at another example. Suppose you said:

He has a mountain of work to do.

We could analyse the image like this:

> Just as a mountain is large and is challenging to climb, so the amount of work he has to do is enormous and will be really difficult.

Now look at an extract from the news article you read on page 172:

> Jonathan Young has big plans for his career. The business analyst at Goldman Sachs is on the autistic spectrum. But this, he says, is not something he allows to hold him back.
>
> 'I'm the company's global go-to guy for all the information used in every single one of our presentations,' he says. 'I'm moving up the ladder every year in terms of responsibility or promotion. My ambition is to maintain this momentum. In 10 years, I want to be someone fairly big.'

Here's an imagery question about this extract:

> Look at the following image: 'I'm moving up the ladder every single year …'.
>
> Explain what this image means and its effect. 3

Here is an answer to the question.

Jonathan Young compares his progress at work to climbing a ladder. Just as climbing a ladder takes you higher, so Young is moving up and being promoted within the company. This shows how much progress he is making.

The question is worth 3 marks, so the student did three things to answer it:

A She stated the comparison: 'Jonathan Young compares his progress at work to climbing a ladder.'

B She analysed the image: 'Just as climbing a ladder takes you higher, so Young is moving up and being promoted within the company.'

C She said what the image shows: 'This shows how much progress Young is making.'

Read this article about a parent who took drastic steps:

I set my daughter a computer curfew

1   At 13, I would spend long vigils beside the home telephone every evening, calling the friends who I had seen all day at school to resume our conversation. Everyone did. It's normal for teenagers to require constant interaction with their peer group, while other figures, like parents, vanish to the margins, and I saw nothing strange about spending hours crouched in our hall, discussing embarrassing teachers and hilarious friends in exhausting detail. Sometimes, an exasperated parent would wrench the phone out of my hand, forcing me to skulk back to my room.

2   Last month I imposed the 21st century equivalent of wrenching the landline from my 13-year-old daughter's hand by imposing a computer curfew. This entailed removing her laptop, phone, Game Boy and all other screens from her room after 9pm at night, about an hour before she goes to sleep. The aim was to allow her this hour to think her own thoughts. An hour of interior life.

3   Our children, like most of their friends, are accessorised with both laptop and mobile phone. As a result, the potential for constant communication with their friends is ever present. Texting begins early morning and lets up last thing at night. Friends wake them up, friends say goodnight and Facebook fills all the gaps in between. The sweet, individualised ring tones that signify when a particular friend is texting beep from 6.30am to 11pm, chirruping their insistent way through supper, homework, bath time and sleep. Technology embraces our children, like ourselves, in a warm electronic sea, and the tide of it comes ever higher.

4   Does this matter?

5   Susan Greenfield, the neuroscientist, thinks it does. Last month she told the BBC Radio 4's *Today* Programme that this 'cyber-lifestyle' is rewiring our brains and even we need at least to acknowledge that there is an issue.

6   Nicholas Carr, in his book *The Shallows: What the Internet Is Doing to Our Brains*, claims that 'loss of concentration and focus, division of our attention and fragmentation of our thoughts', is changing how our minds work, creating shorter attention spans and making reading harder by destroying 'the linear, literary mind'.

7   Sue Palmer, in her new book, *21st Century Girls*, goes all out for total technological cold turkey. 'Allowing electronic strangers into a girl's bedroom before her mid-teens is an extremely bad idea. If parents want their daughters to establish healthy sleeping habits they have to bite the bullet and insist that their bedroom remains a technology-free zone.'

8   Especially for girls, with their intimate, gossipy, social natures, the drive to remain as connected as possible with friends is overwhelming. Yet perversely, floating in an electronic sea has the deeper effect of depriving them of the habit of being alone, developing their own thoughts.

9   Needless to say, my efforts to explain this to my daughter were pretty hapless. I dredged up the example of the hostage Terry Waite who got through years chained to a radiator in Beirut by the sheer strength of his interior life. My daughter listened politely, but her expression was incredulous. When was she ever going to be chained to a radiator in Beirut?

10 As a writer, I had one other, overriding concern. The key thing children miss out on without that moment of solitude before sleep is reading. A generation ago, if you saw a light under a child's bedclothes, it would be a torch illuminating some secretive paperback. Now the light under the bedclothes has changed to the blue phosphorescent glow of a laptop or an iPad or a phone.

11 A report by Professor Keith Topping for this year's World Book Day, which looked at the reading habits of 300,000 students, found that reading ages were actually declining. Increasing numbers of 13 and 14-year-olds opted for books with a primary-school reading age.

12 I don't believe you can overstate the case for literature: reading develops key life skills, including the empathy to place yourself

imaginatively in another mind and the ability to sustain deep concentration.

13   My children would be the first to point out that I'm as bad as any teenager in wasting time on Twitter and Facebook. Those addictive social networks account for at least half an hour of my day that I won't get back. Yet it seems a more grievous thing to rob a child of the chance to read.

14   So here am I with my heavy-handed computer curfew. Luckily, our daughter has taken to it. She reads and loves poetry, but I know I'm just Canute trying to hold back the tide. I can't help envying previous generations of parents who didn't have to face this addictive electronic onslaught in their efforts to give their children a bit of time on their own. The fact remains that, for children, the chance to be alone and read, write, or simply think is vanishing in our connected world. We should do everything we can to help them reclaim a small desert island of their own in the electronic sea.

Adapted from an article by Jane Thynne, *Guardian* website,
27 April 2013, © Guardian News and Media

Active learning

You are going to have a little help to examine the **imagery** in this passage. You will gradually become more independent at doing this. Work through the following questions, using the frameworks to help you. **Each question is worth 3 marks.**

1   Look at the following image:

'vanish to the margins' (paragraph 1)

Explain what the image means and analyse its effect.

State the comparison: *The writer compares the declining importance of parents to …*

Analyse the image: *Just as the margins are at the edges, so …*

Say what the image therefore shows: *This shows that parents …*

2   Look at the following image:

'Technology embraces our children' (paragraph 3)

Explain what the image means and analyse its effect.

State the comparison: *The writer compares technology's influence over children to …*

Analyse the image: *Just as an embrace is a close, enfolding hug, so …*

Say what the image therefore shows: *This shows that technology …*

3 Look at the following image:

'a warm electronic sea' (paragraph 3)

Explain what the image means and analyse its effect.

State the comparison: *The writer compares … to …*

Analyse the image: *Just as the sea …, so …*

Say what the image therefore shows: *This shows …*

4 Look at the following image:

'the tide of it comes ever higher' (paragraph 3)

Explain what the image means and analyse its effect.

State the comparison: *The writer compares … to …*

Analyse the image: *Just as the tide …, so …*

Say what the image therefore shows: *This shows …*

5 Look at the following image:

'Allowing electronic strangers into a girl's bedroom …' (paragraph 7)

Explain what the image means and analyse its effect.

State the comparison: *The writer compares … to …*

Analyse the image: *Just as …, so …*

Say what the image therefore shows: *This shows …*

6 Look at the following image:

'a small desert island of their own' (paragraph 14)

Explain what the image means and analyse its effect.

For answers see page 263.

Active learning

Earlier in this chapter you learned about how to answer questions about **meanings in context**. Now answer these:

7 How does the context help you to understand the meaning of 'exasperated' as used in paragraph 1?   2

8 How does the context help you to understand the meaning of 'entailed' as used in paragraph 2?   2

9 How does the context help you to understand the meaning of 'hapless' as used in paragraph 9?   2

You also learned how to answer questions about **word choice**. Now answer these:

10 Explain what the writer's word choice in the first line of the article conveys about the time she spent beside the home telephone as a teenager. **2**

11 What does the writer's use of 'chirruping' in paragraph 3 suggest about mobile phones? **2**

You also practised questions that ask you **to summarise** in a way that shows your understanding of a writer's overall argument. Now answer this:

12 Referring to the whole article, **in your own words** list the key reasons for concern about the amount of time modern teenagers spend using electronic gadgets. **4**

For answers see pages 264–65.

Link questions

You may be asked a **link question**. These often ask you to say how a sentence **creates an effective link** between one paragraph and another. These questions are usually worth 2 marks and you usually need to answer them in two parts:

- Show how one part of the sentence **links back** to the previous paragraph.
- Show how another part of it **refers forward** to the new paragraph.

For example, a **link question** based on the news article about a teenage computer curfew might be worded like this:

> **How does the sentence 'Needless to say, my efforts to explain this to my daughter were pretty hapless.' form a link between paragraphs 8 and 9?**

To answer this, you need to reread this section of the passage:

8   Especially for girls, with their intimate, gossipy, social natures, the drive to remain as connected as possible with friends is overwhelming. Yet perversely, floating in an electronic sea has the deeper effect of depriving them of the habit of being alone, developing their own thoughts.

9   Needless to say, my efforts to explain this to my daughter were pretty hapless. I dredged up the example of the hostage Terry Waite who got through years chained to a radiator in Beirut by the sheer strength of his interior life. My daughter listened politely, but her expression was incredulous. When was she ever going to be chained to a radiator in Beirut?

A good answer to this question would be:

> The expression 'to explain this' links back to the harmful effects of always being connected as discussed in paragraph 8.
>
> The expression 'my efforts' introduces the writer's attempt to explain the value of having an interior life, which is discussed in paragraph 9.

This answer would get 2 marks because it has two parts to it, one linking back, the other referring forward. We can put this into a **formula for link questions** which, with occasional slight adaptation, should ensure you always get 2 marks for this question.

The word/expression '_____' links back to _____, which was discussed in in paragraph _____.

The word/expression '_____' introduces the idea of _____, which is going to be discussed in paragraph _____.

Read the following news article about government plans to change the rules about childcare:

Has Liz Truss tried looking after six toddlers? I have

Zoe Williams test-drives Liz Truss's theory that one adult should be able to care for six two-year-olds

1   The Conservative MP Liz Truss, like so many in public policy, has noticed that childcare is unaffordable – families in the UK spend nearly a third of their income on it; more than anyone else in the world.

2   Truss is unique, I think, in identifying the problem as over-regulation – specifically, she thinks the current adult-to-child ratios are too stringent. In her plan, one adult would be able to care for six two-year-olds (at the moment it's four).

3   Did anybody test-drive her theory for her, even in its planning stage? I do not think they did.

4   So in the interests of public policy research, I scored myself six toddlers between 9.30am and 1pm. These are not standard nursery hours, so I cannot vouch for the poor humans who would have to do this professionally. I should note here that I don't have any childcare qualifications, though I am educated to degree level. That didn't help.

5   Sid and Sam are twins, Lucas and Ryan are good pals, Harper is my daughter and is actually three, and Gus rounded it up.

6   Ryan was the godsend of the group: fascinated by the taxonomy of the Pixar Cars franchise, he made precisely no demands, apart from 'Where's the red one?', 'Where's the blue one?', 'Where's Sally?' and 'Batteries'. He was also potty trained, along with Lucas, who is a charmer. The twins were in nappies; Gus was not in a good mood.

7   Basically, the Ryan of a gang this size will get precisely no attention at all. He will just occasionally be handed a car. That might be fine. He might be a mini-version of those adults who like to read poetry at parties. But I think the authorities would expect him to have some interaction.

8   On the subject of regulations, these require a carer to take the kids out at least once a day. I want to make a complicated analogy about a horde of ferrets and a motorway, but actually, anybody who thinks an adult could take out six two-year-old children has simply never met a pre-verbal child. It would be the apex of irresponsibility. People would stop you in the street. I couldn't even get them all into the same room at the same time.

9   Gus's mood was not bad, he just wasn't feeling very vivacious and wanted to be in someone's arms the whole time. It's incredibly cute, like having a marmoset, but now I have no arms to look after the other five. They didn't fight with each other; I think they knew on some instinctive level that I wouldn't be able to intervene.

10 The twins are in that call-and-response phase, where they show you something and tell you what it is, but they won't really rest until you show them something else, tell them what

that is, and then you swap. It's not time-consuming so much as concentration-breaking, so you can never follow through on what you're doing, and what you're normally doing is looking for the child you can't immediately see. Quite often, that child will show up in the time it takes you to remember that you were looking for him, but not always, so there is a hell of a lot of running up and down stairs and blind panic. I wasn't going to admit that, because I thought their mothers would freak out. But now I've given them all back alive, I figure it's OK. And because she's three and won't choke, I didn't take any notice of my daughter at all. For all I know, she took off and spent the time in Caffè Nero.

11   Long-term, or rather, for any period longer than three hours, you would basically have to pen them into a smaller space, otherwise you would go mad. That's fine, it's not dangerous, but again, it's not very appropriate. You can't keep kids in a single room for a whole day with no fresh air. Those are battery conditions.

12   Twins poo at the same time, who knew? But you have to prioritise the toddlers who are using a loo, as they seem to have some auto-suggestion and need to go as soon as they smell anything that reminds them of a loo. Building in some time to lose track of what you were doing, I'd put this job at an hour, from poo-alert to the second twin getting a fresh nappy.

13   I want to put you through this in real time, but I've got to pick peas out of the weave of my carpet. This is, on mature consideration, and with no offence meant, the worst idea a person in government has ever had.

Adapted from an article by Zoe Williams, *Guardian* website, 1 February 2013, © Guardian News and Media

Active learning

Answer the following **link questions** about the article:

1 How does the sentence, 'So in the interests of public policy research, I scored myself six toddlers between 9.30am and 1pm' (paragraph 4) form a link at this stage in the article?   **2**

2 How does the sentence, 'On the subject of regulations, these require a carer to take the kids out at least once a day' (paragraph 8) form a link at this stage in the article?   **2**

For answers see page 266.

Active learning

Earlier in this chapter you learned about how to answer questions about **imagery**. Now answer these:

3 Look at the following image:

'a horde of ferrets and a motorway' (paragraph 8)

Explain what the image means and analyse its effect. 3

4 Look at the following image:

'Those are battery conditions.' (paragraph 11)

Explain what the image means and analyse its effect. 3

Now answer these other questions about **particular aspects** of this article:

5 'Childcare is unaffordable.' **In your own words**, explain how examples the writer gives in the first paragraph illustrate this idea. 2

6 Show how the context of paragraph 2 helps you to understand the meaning of the word 'stringent' as used there. 2

7 Discuss the effect of the rhetorical question used in paragraph 3. 2

8 Show how the context of paragraph 8 helps you to understand the meaning of the word 'analogy' as used there. 2

9 Identify two examples of the writer using exaggeration in paragraph 10 and discuss how they add to her argument. 4

You also learned to answer **summarising questions**. Now answer this:

10 Referring to the whole article, **in your own words** list some of the challenging aspects of caring for young children. 4

For answers see pages 266–68.

Tone questions

It is easy to understand what we mean by **tone** if we think of a speaking voice. When you hear someone speaking, you can tell if he/she is angry, confused, excited or afraid. These tones in the speaking voice are created by factors such as the volume, the speed of speech, which words the speaker puts emphasis on and how fluently or hesitantly the words come out.

It is a little harder at first to see how we can identify tone in written English, when there are no sounds, only words. But, skilled writers can create a tone by word choice alone.

Active learning

Four tones have already been mentioned above: *angry, confused, excited* and *afraid*. Draw the biggest speech bubble you can on a page of your notebook. Write those four tones in the bubble, then add as many more as you can think of. After five minutes, compare your answers with the rest of the class. Add to your list as you hear other people's answers.

You should now have a huge list of many tones. Some of the most common ones that crop up in exam questions are *humorous, matter-of-fact, emphatic/definite, critical* and *angry*. Make sure all five of those are in your bubble. Now underline them to remind yourself that these are ones to especially look out for.

The wording of tone questions can vary. Depending how the question is expressed, you will probably have to do a mixture of the following:

1 Identify a tone.
2 Quote words which create that tone.
3 Explain how the words you have quoted create the tone.

Look at this extract from the article on pages 191–93 about childcare:

> Long-term, or rather, for any period longer than three hours, you would basically have to pen them into a smaller space, otherwise you would go mad. That's fine, it's not dangerous, but again, it's not very appropriate. You can't keep kids in a single room for a whole day with no fresh air. Those are battery conditions.
>
> Twins poo at the same time, who knew? But you have to prioritise the toddlers who are using a loo, as they seem to have some auto-suggestion and need to go as soon as they smell anything that reminds them of a loo. Building in some time to lose track of what you were doing, I'd put this job at an hour, from poo-alert to the second twin getting a fresh nappy.
>
> I want to put you through this in real time, but I've got to pick peas out of the weave of my carpet. This is, on mature consideration, and with no offence meant, the worst idea a person in government has ever had.

Here are two possible tone questions on this extract, along with suitable answers. Notice that in one of the questions you have to identify the tone, while in the other you only have to show how it is created:

Q1 How does the writer establish a tone of surprise in the second paragraph?

2

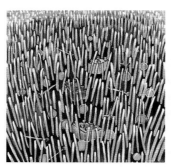

A1 She does so by stating a surprising fact: 'Twins poo at the same time.' She also adds a rhetorical question: 'who knew?'' to point out that the fact is unexpected.

Q2 What is the tone of the first sentence in the final paragraph, and how is this created? 2

A2 The tone is one of exhaustion. It is created by the author describing a task she still has to do: 'pick peas out of the weave of my carpet.'

Active learning

Now try this **tone question**:

11 What is the tone of the final sentence and how is this made clear? 2

For answer see page 268.

Now read this article about the changes technology may bring to all our lives:

Your life in 2033

1 Imagine you are an urban professional living in a western city a few decades from now. An average morning might look something like this:

2 There will be no alarm clock in your wake-up routine – at least, not in the traditional sense. Instead, you'll be roused by the aroma of freshly brewed coffee, by light entering your room as curtains open automatically, and by a gentle back massage administered by your hi-tech bed. You're more likely to awake refreshed, because inside your mattress there's a special sensor that monitors your sleeping rhythms, determining precisely when to wake you.

3 Your apartment is an electronic orchestra and you are the conductor. With simple flicks of the wrist and spoken instructions, you can control temperature, humidity, ambient music and lighting. You are able to skim through the day's news on translucent screens while a freshly cleaned suit is retrieved from your automated closet. You head to the kitchen for breakfast and the translucent news display follows, as a projected hologram hovering just in front of you. You grab a mug of coffee and a fresh pastry, cooked to perfection in your humidity-controlled oven, and skim new emails on a

holographic tablet projected in front of you. Your central computer system suggests a list of chores your housekeeping robots should tackle today, all of which you approve.

4   You pull up notes for a presentation you'll give later that day to important new clients abroad. All of your data – from your personal and professional life – is accessible through all of your various devices, as it's stored in the cloud, a remote digital-storage system with near limitless capacity. You own a few different and interchangeable digital devices; one is the size of a tablet, another the size of a pocket watch, while others might be flexible or wearable. All will be lightweight, incredibly fast and will use more powerful processors than anything available today.

5   As you move about your kitchen, you stub your toe, hard, on the edge of a cabinet – ouch! You grab your mobile device and open the diagnostics app. Inside your device there is a tiny microchip that uses low-radiation submillimetre waves to scan your body, like an x-ray. A quick scan reveals that your toe is just bruised, not broken. You decline the invitation to get a second opinion at a nearby doctor's office.

6   There's a bit of time left before you need to leave for work – which you'll get to by driverless car, of course. Your commute will be as productive or relaxing as you desire.

7   Before you head out, your device reminds you to buy a gift for your nephew's upcoming birthday. You scan the system's proposed gift ideas, derived from anonymous, aggregated data on other hundreds of other nine-year-old boys with his profile and interests, but none of the suggestions inspires you. Then you remember a story his parents told you that had everyone 40 and older laughing: your nephew hadn't understood a reference to the old excuse 'a dog ate my homework'; how could a dog eat his cloud storage drive? You do a quick search for a robotic dog and buy one with a single click. In the card input, you type: 'Just in case.' It will arrive at his house within a five-minute window of your selected delivery time.

8   You think about having another cup of coffee, but then a haptic device ('haptic' refers to technology that involves touch and feeling) that is embedded in the heel of your shoe gives you a gentle pinch – a signal that you'll be late for if you linger any longer.

Adapted from an extract taken from *The New Digital Age* by Eric Schmidt and Jared Cohen, John Murray 2013

Active learning

Answer these **tone questions** about the passage:

1 How do the writers maintain a conversational tone throughout the passage?   2

2 What is the tone of paragraph 6, and how is this created?   2

For answers see page 269.

Just before we leave behind the idea of tone, a word of advice. If you are asked to identify or name a tone, do not ever just say that it is positive or negative. That is far too vague. You need to say something much more exact. What kind of positive tone is it? Praising? Happy? Encouraging? What kind of negative tone is it? Critical? Despairing? Angry?

Active learning

Now answer these **additional questions** based on the passage. They will allow you to practise skills you have learned already.

3 'Imagine you are an urban professional living in a western city a few decades from now.' **In your own words** explain how details the writers use in paragraphs 1 to 6 create the impression that the reader is a professional, **and** that the reader is living in a city.   4

4 What is the meaning of 'roused' as used in paragraph 2, and how does the context help you to understand the meaning?   2

5 'Your apartment is an electronic orchestra and you are the conductor' (paragraph 3). Choose **one** of the two images in this sentence. Explain what your chosen image means and analyse its effect.   3

6 The writers aim to present a positive picture of life in 2033. Referring to the whole article, **in your own words** list ways in which the writers suggest that a life lived then will be a good one.   4

For answers see page 269.

Sentence structure questions

Sentence structure is how a sentence is made and built up. Very often, students get structure questions wrong because they do not actually answer the question. Many students end up rehashing the content of a sentence when they should be examining its structure.

Structure is not the same as content. The structure of a house might be bricks and mortar placed on a strong, deep foundation; its contents will include furniture and people. The structure of the bag you take to school might be canvas, stitched together and then attached with leather straps and metal buckles; its content would probably include books, pens and your iPod.

A number of smaller techniques contribute to sentence structure:

- **Length**: look at whether a sentence is noticeably long, or noticeably short, especially if its length contrasts with the length of other sentences nearby.
- **Listing**: what is being listed and what does this list suggest?
- **Repetition**: what is being repeated, and what does this repetition suggest?
- **Parenthesis**: what is the extra information inside the parenthesis about and what is the effect of this?
- **Word order**: have any words been put in a position in the sentence that particularly creates emphasis?
- **Colons or semicolons**: what do these divide the sentence into? What do colons introduce?
- **Minor sentence**: these ungrammatical (usually short) sentences are used to create some kind of impact, so what impact is it?
- **Questions**: what is the effect of these on the reader?

Look at this extract from the article you have already read about life in 2033 on pages 196–98:

> Your apartment is an electronic orchestra and you are the conductor. With simple flicks of the wrist and spoken instructions, you can control temperature, humidity, ambient music and lighting. You are able to skim through the day's news on translucent screens while a freshly cleaned suit is retrieved from your automated closet. You head to the kitchen for breakfast and the translucent news display follows, as a projected hologram hovering just in front of you. You grab a mug of coffee and a fresh pastry, cooked to perfection in your humidity-controlled oven, and skim new emails on a holographic tablet projected in front of you. Your central computer system suggests a list of chores your housekeeping robots should tackle today, all of which you approve.

Here are two possible sentence structure questions on this extract, along with suitable answers.

Q1 How does the sentence structure of this paragraph contribute to a conversational tone throughout? 2

A1 The writers repeatedly use 'you' or 'your' at the start of sentences. This creates the impression that they are talking directly to the reader.

Q2 Show how the structure of the second sentence suggests that technology will make future life straightforward. 2

A2 The writers list a number of things we will be able to control: 'temperature, humidity, ambient music and lighting'. This suggests that everything in life will be easily controlled, and that life will therefore be straightforward.

Now read this article about how technological change will affect lives around the world.

The connecting world

1   The accessibility of affordable smart devices, including phones and tablets, will be transformative in developing countries. Consider the impact of basic mobile phones for a group of African fisherwomen today. Whereas they used to bring their daily catch to the market and watch it slowly spoil as the day progressed, now they keep it on the line, in the river, and wait for calls from customers. Once an order is placed, a fish is brought out of the water and prepared for the buyer. There is no need for an expensive refrigerator, no need for someone to guard it at night, no danger of spoiled fish losing their value (or poisoning customers) and no unnecessary overfishing.

2   Mobile phones are transforming how people in the developing world access and use information, and adoption rates are soaring. There are already more than 650m mobile phone users in Africa, and close to 3bn across Asia. The majority of these people are using basic-feature phones – voice calls and text messages only – because the cost of data service in their countries is often prohibitively expensive. This will change and, when it does, the smartphone revolution will profoundly benefit these populations.

3   What connectivity also brings, beyond mobile phones, is the ability to collect and use data. Data itself is a tool, and in places where unreliable statistics about health, education, economics and the population's needs have stalled growth and development, the chance to gather data effectively is a game-changer. Everyone in society benefits, as governments

can better measure the success of their programmes, and media and other nongovernmental organisations can use data to support their work and check facts.

4   And the developing world will not be left out of the advances in hi-tech gadgetry. Even if the prices for sophisticated smartphones remain high, illicit markets for knock-off consumer electronics will produce and distribute imitations that bridge the gap.

5   In 'additive manufacturing', or 3D printing, machines can actually 'print' physical objects ultra-thin layer by ultra-thin layer. Communal 3D printers in poor countries would allow people to make whatever tool or item they require from freely available templates. In wealthier countries, 3D printing will be the perfect partner for advanced manufacturing. New materials and products will all be built uniquely to a specification from the internet and on demand by a machine run by a sophisticated, trained operator.

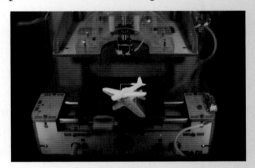

6   As for life's daily tasks, information systems will free us of many small burdens that today add stress and chip away at our focus. Our own mental limits, which lead us to forgetfulness and oversights, will be supplemented by information systems designed to support our needs. Two such examples are memory prosthetics – calendar reminders and to-do lists – and social prosthetics, which instantly connect you with your friend who has relevant expertise in whatever task you are facing.

7   By relying on these integrated systems, we'll be able to use our time more effectively each day – whether that means having a 'deep think', spending more time preparing for an important presentation or guaranteeing that a parent can attend his or her child's football match without distraction.

8   Yet despite these advancements, a central and singular caveat exists: the impact of this data revolution will be to strip citizens of much of their control over their personal information in virtual space, and that will have significant consequences in the physical world.

9   In the future, our identities in everyday life will come to be defined more and more by our virtual activities and associations. Our highly documented pasts will have an impact on our prospects, and our ability to influence and control how we are perceived by others will decrease dramatically. The potential for someone else to access, share or manipulate parts of our online identities will increase, particularly due to our reliance on cloud-based data storage.

10   The basics of online identity could also change. Your online identity in the future is unlikely to be a simple Facebook page; instead, it will be a constellation of profiles, from every online activity, that will be verified and perhaps even regulated by the government. Imagine all of your accounts – Facebook, Twitter, Skype, Google+, Netflix, newspaper subscription – linked to an 'official profile'.

11   Identity will be the most valuable commodity for citizens in the future, and it will exist primarily online. We will see a proliferation of businesses that cater to privacy and reputation concerns. We will even see the rise of a new black market, where people can buy real or invented identities.

12   Without question, the increased access to people's lives that the data revolution brings will give some repressive governments a dangerous advantage in targeting their citizens. Yet demand for tools and software to help safeguard citizens living under such digital repression will give rise to a growing and aggressive industry. And that is the power of this new information revolution: for every negative, there will be a counter-response that has the potential to be a positive. More people will fight for privacy and security than look to restrict it, even in the most repressive parts of the world.

Adapted from an extract taken from *The New Digital Age* by Eric Schmidt and Jared Cohen, John Murray 2013

Active learning

You are going to try some **sentence structure questions** on the passage above, with some support at times.

1 How does the sentence structure of the first paragraph suggest that change is inevitable?   2

   HINT: look for an example of repetition.

2 'Whereas they used to bring their daily catch to the market and watch it slowly spoil as the day progressed, now they keep it on the line, in the river, and wait for calls from

customers' (paragraph 1). How does the structure of this sentence emphasise the idea that life has already improved for African fisherwomen?

2

HINT: look at how the sentence is divided, and how the different parts of it begin.

3 How does sentence structure in the second paragraph make clear what the writers mean by 'basic-feature phones'?

2

4 What is the function of the dash in paragraph 7?

2

5 How does the sentence structure of the final paragraph show that the writers are reaching their conclusion?

2

HINT: look at how the paragraph opens.

For answers see page 270.

Active learning

To give you some further practice in tackling the **summarising questions** that are likely to come up at the end of the exam, answer these two questions:

6 Referring to the whole article, **in your own words** list ways in which the writers suggest that technological change will bring benefits for developing countries.

4

7 Referring to the whole article, **in your own words** list ways in which the writers suggest that technological change and increasing connectivity may have disadvantages.

4

For answers see page 271.

You have seen some examples of what the questions in this exam might be like. Now you have to get as much practice as possible.

Read the article below by a newspaper columnist discussing schooling in Britain.

Children are sent to school too young in the UK

1 It's an eye-catching statistic. Almost 20% of schoolchildren in the UK are registered as having special educational needs, five times higher than the EU average.

2 Some of the suggested solutions, however – more intense and more rigorous education, longer hours at school, more testing, more competition and schools that are more strict and conformist – could actually be an attempt to put out the fire with petrol.

3 As well as this high level of special needs provision, there's another huge discrepancy between the way children are taught in Britain and the way they are taught in the rest of Europe: the age at which formal education begins. This issue is always skulking

around in the background of UK debate, but is somehow never fully discussed or explored, no matter how many experts warn that it is damaging.

4   In most European countries, children usually start formal education at six to seven, rather than our four to five. Finland has the best educational outcomes in the EU, but also has the highest age for beginning formal education – which is seven, a full three years later than many children here.

5   There are many reasons why it's not necessarily a good idea to get children learning in an academic way at too early an age. People tend to think that this puts more pressure on the less bright kids. Actually, it's not terribly good for the majority of children – academically or psychologically. But, interestingly, it can be the brightest children who fare least well, when their natural curiosity about the world, and instinctive eagerness to learn about it, is institutionally curtailed in favour of prescriptive learning.

6   People think that clever kids will always be spotted and always thrive. It's a wrong assumption. The charity Potential Plus UK advocates for 'gifted' children. It argues that such children often underachieve for a variety of reasons, including: an inability to manage time; disorganisation and frequently losing things; lack of motivation to succeed; problems with friendships; bullying; being disruptive, confrontational or disrespectful in class; difficulty concentrating; poor handwriting and overall poor presentation of work, and perfectionist personality type – resulting in resisting work that is deemed more challenging because of the fear of failure.

7   In fact, a talented child can look a lot like a child who has significantly little in the way of talent. Sometimes it's simply because they are tired at school – they often have trouble sleeping because their brains won't stop.

8   Here's another list, this time of learning difficulties that 'gifted' but underachieving children are often misdiagnosed as having: attention deficit hyperactivity disorder; oppositional defiant disorder; depression; bipolar disorder; obsessive-compulsive disorder or obsessive-compulsive personality disorder, and Asperger's syndrome. As far as the last is concerned, Asperger's is frequently misdiagnosed in gifted children.

9   It seems like a ghastly vision, the idea that children are being forced into formal schooling too early, then being diagnosed with learning difficulties when they react badly to the straitjacket that has been laced around their intellect at too tender an age. This must be particularly awful for children whose intellect isn't stimulated enough at home. Imagine. You find yourself in an environment where there are books and toys, other children to play with, adults who engage with you, then just as the possibilities of the world are blossoming like fireworks in your head, you're told to sit down, be quiet, somehow silence that explosion, and concentrate on one thing to the exclusion of everything else. People in Britain don't seem to understand how damaging our desire to get our children into formal education as early as possible can be.

10   Some children thrive on it. Many do not. In the UK, there seems to be little understanding or acknowledgement of the fact that underachievement at school can simply be because our highly standardised education system is inappropriate, not because there is necessarily a learning difficulty.

11   The picture is complicated further because it is also crucial that learning difficulties are addressed. It's significant that Finland is also good at identifying special educational needs. As Finnish education expert Pasi Sahlberg points out, 'up to half of those students who complete their education at 16 have been in special education at some point in their schooling. In other words, it is nothing that special any more for students. This fact significantly reduces the negative stigma that is often brought on by special education.'

12   It's important to note that the Finnish system prizes early intervention, preferring diagnosis 'during early childhood development and care, before children enter school'. This is sensible, since actual developmental difficulties are being identified, rather than a response to a more general antipathy – which is, let's face it, pretty understandable – to the highly artificial and controlling environment that is a classroom. Start the wrong child learning formally at five, and by seven he – and boys do have a bigger problem here – could well have had enough of education to last him a lifetime.

Adapted from an article by Deborah Orr, *Guardian* website, 9 March 2013, © Guardian News and Media

Active learning

Now answer the questions:

1. 'It's an eye-catching statistic.' **In your own words** explain how examples given in the first paragraph illustrate this idea. **2**

2. Look at paragraph 2. **In your own words**, explain some of the suggested solutions to the problem. **3**

3. Show how the context of paragraph 3 helps you to understand the meaning of 'discrepancy' as used in this paragraph. **2**

4. Referring to paragraph 4 in your answer, **in your own words** explain how starting school at a later age may be better for students. **2**

5. How does the first sentence of paragraph 5 act as a link at this stage in the writer's argument? **2**

6. What are some of the reasons why 'gifted' children underachieve? Refer to paragraph 6 in your answer, **using your own words.** **4**

7. How does the writer's use of repetition in paragraph 8 help to show the problems faced by gifted children? **2**

8. Choose one of the following images from paragraph 9:

   - 'a ghastly vision'
   - 'the straightjacket that has been laced around their intellect'
   - 'like fireworks'.

   Explain what your chosen image means and examine its effect. **3**

9. Read paragraph 10. Explain **two** ways in which the writer makes clear her disapproval of starting school at an early age. **4**

10. How does the writer's quotation of Pasi Sahlberg in paragraph 11 support her overall argument? **2**

11. Referring to the whole article, **in your own words** list the key disadvantages the writer believes are caused by starting formal education at too early an age. **4**

Total: 30 marks

For answers see pages 272–76.

You may have noticed that some of the types of questions you have learned about in this chapter did not appear in this final practice task. The examiners always ask the questions they feel passages deserve, and not every sort of question will come up every time. However, you still need to know how to answer every question type, because you do not know when they will come up.

CHAPTER 7 The National 5 Critical Reading Exam

Critical Reading means being able to demonstrate your understanding of texts you have studied in class. You will be tested on this by sitting an exam (sometimes called the question paper) in May of your National 5 year.

The exam is broken down into two parts:

- In **SECTION 1** you will read an extract from a **Scottish text** you have studied in class and answer **questions**. There are **20** marks available for answering these questions.
- In **SECTION 2** you will write **one critical essay** about a text you have studied in class. This text can be drama, prose, poetry, film and television drama or language study. This essay will be given a mark out of **20**.

The entire exam is only **1 hour and 30 minutes** long, so you just have **45 minutes** for each section. That is not long at all! So, you need to be thoroughly prepared before you go into the exam. This means you need to know your texts and to have had practice in exam technique. This chapter will help you to do both these things.

How to use this chapter

The chapter starts by teaching you in detail about two Scottish poems. Then you will learn about the Scottish text questions. These will be based on the two poems in this book. The last part of the chapter will be about critical essay writing. Again, any examples or models will mostly be based on the two poems.

 Warning

The list of poems you will explore may change from time to time. Before you launch into learning everything there is to know about these poems, get your teacher to check if they are still on the list. You might need to study different poems for your exam.

Two poems by Edwin Morgan

The Scottish text options include prose (both short stories and novels) as well as poems. There are also several plays on the Scottish text list. However, we are going to look at poems because these are the shortest types of text, and the easiest therefore to fit in this book. Poems are also ideal for this book because the Scottish text question asks you to compare one part of a writer's work to another. By looking at two poems, we can make this sort of comparison.

The poems are both by Edwin Morgan. Morgan lived a long life, dying in 2010 aged 90. He did not come from a bookish family but loved to read and studied English at university. He was a pacifist who served as a non-fighting member of a medical corps during the Second World War. He lectured in English at Glasgow University from 1947 to 1980.

Edwin Morgan

In his 80s, an age when most people are asking you to turn that noise down, Morgan worked with the Scottish band Idlewild, a group so loud that a critic once described them as sounding like a flight of stairs falling down a flight of stairs. You can hear Morgan on their song *In Remote Part / Scottish Fiction*. Morgan was also gay, something he did not make public until he was in his 70s. This was partly because homosexuality was illegal for much of his life; it was also because he wanted his love poems to feel universal, as if they could apply to anyone in any kind of relationship.

He was a prolific poet, who wrote in all sorts of styles and about many different subjects – including what the Loch Ness Monster would sound like (well worth finding on the internet to listen to) or what might happen if a computer wrote a Christmas card. He translated poetry from many other languages into English. In 2004 he wrote a poem for the official opening of the Scottish Parliament building at Holyrood and the same year was made Scotland's first national poet, or *makar*.

There are six Morgan poems on the set text list. The two that we will study have been chosen because of their similarities, which will help later when we look at the Scottish set text question. They are both about real life encounters. Morgan once said:

> I think of poetry partly as … a special way of recording moments and events … I am very strongly moved by the absolute force of what actually happens.

and that is what he does with these particular poems. He also said he was fascinated by

> the romance of facts

and in these poems we will see him taking factual events and finding the romance and poetry in them.

Both poems are printed in this book, but you need to have copies for yourself, on paper. This way you can underline, highlight and make notes so that you are engaging and interacting with the poems.

'Good Friday'

 Getting in

Before you read the poem, think about these two questions:

1 What do you associate with Easter?
2 In the Christian Easter story, what happens on Good Friday?

 Meeting the text

You are about to read a poem about an encounter. As you read it for the first time, work out the answers to these questions:

1 Where (exactly) does this encounter happen?
2 When does it happen?
3 What happens?
4 Who is involved in this encounter?

Good Friday

Three o'clock. The bus lurches
round into the sun. 'D's this go –'
he flops beside me – 'right along Bath Street?
- Oh tha's right, tha's all right, see I've
5   got to get some Easter eggs for the kiddies.
I've had a wee drink, ye understand –
ye'll maybe think it's a – funny day
to be celebrating – well, no, but ye see
I wasny working, and I like to celebrate
10   when I'm no working – I don't say it's right
I'm no saying it's right, ye understand – ye understand?
But anyway tha's the way I look at it –
I'm no boring you, eh? Ye see today
take today, I don't know what today's in aid of,
15   whether Christ was – crucified or was he –
rose fae the dead like, see what I mean?
You're an educatit man, you can tell me –
- Aye, well. There ye are. It's been seen
time and again, the working man
20   has nae education. He jist canny – jist
hasny got it, know what I mean
he's jist bliddy ignorant – Christ aye,
bliddy ignorant. Well –' The bus brakes violently,
he lunges for the stair, swings down – off
25   into the sun for his Easter eggs
on very
        nearly
            steady
                legs.

 Thinking through

First, share your answers to the 'Meeting the text' questions you were
given at the start of the poem.

Before we start to look at Morgan's ideas, and at the techniques he uses to put them across, it is useful to think about the two characters in the poem. One of them is the **narrator**. We will refer to the other as **the working man** because that is how he describes himself.

Active learning

Draw two stick men or gingerbread men in your notebook. Label them '**the narrator**' and '**the working man**'. Around your two cartoons, write down everything you know already about each character.

Let's get to work

As we study this poem we will look especially at how Morgan's language conveys the two different characters, and how he makes the encounter seem real.

Realism

The opening of the poem is full of **real life detail.** You already thought about this as you answered the 'Meeting the text' questions. We know exactly where the encounter happens: on the top deck of a bus heading along Bath Street in Glasgow. We know exactly when it happens: three o'clock on Good Friday afternoon. We know the weather is sunny.

What Morgan does not do is describe the working man, at all. We do not know how old he is, what he looks like, what he is wearing.

(If you study the other Morgan poem in this book, 'Trio', and also 'In the Snack Bar', you will see that he does sometimes describe characters in vivid detail, even though he chooses not to do so here.)

The character is not really introduced either. He just starts to speak, sits down, and keeps on talking. And yet, he feels very real. This is partly because of how realistically Morgan the poet renders this man's speech. We will cover this idea later. It is also because the start of the poem is so vividly real that everything else in the poem seems real too. Morgan paints enough pictures in our head at the start for us to be able to paint the rest for ourselves.

Morgan also uses tense to create realism. By telling the whole poem in the **present tense** he creates what we call **immediacy**, a sense that the whole thing is unfolding in front of us as we look on.

The narrator

You may have noticed that we have been using the words 'character' and 'narrator'. This might seem a bit surprising, as Morgan's own public statements about his poems suggest that the encounters in them really happened. But, we have to remember that Morgan is a poet. He shapes life into poetry. Also, remember that in his love poems he deliberately hid things from the reader.

We should not assume that the voice of a narrator is the voice of the poet. If you read a poem in which the narrator described killing a 90-foot-long giant squid after a 3-day-long battle in outer space, we would not assume the narrator was the poet, because we know that poem just could not be true. In general, we should not ever assume that the voice of the narrator is the voice of the poet, even when the narrator describes an event in the city where we know the poet lived.

Some parts of the poem 'belong to' the narrator. They come from his voice. Other parts come from the voice of the working man.

- Using the line numbers to help you, write a sentence or two in your notebook to say which parts of the poem come from the narrator's voice.
- Again using the line numbers to help you, write a sentence or two in your notebook to say which parts of the poem come from the working man's voice.

The narrator's language

You should have worked out that these are the narrator's only words:

> **Three o'clock. The bus lurches**
>
> **round into the sun ...**
>
> **he flops beside me**

and

> **... The bus brakes violently,**
>
> **he lunges for the stair, swings down – off**

into the sun for his Easter eggs

on very

nearly

steady

legs.

Everything else in the poem is a monologue by the working man.

- There are five **verbs** in the narrator's language. List them.

These verbs (especially if we include the adverb 'violently' along with 'brakes') all tell us about **active and expressive** movement. Along with the real life detail we saw earlier, they are another way in which Morgan the poet brings the scene to life and makes us feel we can almost see it happening before our eyes.

The narrator's verbs also contrast with those of the other man, as we will see later.

As well as this clever use of verbs, we can see other poetic techniques in what the narrator tells us at the end.

He uses **rhyme** of 'eggs' and 'legs'. It is one of very few rhymes in the poem, and the only **rhyming couplet**, when two lines side by side rhyme with each other.

- Why do you think Morgan the poet saved this technique until the very end? How does it help give the poem an effective ending?

There is a carefully chosen **layout**. The last line 'on very nearly steady legs' is stretched out onto four lines of the page.

- Why do you think Morgan the poet laid the ending out like this? What does the shape of the lines suggest?

He **undermines** his own words. The description 'very nearly' challenges the idea that the working man's legs are 'steady'.

The working man's language
In contrast with the narrator's short, but poetic, speech, the other man's language might seem very unlike poetry. There are no similes or metaphors, no images or personification. Remember though that this man's language is shown to us by being passed through the filter of Morgan the poet. There is technique here too, and it all means something.

First of all, Morgan the poet puts in **a detail we, the readers, need** to help us understand.

- Look at line 6. What do we learn? Why would the working man not need to say this to the narrator?

Next, Morgan makes careful use of **word choice** and of **repetition**.

Active learning

Read the poem again. It will help if you have your own copy to write on. As you read the poem, circle every use each of these words:

see   understand   say/saying   mean

How many uses of each word did you find?

The repeated use of these words seems to suggest that the working man really wants to be taken seriously. He is trying hard to communicate. He wants to be understood and accepted. He does not want to be judged. We can find other evidence of this too.

- How does line 5 show his kindness?
- How do lines 10 and 11 show that he does not want us to judge or condemn his drinking?
- How does line 11 show that he wants to be understood?
- How does line 13 show his need to be accepted?
- How many dashes are there in the poem? Count them.
- What do the dashes suggest about the way the man talks?
- How do the dashes show us that the man wants to be understood?

Active learning

Discuss these questions in your group or with a partner and then share your answers with the class:

1 Why do you the think this man starts talking to the narrator in the first place?

2 Why do you think he feels the need to explain that he has been drinking?

3 Why do you think he tells the narrator that he is going to buy Easter eggs?

4 Why do you think he stresses the fact that the working man is ignorant and uneducated?

One reason the working man may be doing all of this is because he can see that the narrator is 'an educatit man'. He may feel very aware of their differences in social class, or in education. He certainly describes himself as 'bliddy ignorant' and admits to not understanding the Easter story, which he thinks the narrator will be able to explain.

Some of his language does slightly support the idea that he might not be well educated. Sometimes he abandons an idea half-way through:

> … **He jist canny – jist/hasny …**

Sometimes he is quite ungrammatical:

… was he –/rose fae the dead like, …

We already looked at the narrator's use of active verbs. We have also looked at the working man's repetition of certainly carefully chosen verbs.

Quite a lot of those verbs make it look as if he is in control of the conversation. He seems to be telling the narrator how to act or what to think:

see … ye understand … ye'll maybe think … ye see … see what I mean … you can tell me … know what I mean

Actually though, these verbs are again showing us how much the man wants the narrator to listen to him and to understand him.

Morgan the poet also writes in such a way as to show us what the man's voice sounds like.

He puts across the man's Glaswegian **accent**. (Accent means the way in which words sound different if they are spoken by speakers who come from different places.)

- How does Morgan do this? Agree on an answer in your class and write it in your notebook.

He puts across the man's Scottish **dialect**. (Dialect means the way in which speakers who come from different places use different words to mean the same thing.)

- Where does Morgan use dialect? Agree on an answer in your class and write it in your notebook.

Interaction
When you first read it, the poem seems to have a short introduction and conclusion from the mind of the narrator, and then a monologue from the tipsy working man. You might almost think the two characters do not properly interact. Look again.

Active learning

There are a number of places in the poem where it seems that the narrator has said something, or done something, but does not tell us what that is. Work on the extracts below. For each extract:

1 Work out where exactly you think the narrator's words or actions might fit in.

2 Work out either what you think the narrator said or what you think he did.

Extract 1

he flops beside me – 'right along Bath Street?

– Oh tha's right, tha's all right, see I've

got to get some Easter eggs for the kiddies.

Extract 2

ye'll maybe think it's a – funny day

to be celebrating – well, no, but ye see

I wasny working, and I like to celebrate

when I'm no working

Extract 3

But anyway tha's the way I look at it –

I'm no boring you, eh?

Extract 4

You're an educatit man, you can tell me –

– Aye, well. There ye are

Incidentally, you should have noticed that the last line quoted above, '– Aye, well. There ye are' suggests the narrator gave an answer that the man thought was quite deep or clever. That answer was about the meaning of Easter.

Christian ideas in the poem

The title of this poem refers to a particular day on the Christian calendar, Good Friday. This is the day on which Jesus was crucified. The idea of Easter is picked up in the working man's mention of going to buy Easter eggs, and by his questions about the meaning of Easter in the second half of the poem.

If we look closely, we can see other parallels. The opening words of the poem are:

Three o'clock. The bus lurches

round into the sun

The Bible story of Jesus death, as told by a writer called Matthew, says:

From the sixth hour until the ninth hour darkness came over all the land. About the ninth hour Jesus cried out in a loud voice [… and] gave up his spirit.

'The ninth hour' here means about three in the afternoon, as the Jews of biblical times counted their hours from sunrise. So, Morgan in his poem has his bus come out into the sun at the exact same time as the Bible story has the darkness ending and Jesus dying. It is a significant time, standing for the end of darkness and of Jesus' suffering.

You do not need to believe or agree with the Christian story of Easter to enjoy this poem. But, if you understand the Easter story, you will be able to appreciate the poem better – to see what Morgan as a writer is doing.

Christians believe Jesus, also known as Christ, was the son of God, in fact God choosing to live on Earth in human form. He lived a perfectly good life, taught people, performed miracles and finally died. Christians believe that Christ's death has the power to save everybody from their sins, from all the wrong things they have done in life. Those who believe in Jesus and put their faith in him are accepted by God and their sins are forgiven.

- What does the working man in the poem think about the Christian Easter story?
- What does he think about Easter as a time of year? How does he celebrate it?
- The working man says the word 'Christ' twice. Explain the two different ways in which he uses the word.

This gives us two different pictures of Easter, the one believed by Christians, and the one expressed by the man, who seems to have more questions than answers.

What is Morgan the poet saying about Easter?

Perhaps that Easter means different things to different people – the man's celebratory drink and buying of eggs for his children is just as valid as any other way of marking it.

Perhaps that the church has not done a very good job of explaining things, if the man doesn't know 'what today's in aid of'.

Perhaps that the church is not good at reaching ordinary working people. The man in the poem says he is 'bliddy ignorant' about Easter. However, Morgan the poet knows the story in enough detail to be able to refer in his opening lines to the detail about the darkness and the third hour.

It does seem that Morgan is questioning how much Christian beliefs and rituals are relevant in modern life. However, he also shows that we still need something to celebrate. The working man celebrates having a day off work. The poem also, by mentioning the sun twice, at the start and at the end, celebrates spring.

The Christian story of Easter goes on to say that although Jesus was crucified, died, and was buried on Good Friday, that is not the end. On the Sunday morning he came back to life again. This event is called the resurrection. We can apply these ideas to the poem. We could say that the working man was somewhat 'crucified' by drink, but that at the end of the poem he has his own 'resurrection' back out into the sunshine.

This is a good moment to take stock of our work on this poem, before we move on to the next.

> You can carry on the rest of the table yourself. You will need a large piece of paper, maybe two, as you need to add the following techniques:
>
> | | | | | |
> |---|---|---|---|---|
> | active, expressive verbs | rhyme | line layout | undermining | word choice |
> | repetition | being ungrammatical | accent | biblical references | |

You will find another of these revision exercises at the end of the work on the next Morgan poem in this book. The task will not be so fully explained again; you will just get a list of the techniques to revise, but you can look back to this page to remind you what to do. It is time now to go on to our second Morgan poem.

'Trio'

 Getting in

Before you read the poem, think about these two questions:

1 What is the best present anyone ever gave you for Christmas?
2 What is the best present you ever gave someone else for Christmas?

 Meeting the text

You are going to read another poem about an encounter. As you read it for the first time, work out the answers to these questions:

1 Where (exactly) does this encounter happen?
2 When does it happen?
3 What happens?
4 Who is involved in this encounter?

 Thinking through

Do these two tasks as a class or by taking part in a smaller group:

First, share your answers to the 'Meeting the text' questions above.

Then, write down everything you know about the story of the Nativity – what Christians believe happened around the time of the birth of Jesus.

'Trio'

Coming up Buchanan Street, quickly, on a sharp winter evening
a young man and two girls, under the Christmas lights –
The young man carries a new guitar in his arms,
the girl on the inside carries a very young baby,
5   and the girl on the outside carries a chihuahua.
And the three of them are laughing, their breath rises
in a cloud of happiness, and as they pass
the boy says, 'Wait till he sees this but!'
The chihuahua has a tiny Royal Stewart tartan coat like a
                                    teapot–holder,
10   the baby in its white shawl is all bright eyes and mouth like
                                 favours in a fresh sweet cake,
the guitar swells out under its milky plastic cover, tied at the neck
               with silver tinsel tape and a brisk sprig of mistletoe.
Orphean sprig! Melting baby! Warm chihuahua!
The vale of tears is powerless before you.
Whether Christ is born, or is not born, you
put paid to fate, it abdicates
15   under the Christmas lights.
Monsters of the year
go blank, are scattered back,
can't bear this march of three.
– And the three have passed, vanished in the crowd
20   (yet not vanished, for in their arms they wind
the life of men and beasts, and music,
laughter ringing them round like a guard)
at the end of this winter's day.

Let's get to work

As we study this poem we will look especially at how Morgan conveys this scene, including the three characters and what they are carrying. We will go on to examine how he uses these to put across an idea. Throughout all of this, we will see how this poem can be compared to 'Good Friday', which we looked at earlier.

Morgan did not divide the poem into verses. However, to help us study it, we are going to break it down into four sections.

Section 1: the title to the end of line 8 ('Trio … sees this but!')
The title, 'Trio', has a **denotation**, a straightforward dictionary meaning. At the most basic level it just means three of something, in this case the three people the narrator sees.

However, the title also suggests three things. These are the **connotations** of the word – the ideas that the word suggests and sparks off for us when we read it.

1   It suggests three people playing music together in a small group. This idea fits this poem because there is a musical instrument in it, the guitar the young man is carrying. The idea of music goes with the general mood of happiness and celebration in the poem.
2   We would hope that a group playing music together will be in harmony with each other. This ties in with the idea that the three people in the poem are in harmony with each other, that they have a close and loving relationship. By the end of the poem, the narrator uses these three characters to celebrate the possible harmony and togetherness of the whole human race.
3   The three people in the poem may suggest the three kings or three wise men from the Nativity story.

Morgan brings the poem to life straight away by using **realistic details,** and by writing in the **present tense**. (We saw how he does this in 'Good Friday' too. He also uses this technique in another of the set poems, 'In the Snack Bar'.)

● List six details we know from the first two lines of the poem.
● List all the present tense verbs Morgan uses from the title to line 8.

The **opening line** of the poem sounds a little negative. We are told that it is 'winter', that the weather is 'sharp', and we know it must be dark as Morgan says it is 'evening'. This might suggest to us that the poem is going to be a negative one. But it is not. The poem is so happy and positive that it stands as a contrast to that opening line. This might suggest two possible ideas:

Perhaps that Morgan is saying we can find happiness in all sorts of unexpected or unlikely places.

Perhaps that Morgan himself, or his narrator, was feeling rather negative before he saw the three young people, but that seeing them really cheered him up.

Morgan uses **repetition** in these lines:

1 How often does he use the word 'young'?
2 How often does he use the words 'girl' or 'girls'?
3 What effect does he get from repeating these words?
4 How often does he repeat the word 'carries'?
5 What effect does he get from repeating that word?

Morgan uses the **connotations** of one word in particular. He tells us the three young people are 'under the Christmas lights'. In this phrase, 'under' suggests that the people are being watched over and protected. This idea of safety and protection is one we will keep coming back to as we study the rest of the poem.

This word 'under' gives us another idea too. At Christmas we put lights on the tree and we put presents under it. If the young people are under the lights, Morgan is saying that, even though one of them is carrying a present, they themselves also are presents. They are a gift to him because they made him feel so joyful and hopeful.

The 'Christmas lights' in this part of the poem may be a **symbol** – something that is really there in the poem but also stands for another idea. If the three young people stand for the three wise men from the Nativity story then the lights Morgan sees in Buchanan Street may also stand for the star the wise men followed as they took their gifts to the baby Jesus. If you are not convinced, this may help: just like the kings or wise men, each one of these people in the poem is carrying something precious.

There are lots of **suggestions of fragility** in this part of the poem. The guitar is not in a proper musical instrument case. The baby is very young and therefore in need of protection. A chihuahua is a tiny dog.

Morgan also makes careful **word choice** of 'cloud'. The trio's breath 'rises in a cloud of happiness'. The cloud suggests their togetherness because it joins their breath together. The actual, real warmth of their breath compared to the cold air is visible as a real, **literal** cloud of vapour. This cloud also has a metaphorical meaning: it shows us the **metaphorical** warmth between them, their bond of friendship that keeps them together.

Lastly in this section, Morgan uses **Glaswegian dialect** to increase the sense of the poem happening in a real place.

- Quote the line in which this dialect is used.
- Explain how you know this is Glaswegian dialect.

Section 2: lines 9–11 ('The chihuahua ... sprig of mistletoe.')
In just three lines of the poem, Morgan packs in an incredible amount of detail. This tells us how important these lines are to him.

Active learning

You will need three sheets of A4 paper. In the middle of the first sheet, draw the chihuahua as it is described in these lines. In the middle of the second sheet, draw the baby as it is described in these lines. In the middle of the third sheet, draw the guitar as it is described in these lines. Under each picture, write the line of the poem that goes with it.

As you work through the material about these lines, annotate your drawings with notes to help you remember and understand what you have learned. There is going to be a lot of detail, and this will help you keep track.

We have noticed already that the baby, the guitar, and the dog are all **fragile**. Now we see however that they are all **safe**.

- What protects the chihuahua? How do we know it is loved and cared for?
- What protects the baby? How do we know it is loved and cared for?
- What protects the guitar? How do we know the young man is proud of it?

Let us look at the three descriptions in more detail.

The chihuahua is a lovely mixture of foreign and Scottish. It is a Mexican breed of dog, but its tartan coat is very Scottish. So, the dog may be there to show that Morgan believes in a Scotland where foreigners are welcome and can become part of our nation. The little dog might also be there to remind us of the animals in the Nativity story, who gathered round the baby Jesus in the manger.

There is a nice contrast between the dignity of the 'Royal' tartan and the silliness of the 'teapot-holder', like something your granny might have. The teapot-holder also makes us think of warmth and care.

The baby gives us another connection to the Christian Nativity story, reminding us of the baby Jesus. The 'white' colour of the shawl (and probably of the icing on the cake too) has connotations of innocence and purity, which are very special qualities.

The baby's 'bright' eyes tell us it is alert, interested in the world and excited about it. This fits with a poem in which the writer is very alert to what he sees in the world, and feels very positive about it.

The baby's eyes and mouth are said to be 'like favours in a fresh sweet cake'. The words 'fresh' and 'sweet' both have positive connotations. If the cake has favours – little hidden treats – in it, then it is most likely to be a wedding or Christmas cake. Both of these usually have white icing, going back to the idea of innocence and purity. A wedding cake celebrates love and the start of an important new phase of life. A Christmas cake is usually shared with people we love, our family and friends. If you got a favour in your slice of cake it would be a nice surprise, just as seeing these three young people and the things they are carrying is a treat and a surprise for Morgan.

The guitar 'swells out' under its cover. This suggests that the young man carrying it is swelling with pride because he knows he has chosen a wonderful present that will make someone very happy.

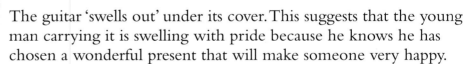

The 'milky' colour of the cover ties in with the idea that babies live on milk. Milk is something natural and very nurturing.

The 'silver' colour of the tinsel tells us the guitar is being treated as something precious and valuable. This is not because of how much it might have cost, but because of the happiness it will bring.

The 'mistletoe' makes us think of love, and the description of the sprig as 'brisk' suggests life and energy that ties back in with all the ideas earlier in the poem about youth and newness.

You should also have noticed that these three lines about what the people are carrying are the longest three lines in the poem. Morgan does not break them up or shorten them because he wants to show that love, happiness and generosity should not be restricted.

Section 3: lines 12–18 ('Orphean sprig! … march of three.')
In the first line here Morgan uses three **exclamation marks**. It is as if he is almost shouting out with joy. Seeing this everyday, even slightly comical, scene gets him celebrating life. It is so uplifting that he feels optimistic.

The poem shows that we can find real happiness in very ordinary things, even in things we have only seen and not actually experienced:

Morgan is only watching these people, he is not one of them. It also shows us what good poets do – they look at life in a special way and find the poetry in it.

The poet uses an **allusion** to the Greek myth of Orpheus. An allusion is when a writer refers to something he expects his readers to recognise and understand.

Orpheus was a poet and musician. He was so talented that he could charm all living things, and even inanimate objects such as stones, with his music. When his lover Eurydice got trapped in Hades, the ancient Greek version of Hell, Orpheus led her back out from the underworld by getting her to follow the music from his lyre (a kind of small harp).

So, when Morgan calls the sprig around the guitar 'Orphean' he is saying music has the power to charm us, and even to lift us out of Hell.

There is humour in this line too – 'Melting baby!' and 'Warm chihuahua!'

Morgan's next phrase, 'The vale of tears' is another **allusion**, this time one that has become a well-known phrase, and which originally came from a hymn. The vale of tears means all the problems and troubles that are an unavoidable part of human life. The hymn says that only Jesus can help people cope with the vale of tears. Morgan however says that the sprig, the baby and the dog have enough joyful power to defeat the vale of tears.

This ties in with the note of doubt in the next line. It is Christmas, but Morgan, or his narrator, is not totally sure about what to believe.

- Quote the words that show us this uncertainty.
- How does this remind us of some lines in 'Good Friday'? Quote those lines again.

This lack of sureness does not matter, because Morgan is so sure of the power of the sprig, baby and chihuahua. His **word choice** shows us this. He says fate 'abdicates'. This is a word that is only ever used about kings and queens, powerful and important people. To abdicate is to completely and utterly give up your power, to step down and know you can never step back up again. It also something the king or queen decides to do willingly. (If they are forced out of power, we would say they had been deposed.) Fate, faced with these three things, just decides to give up.

This is supported by his **line layout** too. In 'Good Friday' we saw how the layout of the last few lines suggested the working man's unsteady legs. Now Morgan gets his line to look like this:

Whether Christ is born, or is not born, you

put paid to fate, it abdicates

under the Christmas lights.

The last line itself almost abdicates, gives up and walks away.

Morgan goes on to make the baby, the sprig and the dog seem almost magical or supernatural because they defeat 'monsters'. This part of the poem again goes in threes. He talks about the 'march of three' and the monsters give up in three ways: they 'go blank', they 'are scattered back' and they 'can't bear' it.

The word 'march' has two meanings. We call this **ambiguity**, which means that we have to keep both meanings in our head at once because the poet does not tell us that one is more right than the other. It makes us think of an army marching, which shows us how powerful these three are. But a march is also a kind of music, which ties in with the idea of a musical trio, and the fact that one of the three things being carried is a guitar.

Section 4: line 19 to the end ('– And the three ... this winter's day.') These lines begin with a **dash**. Did you even notice it? This dash is in fact the end of a **parenthesis** that began with an earlier dash at the end of line 2. Did you notice that one? In between these dashes we see the three young people and the things they are carrying.

There are two reasons Morgan encloses this main section of the poem in dashes.

1 The dashes **enclose** the whole encounter. They remind us how brief Morgan's sight of the trio is. In fact, he probably spent much less time looking at them than it takes us to read about him looking at them.

2 The dashes **protect and surround** the trio. The trio is powerful, but because joy is so rare in this world they should be protected as something precious.

There is another **parenthesis** in this last section of the poem, this time one made by the use of **brackets**. You'll find it in lines 20 to 22:

> (yet not vanished, for in their arms they wind
>
> the life of men and beasts, and music,
>
> laughter ringing them round like a guard)

Once again the parenthesis protects these words. Very cleverly, this time the words are actually *about* protection. We are told that their laughter is 'like a guard'. It is also 'ringing round them', which is another example of **ambiguity**. The laughter is 'ringing' in the sense that it makes a ringing sound, it rings out. The laughter also surrounds them, goes around them in a ring, again protecting them. We might even see a hint of a wedding ring here, just like we saw a hint of a wedding cake earlier.

This bracketed parenthesis also gives Morgan a chance to contradict himself. He has just told us in line 19 that 'the three have passed, vanished in the crowd'. But now he tells us they have 'not vanished'. They may be lost in the crowd but their effect on him is lasting. We know it lasted because he went away and eventually wrote a poem about it. People are still reading that poem nearly 50 years later. The trio certainly have 'not vanished'.

So what can we say about this poem overall. What is Morgan's message? How about:

> Human life and love are special and sacred, with or without religion.

Active learning

Work in a group. Copy the above statement down in the centre of a sheet of paper. Around this, give all the proof from the poem that you can find to back up this statement. Your evidence might be quotations from the poem or notes in your own words.

Active learning

Technique revision

Now that you have worked your way through all the work on 'Trio' you should know the poem very well. Now revise your knowledge of Morgan's techniques.

You are going to carry out the same exercise that you did at the end of the 'Good Friday' work (see page 218). (Look back to it now if you need to be more fully reminded of the instructions.) Take a large piece of paper and mark it up into a **PEE** grid. For every technique, fill in a quotation from the poem, and explain the effect it has on the reader. For a grid about 'Trio' you need to work with the following techniques in the box below.

Deal separately with the connotations of each of these words: *trio, under, cloud, white, bright, favours, fresh, sweet, cake, swells, milky, silver, mistletoe, bright, abdicates.*

realistic details	present tense	symbol
repetition of 'young' and 'girl(s)'	repetition of 'carries'	negative-sounding first line
Glasgow dialect	ideas of fragility	ideas of safety and protection
very long descriptive lines	exclamation marks	humour
allusion to the myth of Orpheus	allusion to the Nativity story	allusion to hymn words
ambiguity of 'march'	ambiguity of 'ringing'	parenthesis made of dashes
parenthesis made of brackets	line layout on page	

Finally, make sure that you finished annotating your drawings of the three long descriptive lines with all your notes about them.

That is the end of our work on these two poems about Glaswegian encounters. Although it is not on the set text list, you might want to take a quick look at a much bleaker poem Morgan wrote about an event in a Glasgow street – 'Glasgow, 5th March 1971' — which presents a far nastier, but sadly still truthful, picture of city life.

There are four other Morgan poems on the National 5 list. You will need to study them **all** if you hope to use them for the Scottish set text question. If you are doing this, I recommend you go next to 'In the Snack Bar', which is about another real-life encounter in Glasgow. Remember, your teacher should double check if these poems are still on the set list at the time when you are using this book.

If Edwin Morgan has been taken off the Scottish text list by the time you take this course, you could still study 'Good Friday; and 'Trio' as texts for the critical essay. If you do that, your Scottish set texts will need to come from a different genre, not poetry but either prose or drama.

The Scottish text questions

Warning

The Scottish set text questions are in the first section of your Critical Reading exam paper. If your teacher has taught you more than one of the set text authors, for example the poems of Morgan and a play by Alan Spence, then you should look at the Scottish text section of the exam paper **first**, to choose which author you will answer on. This will let you know which genres to look at for the critical essay questions in the second section.

What you will be assessed on

In this part of the exam you will read an extract – or in the case of poetry, probably a whole poem – from a Scottish text you have previously studied in school and then answer some questions.

There will be several questions focusing on the extract, or poem, itself. These questions will each be worth 2, 3 or 4 marks. There will be a total of 12 marks worth of questions about the extract or poem.

The last question will be a far weightier one, worth 8 marks. This question will require you to compare the extract, or the poem, to the rest of the work you have studied. For example:

- If your Scottish text is a play or novel, and the extract focused on one character, you might be asked to look at how that character develops over the course of the text.
- If the extract touched on a particular theme, you might be asked how that theme is explored and developed in the rest of the text.
- If you have studied poetry, the final question may ask you how the ideas and language of the poem printed in the exam paper compare to other poetry you have studied by the same writer.

Warning

You will need lots of practice at this task before your exam. This book can only help you begin that process and can only give you an example of what the Scottish set text questions might be like.

Active learning

Your teacher may want you to work on your own, or perhaps with a partner or in a group. Start by reading 'Trio' on page 220 again. Then attempt each question. If you are working with someone else, make sure you write down your answers as you would in an exam. Once you have finished, give your work to your teacher to mark.

1 The author gives this poem a sense of reality. Show how this is achieved in the first eight lines. ('Coming up … sees this but!') **2**

2 In lines 9–11 ('The chihuahua has … sprig of mistletoe') Morgan describes what the young people are carrying. What mood or atmosphere is created by the writer, and how does he use language effectively to create this mood? **3**

3 Many of the main ideas in the poem come across clearly in lines 12–18 ('Orphean sprig! … this march of three'). Identify at least **one** of Morgan's main ideas from these lines. Show how **one** example of the poet's language in these lines helps to clarify or illustrate his meaning. **3**

4 Show how two examples of the poet's use of language in lines 19–23 ('– And the three … this winter's day.') help to clarify or illustrate his ideas in these lines. **4**

For answers go to page 276–78.

You have now done the first four questions for this task. These questions are specifically about 'Trio'. Either mark these yourself, or give them to your teacher to mark. Do not go on to the next task until you know how well you got on with questions 1 to 4.

Before we go on to look at the final question, the one that gets you to place this poem in the wider context of Morgan's other work, there is something you need to do.

Active learning

Work with a partner or a small group. Get a large sheet of paper and divide it in two. Mark one side **Similarities** and the other side **Differences**. Compare and contrast 'Good Friday' and 'Trio' and use the sheet to create a record or poster of your discoveries. The first few have been done for you.

SIMILARITIES

- Set in Glasgow.

- About unexpected encounters with people.

DIFFERENCES

- 'Good Friday' is mainly the speech of the working man; 'Trio' is nearly all description by Morgan/narrator.

- The working man in 'Good Friday' interacts with the narrator; the young people in 'Trio' are probably unaware of him.

Carry on finding more answers in your group. If you push yourself to think of the techniques Morgan uses, and then also to think of the ways in which he uses these techniques, you should be able to get at least ten similarities and at least ten differences.

Active learning

Now answer the final question. This is worth 8 marks and needs a much longer answer. You could, if you wish, tackle this as a kind of mini-essay. It is, however, perfectly all right if you approach this question by giving a set of bullet-pointed answers that all fit together to form a complete response.

Here is the question:

5 With close textual reference, show how the ideas and/or language of this poem are similar to another poem or poems by Morgan that you have read.   **8**

When you have written your answer, give it to your teacher to mark.

For answer go to page 279.

Active learning

Now you are going to try a similar task to the one above, working this time on 'Good Friday'. This time you should work on your own. You should attempt this task once your teacher has marked your 'Trio' questions. Start by reading 'Good Friday' on page 210. Then answer each question in writing. Once you have finished, give your work to your teacher to mark.

1 The author gives this poem a sense of reality. Show how this is achieved in the first three lines. ('Three o'clock … Bath Street?')   **2**

2 How does the writer's use of language in lines 6 to 16 ('I've had a wee drink … see what I mean?') show the man's need to communicate?   **3**

3 With close reference to lines 6 to 23 (I've had a wee drink … bliddy ignorant. Well –') explain how the poem shows at least one belief Morgan has about Easter and/or the church   **3**

4 Show how two examples of the poet's use of language in lines 23 to end ('The bus brakes … steady legs') create an effective ending to the poem.   **4**

5 With close textual reference, show how the ideas and/or language of this poem are similar to another poem or poems by Morgan that you have read.   **8**

For answers see page 280.

That brings us to the end of our work on the Scottish set text question. Remember that you will need much more practice than this. Past papers and other material that your teacher will have will all help you with this.

The critical essay

You have written critical essays before of course, but in National 5 you will write them under exam conditions for the first time. So, it is important to understand what you are being asked to do.

A critical essay **is not**:

- a chance for you to write everything you know about a text
- a chance to explain your favourite things about a text
- a chance to tell the marker about the bits you understand best, or find easiest to explain
- an invitation to write a commentary on the whole text from start to end.

A National 5 Critical Essay is a kind of test. It tests your ability to select from your knowledge of a text, and to use that selected knowledge to answer a specific question.

What you will be assessed on

In Section 2 of the exam you will be given a choice of questions. These questions will be divided into five parts. Each part contains questions about a different genre:

- Drama
- Prose
- Poetry
- Film and television drama
- Language

There will be two questions for each genre. These questions will not name any specific texts. Instead, they will be quite broad and general questions that are likely to suit many texts from that genre.

All these questions are designed to test your familiarity with the text, your understanding of the ideas in it, and your awareness of the writer's use of techniques.

You will have about 45 minutes to write the essay in, and it will be marked out of 20.

The next few pages will teach you how to do this. As we have studied two Morgan poems, most of our examples will come from the poetry section. The techniques you will learn should help you to write about any kind of text that you have studied this year. Whichever texts you have studied in class, you will need to know everything there is to know about them, so you can pick the right details from that knowledge to use in the exam.

The examiners are looking at four different areas of your essay-writing skill: **familiarity, understanding and relevance; analysis; evaluation; your use of language.**

- **Familiarity, understanding and relevance** means how well you understand and know the text you have studied, and how well your essay answers the question you have been asked.
- **Analysis** means being able to examine and explain the way the writer writes and the techniques he/she uses.
- **Evaluation** means having a personal response to and a personal opinion about what you have read. You will be able to show what you have enjoyed in the text and what you have gained from it.
- **Use of language** is how clearly you put across your ideas. This includes your spelling, grammar, paragraphing and punctuation. It also means that your essay has to be well structured

As you work through this chapter you will learn to produce essays that display all these skills.

Choosing an essay

At the top of the first page of Section 2 you will find a general instruction:

> **Attempt only ONE question from this Section of the paper, choosing from Drama, Prose or Poetry, Film and Television Drama, or Language.**
>
> **You may use a Scottish text but not the one used in Section 1.**
>
> **Your essay should be on a different genre to the one used in Section 1.**

You **must** make sure you do not write on either the same text or the same genre as you do in the Scottish text part of the exam. In the first few minutes of your exam you need to weigh up your choices quickly but carefully, so that you can do your best work overall and earn as many marks as possible.

How will you choose the best question?

To begin to work this out, we need to look at the way the individual questions are worded. All the essays tasks follow the same pattern. They are set out in two paragraphs. For example:

> **Choose a poem that features an encounter or an incident.**
>
> **By referring to appropriate techniques, show how the poet's development of the encounter or incident leads you to a deeper understanding of the poem's central concerns.**

To choose which essay to write, you are going to look at just the **first** paragraph of the essay topic.

As soon as you see these words, you need to run through a quick mental checklist. Let's assume you go into the exam having studied Edwin Morgan. You can ask yourself:

> **Have I studied any poems?**

To which the answer would be:

> **Yes.**

So, you **might** be able to write this essay. Now it is time to focus in even tighter on that first paragraph and look at **what kind of poem** the examiners want you to write about.

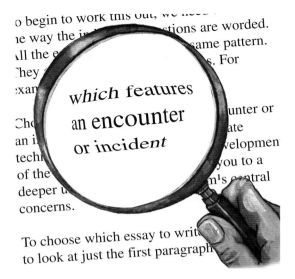

o begin to work this out, we need
the way the ____tions are worded.
All the e____ ____ ____same pattern.
They ____
____xam____

Ch____
an i____
tech____
of the____
deeper u____
concerns.

which features
an encounter
or incident

____unter or
____ate
____velopmen
____ou to a
____m's central

To choose which essay to writ____
to look at just the first paragraph

So now you need to ask yourself:

- Do any of the poems I have studied feature an encounter or incident?

This essay question turns out to be quite a good one, because you get two quite positive answers:

> In 'Good Friday' the narrator encounters a drunk and chatty working man on a bus.

> In 'Trio' the narrator encounters a group of three young people in Buchanan Street at Christmas.

(If you have also studied Morgan's 'In the Snack Bar' you will have a third option, as this poem is also about an encounter.)

It is time to narrow down your choice. To help you do this, take another look at the words in **the second paragraph** of the task. This paragraph is where the examiners tell you how they actually want you to tackle the essay. The words of the second paragraph give you instructions that you must follow. If you do not obey the instructions in the second paragraph of the task, you are not answering the essay question and you will certainly not pass.

For this essay, these words in paragraph 2 are important:

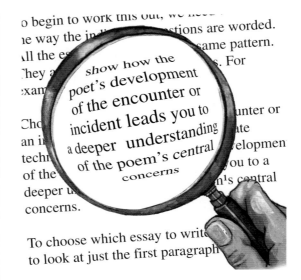

o begin to work this out, we nee...
...e way the in... ...tions are worded.
...ll the e... ...same pattern.
They a... ...s. For
...exam...

show how the poet's development of the encounter or incident leads you to a deeper understanding of the poem's central concerns

Cho...
an i...
techn...
of the...
deeper u...
concerns.

To choose which essay to writ...
to look at just the first paragraph...

Now you can narrow down your options by asking yourself:

- Does one of these poems more clearly use the encounter to express a central idea or concern?

Although both poems have obvious ideas in them, it is perhaps easier to identify Morgan's central idea in 'Trio' than it is in 'Good Friday'. In 'Good Friday' the voice is mostly that of the working man, who does not quite seem to know what he thinks. In 'Trio' however, we can see much more clearly what Morgan is saying – that human life and love are still special, with or without religion.

At this stage you could decide to write your critical essay on Edwin Morgan's 'Trio', or you could carry on looking through the relevant sections of the exam paper until you find a different essay that appeals to you more. Remember, if Morgan is the only author you have studied for the Scottish set text, you cannot do your critical essay on him too. And, remember your essay question must come from a different genre than your Scottish set text.

Active learning

Below you will see just the first paragraph from a number of essay tasks. Some of them fit the two Morgan poems we have studied. Some do not.

For each question, decide if it fits one of these poems. If it does, say which poem it fits. Be careful! Some of the questions may look as if they might work, but actually there would not be enough in the poem to write a whole essay on this idea.

1 Choose a poem in which a particular place is described, either in the town or in the country.

2 Choose a poem in which you find the ending particularly interesting or surprising or satisfying.

3 Choose a poem which takes an optimistic view of life.

4 Choose a poem which tells an exciting or frightening story.

5 Choose a poem which describes a positive experience.

6 Choose a poem which deepens your understanding of human nature.

7 Choose a poem which seems to be about an ordinary, everyday experience but which actually makes a deeper comment about life.

8 Choose a poem which creates pity or sympathy in you.

9 Choose a poem about a strong relationship – for example between two people, or between a person and a place.

Writing your introduction

The first paragraph you write in the essay will be your introduction. Whenever you write a critical essay, the same three things should appear in the opening sentence:

1 the title of the text you read
2 the name of the author
3 a clear indication of what you will be writing about.

As we have already seen, the first paragraph of the essay task helps you to choose which task you are going to do. Once you have chosen an essay to tackle, that same first paragraph of the task instructions is also useful for something else. It helps you to write the introduction to your essay. To do this, you are going to **recycle** many of the words from that paragraph.

Let us assume that you have chosen to do the essay task we looked at in detail earlier, and that you are going to write about 'Trio'. Here is the first paragraph from the essay task we saw earlier on. Look at the words printed in bold type.

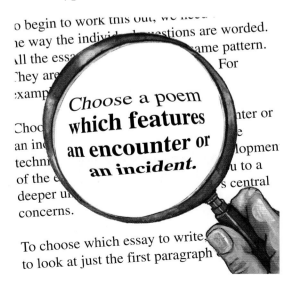

o begin to work this out, we nee...
ne way the individual questions are worded.
ll the essa... ame pattern.
They are For
example

Choo...
an in...
techni...
of the ...
deeper u...
concerns.

Choose a poem **which features an encounter or an incident.**

...nter or
...e
...lopmen
...u to a
...s central

To choose which essay to write,
to look at just the first paragraph

You can recycle all of those words in the first sentence of your essay. Those words help you to give a clear indication of what you will be writing about. You still need to add the title and author to these to have a complete first sentence, which would end up looking like this:

> One poem which features an encounter is 'Trio' by Edwin Morgan.

Can you see the words that have been recycled from the task instructions? Did you also notice that the student missed out the words 'or incident'? Whenever you get the word 'or' in any essay question, you are being invited to make an immediate choice. The way that you write your introduction will show that you have made that choice. This poem is more about an encounter – meeting or noticing some people – than it is about an incident, about something happening. So, the student has focused on the idea of encounter right away, in the introduction.

Active learning

Go back and look at the list of nine opening paragraphs for essay tasks on page 236. You have already worked out which of these you thought suited one of the Morgan poems. Now turn each one of the suitable openings into the opening sentence of an essay. Start each time with

One poem (in) which …

After the opening sentence, it is a good idea to continue your introduction by writing a **short** summary of your text. Teachers can choose to teach any texts that they enjoy, and that they think their students will like. This means that you may end up writing your critical essay about a text that the exam marker has never read, or maybe even never heard of. Writing a **short** summary will give the marker a little bit of context and background, making it easier for him/her to understand comments you make about that text in your essay.

 Warning

Take care! You will have noticed two bold type reminders that you should be writing a **short** summary. The summary itself does not earn you any marks. It just helps you and the exam marker to get your heads clear. You must not waste precious exam time by waffling.

Here is a summary of 'Good Friday'.

> In this poem the narrator is on a bus in Glasgow when a rather drunk man sits down beside him. This man freely shares his thoughts, and doubts, about life, Easter, and the Scottish working man.

That summary is just 36 words long. It should be easily possible to summarise most texts in fewer than 50 words.

Active learning

First complete these two tasks.

1 Write a brief summary of 'Trio'.

2 If you have also studied other literature or media texts in your National 5 course, write a brief summary for each of them.

Now swap your summaries with another student.

Read and mark each other's work. Try to make each other's summaries as brief, clear and efficient as possible.

The main body of your essay

Once you have written the introduction and summary, it is time for the main body of your essay. This main body will be made up of several paragraphs – four or five will be enough.

We have already looked carefully at the fact that the first paragraph of the essay instructions tells you what sort of text to write about. The second paragraph of the essay instructions tells you **what you are actually going to do** in your essay. Remember, if you do not do what that second paragraph tells you to do then you are not answering the question and you will never pass the essay. Here is the whole of an essay question that could suit 'Trio'.

> **Choose a poem which made a lasting impression on you.**
>
> **Explain briefly what the poem is about, then, by referring to appropriate techniques, show how the poem has made this lasting impression.**

If you look at this instruction carefully, you will see that in this essay you have two main things to do:

1 **Explain briefly** what the poem is about.
2 **Say how** the poem made a lasting impression on you.

Many of the critical essays you will find in past papers or in the exam give two things to do.

Active learning

You are going to see some essay questions in full. These questions are on a variety of genres, not just poetry. From each second paragraph, pick out the two things you have to do in the main body of the essay.

1 Choose a play in which one of the man characters has to overcome difficulties in the course of the action.

State what the difficulties are and, by referring to appropriate techniques, show how the character's strengths allow him or her to overcome them.

I have to …
Then I have to …

2 Choose a film or television drama which deals with the subject of good versus evil.

Briefly explain the struggle and, by referring to appropriate techniques, show how your sympathy was engaged on one side or the other.

I have to …
Then I have to …

3 Choose a novel or a short story which has an incident or moment of great tension.

Describe briefly what happens at this point in the story and, by referring to appropriate techniques, go on to show how it is important for the outcome of the story as whole.

I have to …
Then I have to …

4 Choose a film in which the closing sequence makes use of a variety of film techniques to make its dramatic impact.

Briefly state what happens in the closing sequence and, by referring to appropriate techniques, show how the ending is made dramatic.

I have to …

Then I have to …

5 Choose a poem which describes a positive experience.

Describe what happens in the poem and, by referring to appropriate techniques, show how the poet has made the positive nature of this experience clear to you.

I have to …

Then I have to …

Not every critical essay task gives you two things to do. For example, you may find one like this:

Choose a play which has a tragic ending.

By referring to appropriate techniques, show how the ending of the play results from the weaknesses of the main character(s).

In this task you do not have two different things to do, you just have to look, in a proportionate way, at the important weaknesses of the main character or characters. The important thing you must always do is read the question to find out exactly what you have to do and what you have to write about.

In the essay tasks above, did you notice one particular phrase that appears in every question? It is this one:

by referring to appropriate techniques

and it is very important. We will come back to it when we look at using the PEE technique. For now, you just need to know that this phrase is in every essay question.

So, now that you know what you are supposed to do, how are you going to do it? Let us take a look at an essay task we thought would be good for 'Trio'. Here is the question in full. The words that tell you what to do have been picked out in bold.

Choose a poem which made a lasting impression on you.

Explain briefly what the poem is about, then, by referring to appropriate techniques, **show how** the poem has made this lasting impression.

A good way to tackle this essay is to write just one paragraph dealing with the first main point, explaining what the poem is about. We know that one paragraph will be enough here as you have been told to explain 'briefly'. Then you could write four more paragraphs showing how the poem made a lasting impression on you.

As you write these paragraphs:

- Every one of the main body paragraphs must help you to do what your chosen task tells you to do.
- Every one of the main body paragraphs must use evidence from the text.

Active learning

Here is an example of a paragraph that does the two things mentioned above. Read it carefully and decide:

1 Does this paragraph come from the 'Explain briefly what ...' section of the essay or from the, 'Show how ...' section?

2 Which words in the paragraph show that this student is trying to stick to the chosen task?

3 Which words in the paragraph show the student is using evidence from the text?

The answers are at the end of the paragraph. Do not look until you have worked them out for yourself.

One way in which the poem makes a lasting impression is through Morgan's use of vivid descriptions, which turn out to be full of meaning. For example, we are told:

'The chihuahua has a tiny Royal Stewart tartan coat like a

teapot-holder'

Firstly, this description brings the little dog to life and helps the reader to picture it very clearly. The details within this description also each mean something. The fact that we are told it is a 'chihuahua', a Mexican breed of dog, but is wearing a Scottish 'tartan' coat shows that Morgan believes in a Scotland where those from overseas are welcome and can fit in. The coat also shows that this tiny dog is safe and protected, as are the guitar and baby in the poem. Morgan also creates contrast between the dignity of the coat's tartan being 'Royal' and the fact that it looks like the kind of 'teapot holder' a granny might use.

Did you manage to answer the three questions?

> 1 This paragraph comes from the 'Show how ...' section of the essay.
>
> 2 The words in the paragraph that show this student is trying to stick to the chosen task are:
> *One way in which the poem makes a lasting impression is through Morgan's use of vivid descriptions, ...*
>
> 3 The words in the paragraph that show the student is using evidence from the text are:
> *The chihuahua has a tiny Royal Stewart tartan coat like a teapot-holder*
> and the shorter individual quotations of words from within this longer one.

Did you notice how this student set out the quotation? When the whole line is quoted it goes on a new line, and it is indented – moved away a little from the left-hand side of the page – to make it stand out. But, you do not need to skip a line above or below the quotation. You are not starting a new paragraph: the quotation is part of the paragraph. The student also used quotation marks.

Let us focus a bit more carefully on how to write the paragraphs in the main body of your essay. There are two things you should do in these paragraphs so that they will be well written and help you to achieve the task you have chosen.

1 You should begin the paragraph with a **topic sentence**.
2 You should use the **PEE structure**.

Topic sentences
Topic sentences are called this for two reasons:

1 They tie in with the topic of your essay.
2 They let the reader understand the topic of the paragraph you are on.

Using a topic sentence at the start of the paragraph sets you off in the right direction.

Active learning

You are going to see again the five essay tasks you examined on pages 240–41. After the tasks you will see a list of sentences. Each one is a topic sentence from one of the five essays. Can you decide which essay each topic sentence belongs to?

Here are the essay topics:

1 Choose a play in which one of the main characters has to overcome difficulties in the course of the action.

State what the difficulties are and, by referring to appropriate techniques, show how the character's strengths allow him or her to overcome them.

2 Choose a film or television drama which deals with the subject of good versus evil.

Briefly explain the struggle and, by referring to appropriate techniques, show how your sympathy was engaged on one side or the other.

3 Choose a novel or a short story which has an incident or moment of great tension.

Describe briefly what happens at this point in the story and, by referring to appropriate techniques, go on to show how it is important for the outcome of the story as a whole.

4 Choose a film in which the closing sequence makes use of a variety of film techniques to make its dramatic impact.

Briefly state what happens in the closing sequence and, by referring to appropriate techniques, show how the ending is made dramatic.

5 Choose a poem which describes a positive experience.

Describe what happens in the poem and, by referring to appropriate techniques, show how the poet has made the positive nature of this experience clear to you.

Here are the topic sentences. Can you match each one to the right essay topic? It does not matter if you do not know the text the topic sentence is about. You are just looking at how well it ties in with the essay question.

a One way in which this moment is important to the story as a whole is that it causes the eventual ending.

b One way the author makes the positive nature of the experience clear is by his use of multiple exclamation marks close together.

c One way in which Alec overcomes his difficulties in life is by putting great effort into his education.

d One technique that makes the ending dramatic is very fast cutting between many brief shots.

e Our sympathy for Moriarty is engaged when we see that he acts so wickedly partly because he is bored and needs stimulation.

The PEE structure

The PEE structure helps you to remember what should be in each paragraph.

- **P** – tells you to make a **P**oint about the writer's technique. In other words, mention something you can see the writer deliberately doing.
- **E** – tells you to give **E**vidence: this will nearly always be by quoting from the text, though just occasionally it may be easier to give evidence by referring to something in the text.
- **E** – tells you to **E**xplain the **E**ffect of this, to show what the writer is doing to us, the readers.

The **P** part of this is also the topic sentence of the paragraph, so there is a bit of an overlap between the idea of using a topic sentence, and the idea of following the PEE structure.

Active learning

Copy the following paragraph into your notebook. Once you have copied it out, do these three things:

1. Underline the **P** part with a straight line.
2. Underline the **E for Evidence** part with a wiggly or jagged line.
3. Draw a box round the **E for Explanation** part.

One way in which Morgan makes his ideas memorable is by saying the same thing in three ways at once. He tells us that when faced with the guitar, the baby, and the chihuahua:

> 'Monsters of the year
> go blank, are scattered back,
> can't bear this march of three.'

If the 'monsters' go 'blank' then they must have no ideas and nothing to say for themselves. If they are 'scattered' then they are separated and no longer any kind of force compared to the three who 'march' in an organised and powerful way. The overall repetition of the fact that the 'monsters' can no longer cope shows how powerful the three simple things are.

Did you notice how the student laid out the long quotation? It is **indented** and **inside quotation marks**, as we saw already. Also, because he was quoting three lines from the poem, he laid them out to match the way they were laid out in the original poem.

You should also have spotted that the student is writing in the **present tense**. You should do this whenever you write about what you have read.

Active learning

Read the essay extract again. Pick out all the verbs which show that the student is writing in the present tense.

Writing about techniques

On the exam paper, above each set of essay tasks, you will see a paragraph of advice. The wording of this paragraph follows a pattern.

Active learning

To get you to spot the pattern of this paragraph in the essay instructions, you are going to see the advice for two different types of essay. The first one is for **poetry** essays; the second one is for **prose** essays. Read the two paragraphs and then answer the two questions below.

Answers to questions in this part should refer to the text and to such relevant features as: word choice, tone, imagery, structure, content, rhythm, theme, sound, ideas …

Answers to questions in this part should refer to the text and such relevant features as: characterisation, setting, language, key incident(s), climax, turning point, plot, structure, narrative technique, theme, ideas, description …

1 Which words are always used at the **start** of the advice above the essay tasks?

2 What do you always see at the **end** of the advice above the essay tasks? What do you think this means?

What this paragraph of advice does is just remind you to write about some of the techniques the author uses, or some of the things that made that text worth studying in the first place. Remember that **a technique is anything a writer deliberately chooses to do.** While some techniques have simple names like *simile, metaphor, alliteration* and so on, anything a writer does on purpose to have an effect on the reader is a technique.

You do not actually have to write about the techniques named in the paragraph, because the three dots at the end of that paragraph allow you to write about whichever techniques and features you think are important for the text and task you have chosen.

What does matter is that you should deal with the writer's techniques, and you should make clear in your essay that you are doing so, because of that instruction in every essay question about **referring to appropriate techniques**.

For example, suppose you were writing an essay on 'Good Friday'. Depending on which essay you chose, you could pick any of the following techniques and features that we looked at as we studied the poem, none of which are on the list in the box in the exam paper:

active, expressive verbs	title	realism
line layout	undermining	present tense
repetition	being ungrammatical	Scottish dialect
accent	biblical references	

as well as these two techniques which are named in that box on the exam paper:

rhyme	word choice

The way that you write about techniques is all tied in with that important **PEE** structure. The **P** part, remember, is where you make a **P**oint to introduce the technique. The first **E** part has you quoting **E**vidence of that technique being used by the author. When you get to the second **E** part of the structure you are **E**xplaining how the writer creates an **E**ffect – how he/she achieves what he/she set out to.

There are words and phrases you can use to show that you are dealing with the writer's techniques.

The following words and phrases describe **what the writer does**, or **what part of the text does**. They will help you to show that you are **analysing** the author's work.

has connotations of	suggests	shows	demonstrates
creates mirrors	establishes	underlines	echoes
reinforces	emphasises	highlights	reveals
foreshadows	exemplifies	explains	hints

The following words and phrases describe **how the reader feels,** or **how the text affects us** as we read. They will help you to show that you are **evaluating** the author's work, and the way that it has an effect upon us.

thought-provoking	inspiring	horrifying
hard-hitting	stimulating	pivotal moment
key idea(s)	fast-paced	effective
gripping	skilful(ly)	perceptive
moving	profound	striking
important	intelligent	thoughtful

Active learning

Work with a group. You should be quite familiar with this essay task by now.

First think of four more ways that Morgan makes his ideas memorable in 'Trio'.

Then compare your own group's answers with those from the rest of the class.

Agree on the best answers for building paragraphs for the essay. You need as many good ideas as the number of groups in the class.

Work just with your own group again. Take one of the paragraph ideas your class agreed on. Write it up into a paragraph for this essay. Remember to:

- Use quotations from the text and to indent the words that you quote.
- Make sure you start with a topic sentence and that the topic sentence works as the **P** part of the **PEE** structure in your paragraph.
- Use some of the key words and phrases from the boxes above.

Read your paragraphs aloud in class or give them to your teacher for marking.

The conclusion

After your introduction, summary and main body, you need to finish off your essay with a conclusion. The conclusion needs to do two things:

1 Sum up and round off what you have written.
2 Give your personal response.

Summing up just means reminding the examiner what you have written about. It should be only one sentence long and could sound something like this:

Clearly, Morgan uses the encounter with the three young people to give the reader a deeper understanding of his ideas about the importance of human life and love.

Giving your personal response takes a little more thought. Earlier in your school career your personal responses were probably a bit like this:

I liked the poem because the writer used nice descriptions. I would recommend it to other students to read.

You have to do something a little more complicated now, because at National 5 level your personal response, just like everything else in your essay, should fit your chosen task, as well as fitting the text you are writing about.

This task was about how Morgan uses the encounter to put across the poem's central concerns and ideas. Your personal response should say something about how well you think he does this. You could say whether you think his ideas are clear. Here is one example of how a student tackled it.

Morgan's ideas in the poem are clearly expressed. He makes it absolutely obvious that the difficulties of human life have been banished by this encounter. While it may seem odd at times that he attributes so much power to the baby, the dog and the guitar, it is clear in the end that the togetherness of the three young people, and their laughter, has the force to defeat sadness.

So, that is it. You know how to write an essay. If you have worked through this chapter you will have found out step by step how to tackle this part of the exam. Before you go into the exam, your teacher will give you lots of chances to practise essay writing in class.

Active learning

You are going to see the whole of the wording for that essay task on 'Trio' again.

First of all, above the essay choices for poetry, the exam paper has this wording:

Answers to questions in this part should refer to the text and to such relevant features as: word choice, tone, imagery, structure, content, rhythm, theme, sound, ideas …

Then you see this essay task:

Choose a poem which features an encounter or an incident.

By referring to appropriate techniques, show how the poet's development of the encounter or incident leads you to a deeper understanding of the poem's central concerns.

Now, using all the advice from this chapter and everything you have learned, write this essay. Remember you need to have:

- an introduction
- a short summary
- about five main body paragraphs beginning with good topic sentences and using the **PEE** pattern
- a conclusion in which you summarise the essay and give your personal response.

Check over your essay and then hand it in to your teacher for marking. Do not just check your content, look at your language too: your spelling, grammar, paragraphing, punctuation and expression.

Essay writing in the exam

During the National 5 course you will get lots of chances to write essays about the texts you study. At first your teacher may support you in some of the following ways:

- giving you a plan to follow
- making a plan with the class
- letting you plan in groups or pairs
- letting you use your texts and notes while you write the essay
- giving you as long as you need to finish the essay
- letting you take the essay home to finish it.

However, by the time you get to the exam you need to be able to choose, plan and write your essay, all in 45 minutes. Two things will help you with this.

First, you need to know your texts really well before you go in to the exam, and you need to know all your notes and materials about those texts. That way you can pick out the right material to use to answer the essay question you have chosen.

Think of it like this. You probably own several different bags. If you know what you have got to carry, and you know what you are about to do, you can pick out the right bag for the situation. The bag you could choose to take all your gear for camping at a music festival would not be the same one you would bring to school.

Similarly, the information you use to write an essay about how the author makes you feel sympathy for a character might not be the same information you would use to write an essay about how the writer deals with a particular theme or issue.

Second, you need to make a quick plan in the exam before you write your essay. It can be a list of the five key ideas you want to base your main body paragraphs on, or a mind map or spider plan with a leg for each main body paragraph. However you do it, you need to know what you are going to say to answer the question.

Sometimes students go into the exam and panic. No matter how scared you are, do not be tempted to write about the Film and Television Drama option if you have not been taught that in class. Even if you are Scotland's biggest *EastEnders* fan, do not write about what you have not been trained to write about. The same applies to the language section. There might well be a question in there about teenage slang, and you may be a slangy teenager, but do not try to write about it if you have not been taught it.

Another danger in the exam is that you might write the essay you want to write, and not the one the examiners want. It is really important to learn essay skills – and that is what this whole chapter has been about – but there is no point trying to learn a particular essay off by heart, even if it is one you got a good mark for in class. You can only write about what the examiners want on that day.

CHAPTER 8

Answers and mark schemes

Chapter 1: mark schemes

Below are the **mark schemes** for the reading tasks in Chapter 1 (The Analysis and Evaluation Unit).

Markers are reminded that candidates do not need to get every question right. Nor must every part of a particular question necessarily be answered correctly. Markers should holistically assess whether candidates have demonstrated their understanding of the areas of purpose and audience; main ideas and supporting details; meaning and effect of language.

Boy who ran up £1700 bill playing a game on his parents' iPad (page 8)

1a Who do you think would like to read this article? Choose one:
  - parents
  - teenagers
  - computer experts.

1b Give a reason why this person **would want** to read the article.

1c Give a reason why one of the other possible people **would not** be interested in reading the article.

Candidates must give at least one plausible reason across the two questions 1b and 1c, in order to support their chosen answer to 1a.

2a What is the purpose of this article? Choose one:
  - to make readers feel sorry for this family
  - to make readers laugh at this family
  - to warn readers about the risk of this kind of thing.

2b Explain how you know that this is the purpose of the article. Give evidence from the text to support your answer.

For question 2, candidates should plausibly support one chosen purpose.

3 The article shows that huge sums can be spent very quickly, and very easily. Give **two details** that prove this.

Candidates should correctly give one of the following three answers: the boy ran up a £1700 bill; it took just 10 minutes; the child placed the orders innocently/accidentally.

4   Look at paragraph 4. Which **two** expressions suggest that Danny nagged his parents?

Candidates should correctly identify one of: pestering; kept saying.

5a How does Mrs Kitchen's language in paragraph 7 show us that Danny is a very young child? You should **quote** something she says and **explain** why you have chosen this quotation.

Candidates should correctly give one of the following answers, or similar:

Use of 'Daddy' suggests she is talking to a young child.

'... run and hide' suggests a childish approach – almost like a game, or being scared of a monster.

'... ready for bed ... before Daddy got home' suggests Danny is a young child who goes to bed early.

'... he turned back' suggests he took his mother literally and had started to run – a childlike understanding.

He was crying – 'through his tears' suggests a young child – more easily upset.

5b How does Mrs Kitchen's language in paragraph 7 show us that she felt some sympathy for Danny? You should **quote** something she says and **explain** why you have chosen this quotation.

Candidates should correctly give one of the following answers, or similar:

'Bless him' shows her fondness; she felt sorry for him; she found him sweet/cute; felt sympathy.

'... that stopped me being angry' shows she felt sorry/could not remain angry.

6   Explain one way the Apple company is made to seem unfriendly or unhelpful in paragraph 10.

Candidates should correctly give one of the following answers, or similar:

'spokesman' — we do not know the person's name

seems to put blame/responsibility on parents

the company sent an email — no human contact/did not speak to the family

use of formal language

Policeman father reports his own son (page 10)

1a Who would be likely to read this article? Think about:
- age and/or
- interests and/or

- gender and/or
- another audience you can identify.

1b Explain, by making reference to the passage, how you reached this conclusion.

Candidates must give at least one plausibly supported audience.

2a What is the purpose of this article?

2b Support your answer with evidence from the text.

Candidates must give at least one plausibly supported purpose.

3a What has Cameron done?

3b What has been his father's reaction to this?

3c What has been Apple's reaction?

Candidates should identify the main idea, that Cameron has run up a huge (emphasis required) bill playing iPad games.

Candidates should identify at least one of the two supporting details: that his father has reported his son for fraud; that Apple has refused to cancel the bill/has blamed the parent/has put the responsibility back on the parent/has refused to help/been unhelpful.

4a Identify one example of informal language from the first two paragraphs. Why has the writer used informal language here?

Candidates should quote one of: 'shopped', 'ran up', 'blown', 'small fortune', 'scrap'.

Suggested reasons for use may be because a teenager is involved/to help readers relate to the story/because the story is about games, which are informal. Other answers are possible.

4b Identify one example of formal language used in paragraphs 3 and 4. Why has formal language been used here?

Candidates should quote one of: 'recouping', 'as being fraudulent', 'crime reference number', 'had no intention', or a number of other possible formal expressions.

Suggested reasons for use may be because this is now a legal matter/because the situation is serious/because the police are involved. Other answers are possible.

5 Read paragraphs 6–9. Explain, with reference to the text, two ways in which these paragraphs make Cameron seem innocent.

Candidates should refer to and explain at least ONE of:

- *Only had iPad since December – probably unused to it.*
- *iPad was given to him by school – not his choice of device.*

- *Father logged credit card details – his fault son was able to make purchases.*
- *Games free to download – users may not realise extras are subject to charge.*
- *Cameron quickly confessed – implies no intention to do (or cover up) harm.*

6 What impression of Apple is created by the final paragraph? How is this impression created?

Candidates should be aware that Apple seems uncaring / unconcerned / unhelpful and make some reference to 'declined to comment'.

'Out, out' (page 13)

1a Who do you think would like to read this poem? Choose one:
- parents
- teenagers
- farm workers.

1b Give a reason why this person **would want** to read the poem.

1c Give a reason why one of the other possible people **would not** be interested in reading the poem.

Candidates must give at least one plausible reason across the two questions 1b and 1c, in order to support their answer to 1a.

2a What is the purpose of this poem? Choose one:
- to make readers feel sorry for this boy
- to make readers criticise this boy for being careless
- to warn readers about the risk of farm accidents.

2b Explain how you know that this is the purpose of the poem. Give evidence from the text to support your answer.

For question 2, candidates should plausibly support one chosen purpose.

3a Read lines 1–16. The writer makes the saw sound as if it is alive. Explain two ways he does this.

Candidates should give two of the following answers: it is described as snarling / reference to saw making dust / reference to saw dropping sticks / reference to saw having to bear load / reference to saw understanding what supper meant / reference to saw leaping.

3b Read lines 1–16. The writer makes the saw sound dangerous. Explain two ways he does this.

Candidates should correctly give two of the following answers: reference to saw snarling / snarling makes it sound like dangerous animal / repetition of snarled (and rattled) / reference to saw leaping out at boy's hand.

4 The boy does not seem to understand what has happened to him. Give two pieces of evidence from lines 19–27 that show this.

Candidates should correctly give two of the following answers: boy laughs at first/boy holds up hand in appeal/boy tries to keep life from spilling/boy begs sister not to let doctor cut his hand off/boy repeats plea that hand not be cut off/boy does not understand that his hand is gone already.

5a The writer, Robert Frost, often uses repetition. Give one example of this.

5b Explain why you think he used repetition in this case.

Candidates should give one example of repetition from anywhere in the poem and support this with a plausible reason. Candidates may refer to examples that have already appeared in their previous answers.

6 This poem features a number of characters. We see the boy, his sister, and the doctor. There are also other farm workers in the poem. Read lines 9–12 and 33–34. Explain one way Frost makes us feel dislike for these other farm workers.

Candidates should correctly give ONE of the following answers: they do not 'call it a day'/they do not let the boy finish work half an hour early/they do not please the boy by letting him finish work early/reference to workers turning to their own affairs/reference to workers seeming not to care 'since they were not the one dead'.

'Tryst'/'Pacepacker' (page 15)

1a Who would be likely to read this poem? Think about:
- age and/or
- interests and/or
- gender and/or
- another audience you can identify.

1b Explain, by making reference to the poem, how you reached this conclusion

Candidates must give at least one plausibly supported audience.

2a What is the purpose of this poem?
2b Support your answer with evidence from the text.

Candidates must give at least one plausibly supported purpose.

This pair of poems can be divided into three distinct sections.

3a Who is narrating the first section? What is this section about?

Accept all plausibly expressed answers, e.g narrated by girl/young woman; she is describing her relationship with her boyfriend.

3b Where do the words of the second section come from? What is this section about?

Accept all plausibly expressed answers, e.g machine instructions/instructions for the machine Gib works on; explains how to (safely) use the Pacepacker.

3c Whose 'voice' do we hear in the third and final section? What is this section about?

Accept all plausibly expressed answers, e.g voice of poet/the poem/omniscient narrator; describes (the aftermath of) an accident Gib had with the machine.

3d What is the connection between the first poem 'Tryst' and the second poem, 'Pacepacker'?

Accept all plausibly expressed answers, e.g first poem is girl talking about her relationship with Gib, second poem is about an accident Gib has at work. Stronger candidates may mention how the accident will put an end to the dreams and hopes expressed by the narrator of 'Tryst'.

Neither the narrator of the first section, nor her boyfriend Gib, seem very intelligent.

4a By making close reference to the text and/or its language, give at least one piece of evidence to show that the girl is not very intelligent.

Candidates should correctly give ONE of the following answers: thinks it is great to deface gravestone; does not understand relatives of person in vandalised grave may be upset; any reference to or explanation of mistakes in her use of language; is impressed Gib runs Pacepacker alone when machine instructions clearly say only one operator is needed; any reference to lack of vocabulary, e.g. 'marble things', 'Packer-thing'; reference to lack of assertiveness/articulacy in letting Gib do what he wants. Other answers may also be possible – mark on merit.

4b By making close reference to the text and/or its language, give at least one piece of evidence to show that Gib is not very intelligent.

Candidates should correctly give ONE of the following answers: gets enjoyment from defacing gravestone; does not understand relatives of person in vandalised grave may be upset; finds amusement in pretending to be the Ripper; does a job that is physical, not mental; does a job that is simple and repetitive; has accident at work despite clear instructions on how to use machine safely. Other answers may also be possible – mark on merit.

The narrator of the first section seems to have mixed feelings about Gib.

5a By making close reference to the text and/or its language, give at least one piece of evidence to show one **positive** feeling she has about Gib.

Candidates should identify at least ONE of: impressed by his muscular, tattooed arms; likes fact he has 'TRUE LOVE' tattoo; impressed that he runs the Pacepacker by himself; looking forward to getting married to him; sympathises with his poor pay; sympathises with him lifting heavy sacks. Other answers may also be possible – mark on merit.

5b By making close reference to the text and/or its language, give at least one piece of evidence to show one **negative** feeling she has about Gib.

Candidates should identify at least ONE of: reference to 'he makes me squiggle'; reference to his pretence of being the Ripper; reference to his hands feeling 'like scurrying rats'. Other answers may also be possible – mark on merit.

6 By making close reference to the text, give at least one example of how the middle section of the poem ('THE *PACEPACKER* NEEDS … CONVEYER BELT') is made to sound commanding.

Candidates should identify at least ONE of: use of capitals/commanding verbs; verbs placed at start of sentences; repeated use of commands. Other answers may also be possible – mark on merit.

Think about the whole poem.

7a By making close reference to the text and/or its language, explain at least one way the author makes us feel sympathy for the girl.

Candidates should identify at least ONE of: reference to need to conduct love life in graveyard; reference to some of her negative feelings about Gib or their love life; reference to unlikeliness of her fulfilling her dream; reference to loss of Gib after his accident. Other answers may also be possible – mark on merit.

7b By making close reference to the text and/or its language, explain at least one way the author makes us feel sympathy for Gib.

Most likely answer is one based on the accident. Other answers may also be possible – mark on merit.

Chapter 5

Using speech, page 130

'I need a doctor!' screamed the woman as she rushed into Casualty.

'I'm a doctor!' yelled Dr Brown, hurtling down the hospital corridor. 'What seems to be the problem?'

'I've gone deaf,' said the woman. 'I woke up this morning and I wasn't able to hear anything out of my right ear. And,' she went on, 'it tickles.'

'Oh dear,' said Dr Brown. 'That does sound nasty. Let me take a look at it.'

He led her into a consulting room and shone a bright light in her ear. 'Hmm, yes,' he muttered. 'Do you have any children madam?'

'I have a little boy, Liam. He's only four. But what has that got to do with my ears?'

'Did you make him have peas for dinner last night?'

The woman nodded. 'I did, but I still don't see what this has got to do with me going deaf.'

'And does he hate peas?'

'Yes, but I still don't understand the connection.'

'Keep quite still,' said Dr Brown. 'You may feel an odd sensation but it shouldn't hurt.'

'Ow!' yelled the woman, who certainly appeared to think that it had hurt.

'Aha!' exclaimed Dr Brown. He showed her the point of a pen lid, on which perched a slightly waxy-looking pea. 'I think your son got his revenge while you were asleep.'

Chapter 6

'Autism doesn't hold me back'

Answers to understanding questions, page 175

1   Penny Andrews 'believes she has proved herself to be the best candidate'. **In your own words**, explain how paragraph 9 illustrates this idea.   2

2   What are some of the advantages for companies who hire members of staff with autism? Refer to paragraph 10 in your answer, **using your own words**.   4

3   **In your own words**, explain in what ways 'there is a lot of ground to make up' for people with autism in the workplace. Give evidence from paragraph 11 to support your answer.   3

4   Read paragraph 15. Identify Salina Gani's attitude to employing young people with autism and give evidence to support your answer.   2

Q	Expected response	Additional guidance
1	Candidates should demonstrate an understanding of Penny Andrews' qualities and/her employers desire to hire her. Any two ideas from the Additional guidance column for 1 mark each.	• She beat 200 other candidates. • She performs a useful task. • She does this task well. • She was employed a month before finishing her degree.
2	Candidates should demonstrate an understanding of hiring staff with autism. Any four ideas from the Additional guidance column for 1 mark each.	At least some attempt at own words gloss of: • 'focused' • 'intense' • 'honest' • 'do things thoroughly' • 'pay proper attention to detail' • 'always switched on'.
3	Candidates should demonstrate an understanding of the extent to which people with autism are still under-represented or disadvantaged in the workplace. Any three ideas from the Additional guidance column for 1 mark each.	At least some attempt at own words gloss of: • 'Just 15% of those with autism have full-time jobs' • '9% work part time' • 'More than a quarter of graduates with autism are unemployed' • Unemployment among graduates with autism is at 'the highest rate of any disability group'.
4	Candidates should identify a suitable attitude and support this with evidence. Any suitable attitude supported by one item of reasonable evidence for 1 + 1 mark.	Possible attitude: • positive Evidence: • She would gladly take these staff on full time. • She would gladly increase the number of people with autism working for the company. • The nature of work in the service industry (e.g. repetitive, structured) is ideally suited to people with autism. Possible attitude: • pleasantly surprised Evidence: • Thought there would be limits to what these staff could achieve but had been proved wrong.

Answers to context questions, page 177

5   Look back at the two-paragraph extract again. Using the formula given above, show how the context helps you to understand the meaning of the word 'accommodate' as it is used here.   2

6   Look back at the two-paragraph extract again. How does the context of these paragraphs help you to understand the word 'intern' as it is used there?   2

Q	Expected response	Additional guidance
5	Candidates should demonstrate understanding of the meaning of the word and provide contextual evidence of how they arrived at this for 1 + 1 marks.	Meaning: to make allowances/adjustments for someone/to make it easier for someone to fit/settle in etc. Context: reference to idea of, or explanation of details of, changes made to accommodate staff with autism.
6	As above.	Meaning: person working to get experience (rather than for a wage). Context: reference to or quotation of 'work experience' in paragraph 1.

Answers to summarising question, page 178

7   Referring to the whole article, both the main section and the later, short extract, list **in your own words** the key advantages for employers in hiring staff who have autism.   4

Q	Expected response	Additional guidance
7	Candidates should summarise the advantages of hiring people with autism, according to the article. Any four points from the Additional guidance column (may be in bullet point form or in continuous prose).	Key points: • They are very focused on their work/they concentrate well. • They are honest. • They work thoroughly. • They pay attention to detail. • They think about the job even when they are not at work. • They have unique skills. • Their skills bring a measurable benefit to their employers. • They have good analytical skills. • They will work even better if their job coincides with an area of specialist interest. • They are good timekeepers. • They are rarely off work. • They are loyal. • They will enjoy jobs which others find boring. • They are ideally suited for work in the service industry/work which is repetitive and structured.

Paraguayan landfill orchestra

Answers to word-choice questions, page 182

1   How does the word choice in paragraph 3 suggest that there is a lot of rubbish?   2

2   What does the word choice of paragraph 4 imply about the environment of the rubbish dump?   2

3   How does the word choice in paragraph 8 give the impression that Gómez is a skilled maker of musical instruments?   2

4 Show how the word choice in paragraph 10 creates an unpleasant picture of the *gancheros'* living conditions. 2

5 What does the word choice in paragraph 12 show about parents' attitudes to their children learning to play music? 2

6 Explain how the word choice of paragraphs 14 and 15 conveys the sisters' feeling about their instruments. 3

Q	Expected response	Additional guidance
1	Candidates should quote an example of word choice for 1 mark and for a second mark explain how this creates the given effect.	'mounds' + explanation
2	As above.	'flies' and/or 'stench' + explanation
3	As above.	Any of 'shapes', 'form', 'engineers', 'sculpted' + explanation
4	As above.	'slums' and /or 'swamps' + explanation
5	As above.	'struggle to see the advantage' and/or 'a violin can't feed you' and/or 'need to work to eat' + explanation
6	As above.	'clutching' AND 'treasure' + explanation

Answers to meaning in context questions, page 183

Show how the surrounding context helps you to understand the meaning of the following words: **2 marks per answer**

7 '*gancheros*' in paragraph 2
8 'landfill' in paragraph 3
9 'tutelage' in paragraph 6
10 'monetary' in paragraph 7
11 'adverse' in paragraph 11

Q	Expected response	Additional guidance
7	Candidates should demonstrate understanding of the meaning of the word and provide contextual evidence of how they arrived at this for 1 + 1 marks.	Meaning: those who make their living from rubbish dumps. Context: reference to/quotation of suitable detail from paragraphs 1 and 2.
8	As above.	Meaning: things found in/deposited at rubbish dumps. Context: reference to/quotation of suitable detail from paragraph 3.
9	As above.	Meaning: teaching/tuition. Context: reference to/quotation of suitable detail from paragraph 5, e.g. conducting a youth orchestra, teaching music to *gancheros'* children.

10	As above.	Meaning: financial/about money. Context: reference to/quotation of suitable detail from paragraph 7, e.g. violin worth more than house, possibility of violin being sold/traded.
11	As above.	Meaning: difficult/challenging. Context: reference to/quotation of suitable detail from paragraphs 10 and 11, e.g. living in slums, poverty, worry about meeting daily needs.

Answers to understanding questions, page 183

12 In your own words, explain why Chávez decided to make instruments from rubbish. Refer to paragraph 7 in your answer.　2

13 Referring to the whole article, **in your own words** explain the advantages for the *gancheros'* children of learning music.　3

Q	Expected response	Additional guidance
12	Candidates should demonstrate their understanding of Chávez's decision. Any two points from the Additional guidance column for 1 mark each.	At least some attempt at own words gloss of: • 'A violin is worth more than a recycler's house'. • 'We couldn't give a child a formal instrument as it would have put him in a difficult position.' • 'The family may have looked to sell or trade it.' • 'It was fine to hand these out as they had no monetary value.'
13	Candidates should summarise the advantages for *gancheros'* children of learning music, according to the article. Any four points from the Additional guidance column (may be in bullet point form or in continuous prose).	Key points: • They have had worldwide acclaim. • They have had the opportunity to travel abroad. • It gives them something to do rather than playing in the rubbish. • It helps them develop a mentality that could lift them out of poverty. • Practising music teaches them self-discipline/teaches them to plan. • It gives them the chance of a better future. • Going abroad opens their minds

I set my daughter a computer curfew

Answers to imagery questions, page 188

Look at the following images. Explain what each image means and analyse its effect.　**3 marks per answer**

1 'vanish to the margins' (paragraph 1)
2 'Technology embraces our children' (paragraph 3)
3 'a warm electronic sea' (paragraph 3)
4 'the tide of it comes ever higher' (paragraph 3)
5 'Allowing electronic strangers into a girl's bedroom' (paragraph 7)
6 'a small desert island of their own' (paragraph 14)

Q	Expected response	Additional guidance
1	Full analysis of the image – 3 marks. Clear analysis of the image – 2 marks. Weak analysis of the image – 1 mark. Misunderstanding of the image – 0 marks.	For 3 marks, candidates should state the comparison and show how it is linked to the example used in the passage. This would be considered a full analysis. For example: The writer compares the declining importance of parents to something being pushed to the margins. Just as the margins are at the edges, so parents are no longer central to their children's lives. This shows that parents are less important to teenagers than friends are.
2	As above.	As above. For example: The writer compares technology's influence over children to an embrace. Just as an embrace is a close, enfolding hug, so technology has a tight hold of teenagers. This shows that technology is very important to teenagers.
3	As above.	As above. For example: The writer compares electronic communication to the sea. Just as a swimmer has the sea all around them, so teenagers are surrounded on every side by technology. This shows that they are in danger of being overwhelmed by the technology in their lives.
4	As above.	As above. For example: The writer compares technology to a rising tide. Just as a rising tide cannot be stopped, so the amount of technology in life keeps increasing. This shows we cannot stop technology coming into teenage lives.
5	As above.	As above. For example: The writer compares using technology in your bedroom to letting strangers in. Just as letting strangers into a girl's bedroom would be dangerous and stupid, so letting her use technology in there is unwise and risky. This shows the risks of technology.
6	As above.	As above. For example: The writer compares being cut off from technology to being on a desert island. Just as a desert island is cut off and peaceful, so being disconnected from technology would give teenagers time alone. This shows that time away from electronic devices allows people to have some peace.

Answers to meaning in context questions, page 189

7 How does the context help you to understand the meaning of 'exasperated' as used in paragraph 1?   2

8 How does the context help you to understand the meaning of 'entailed' as used in paragraph 2?   2

9 How does the context help you to understand the meaning of 'hapless' as used in paragraph 9?   2

Q	Expected response	Additional guidance
7	Candidates should demonstrate understanding of the meaning of the word and provide contextual evidence of how they arrived at this for 1 + 1 marks.	Meaning: annoyed, frustrated. Context: reference to/quotation of suitable detail from paragraph 1, e.g. parent wrenching phone from teenager's hand.
8	As above.	Meaning: involved, consisted of. Context: reference to/quotation of suitable detail from paragraph 2, e.g. explanation of how parent removed gadgets, listing of items removed.
9	As above.	Meaning: useless, unsuccessful, ineffective. Context: reference to/quotation of suitable detail from paragraph 9, e.g. story of Terry Waite making no sense to daughter.

Answers to word choice, page 190

10 Explain what the writer's word choice in the first line of the article conveys about the time she spent beside the home telephone as a teenager.   2

11 What does the writer's use of 'chirruping' in paragraph 3 suggest about mobile phones?   2

Q	Expected response	Additional guidance
10	Candidates should quote an example of word choice for 1 mark and for a second mark explain how this creates the given effect.	'vigils' + explanation
11	Candidates should explain what the word choice suggests. Any two details for 1 mark each.	Details referring to: • quality of sound, e.g. sharp, shrill, attention grabbing • volume • persistence • comparison to sound of bird or insect.

Answers to summarising question, page 190

12 Referring to the whole article, **in your own words** list the key reasons for concern about the amount of time modern teenagers spend using electronic gadgets.   4

Q	Expected response	Additional guidance
12	Candidates should summarise the key reasons for concern about the amount of time modern teenagers spend using electronic gadgets, according to the article. Any four points from the Additional guidance column (may be in bullet point form or in continuous prose).	Key points: • It gives them no time for thought/reflection/an interior life. • Rings tones etc. demand teenagers' constant attention. • Such a lifestyle may be rewiring teenage brains. • Technology causes loss of attention/focus. • It fragments thought. • It makes reading harder. • It prevents linear thought. • It prevents literary thought. • It allows strangers into teenagers' bedrooms. • It interferes with/prevents development of good sleep patterns. • They lose the habit of being alone. • They read less. • What they do read is less challenging.

Has Liz Truss tried looking after six toddlers? I have

Answers to link questions, page 193

1   How does the sentence, 'So in the interests of public policy research, I scored myself six toddlers between 9.30am and 1pm' (paragraph 4) form a link at this stage in the article?   2

2   How does the sentence, 'On the subject of regulations, these require a carer to take the kids out at least once a day' (paragraph 8) form a link at this stage in the article?   2

Q	Expected response	Additional guidance
1	Candidates should, by quotation and explanation, show what idea is being linked back to, and what new idea is being introduced.	'research' links back to rhetorical question in paragraph 3 about whether anyone had test-driven the theory. 'I scored myself six toddlers' introduces the day of childcare she is about to describe.
2	Candidates should, by quotation and explanation, show what idea is being linked back to, and what new idea is being introduced.	'On the subject of regulations' links back to the above mention of the authorities. '… take the kids out at least once a day' introduces the idea of how complex this would be to achieve.

Answers to imagery questions, page 194

3   Look at the following image:

'a horde of ferrets and a motorway' (paragraph 8)

Explain what the image means and analyse its effect.   3

4   Look at the following image:

'Those are battery conditions' (paragraph 11)

Explain what the image means and analyse its effect.   3

Q	Expected response	Additional guidance
3	Full analysis of the image – 3 marks. Clear analysis of the image – 2 marks. Weak analysis of the image – 1 mark. Misunderstanding of the image – 0 marks.	For 3 marks, candidates should state the comparison and show how it is linked to the example used in the passage. This would be considered a full analysis: The writer compares taking a lot of young children out together to taking ferrets on to a motorway. Just as ferrets on a motorway would run around out of control and cause danger, so lots of children outdoors together would be hard to care for and might get hurt. This shows that taking lots of children out would be difficult and risky.
4	As above	As above. For example: The writer compares children kept indoors all day to hens in a battery farm. Just as battery hens are confined in unpleasant conditions, so children kept indoors together would be unhappy. This shows that it is wrong to keep lots of children together indoors all day.

Answers to particular aspects questions, page 194

5 'Childcare is unaffordable.' **In your own words**, explain how examples the writer gives in the first paragraph illustrate this idea.　　　　2

6 Show how the context of paragraph 2 helps you to understand the meaning of the word 'stringent' as used there.　　　　2

7 Discuss the effect of the rhetorical question used in paragraph 3.　　　　2

8 Show how the context of paragraph 8 helps you to understand the meaning of the word 'analogy' as used there.　　　　2

9 Identify two examples of the writer using exaggeration in paragraph 10 and discuss how they add to her argument.　　　　4

Q	Expected response	Additional guidance
5	Candidates should show they understand the meaning of the phrase by referring to examples that illustrate the idea. Any two ideas from the Additional guidance column for 1 mark each.	At least some own words gloss of: '… families in the UK spend nearly a third of their income on it' '… more than anyone else in the world'
6	Candidates should demonstrate understanding of the meaning of the word and provide contextual evidence of how they arrived at this for 1 + 1 marks.	Meaning: strict, restrictive, severe, etc. Context: quotation of or reference to 'over-regulation'/Truss's plan to allow each adult to care for more children than currently allowed.
7	Candidates should identify the rhetorical question and discuss its effect.	'Did anybody test-drive her theory for her, even in its planning stage?' Plus effect of the question, which is to question the common sense/feasibility of the idea (that one adult can care for six toddlers).

| 8 | Candidates should demonstrate understanding of the meaning of the word and provide contextual evidence of how they arrived at this for 1 + 1 marks. | Meaning: example, comparison, etc.

Context: quotation of or reference to idea of 'a horde of ferrets and a motorway'. |
| 9 | Candidates should identify an example of exaggeration and discuss its effect.

Any two correctly identified examples of exaggeration supported by relevant explanation for 2 marks each. | Possible examples:
• 'a hell of a lot'
• 'blind panic'
• 'freak out'
• 'now I've given them all back alive'
• 'because she's three and won't choke'
• 'didn't take any notice of my daughter at all'
• 'took off and spent the time in Caffè Nero'
+ suitable explanation of effect. |

Answers to summarising question, page 194

10 Referring to the whole article, **in your own words** list some of the challenging aspects of caring for young children.   4

Q	Expected response	Additional guidance
10	Candidates should summarise the key challenges in caring for young children, according to the article. Any four points from the Additional guidance column (may be in bullet point form or in continuous prose).	Key points: • Children who do not demand attention will not get it. • Taking children outdoors is too difficult. • Children who cannot speak are hard to take care of. • It is hard to even keep them all in the same room. • If one child needs lots of affection/attention, others will be ignored. • Interacting with children stops you concentrating on anything else. • Not being able to see children/not knowing where they are leads to anxiety. • The only way to cope with more than a few hours' care is to keep them in a confined space. • Keeping children shut up like this is unfair – battery hens analogy. • They need help with nappies/toilet use. • Help with toileting/nappies is very time-consuming. • They leave dirt/mess (peas in carpet example).

Answer to tone question, page 196

11 What is the tone of the final sentence and how is this made clear?   2

Q	Expected response	Additional guidance
11	Candidates should correctly identify a tone for 1 mark and provide evidence by reference or quotation to support this tone for a second mark.	Tone: critical/angry/definite + suitable explanation.

Your life in 2033

Answers to tone questions, page 198

1 How do the writers maintain a conversational tone throughout the passage?　　2

2 What is the tone of paragraph 6, and how is this created?　　2

Q	Expected response	Additional guidance
1	Candidates should give evidence, by reference or quotation, of how the tone is created, and should then explain the effect of this. One item of evidence for 1 mark, explanation for a second mark.	Evidence: use of 'you' + suitable explanation, e.g. feels as they are talking to the reader.
2	Candidates should correctly identify a tone for 1 mark and provide evidence by reference or quotation to support this tone for a second mark.	Tone: reassuring. Evidence: 'of course'/'as productive or relaxing as you desire'.

Answers to additional questions, page 198

3 'Imagine you are an urban professional living in a western city a few decades from now.' **In your own words** explain how details the writer uses in paragraphs 1 to 6 create the impression that the reader is a professional, **and** that the reader is living in a city.　　4

4 What is the meaning of 'roused' as used in paragraph 2, and how does the context help you to understand the meaning?　　2

5 'Your apartment is an electronic orchestra and you are the conductor.' Choose **one** of the two images in this sentence. Explain what your chosen image means and analyse its effect.　　3

6 The writers aim to present a positive picture of life in 2033. Referring to the whole article, **in your own words** list ways in which the writers suggest that a life lived then will be a good one.　　4

Q	Expected response	Additional guidance
3	Candidates should give in their own words one detail from the passage to imply that the reader is a professional, and one that implies the reader lives in a city. 1 mark for each detail + 1 mark for explanation of the given detail.	Professional: giving a presentation at work. Urban: living in an apartment. Other details may be possible. + suitable explanation.
4	Candidates should demonstrate understanding of the meaning of the word and provide contextual evidence of how they arrived at this for 1 + 1 marks.	Meaning: woken up. Context: quotation of or reference to idea of 'wake-up routine'/'alarm clock'/'awake'/'(when to) wake (you)' It may also be possible to evidence this with explanation of the likely wakeful effect of smell of coffee/daylight/back massage.

5	Full analysis of the image – 3 marks. Clear analysis of the image – 2 marks. Weak analysis of the image – 1 mark. Misunderstanding of the image – 0 marks.	For 3 marks candidates should state the comparison and show how it is linked to the example used in the passage. This would be considered a full analysis: The writer compares a 2033 apartment to an orchestra. Just as an orchestra has many parts that work together under the guidance of a conductor, so the 2033 apartment will have many gadgets that can all be controlled by the person who lives there. This shows that a 2033 apartment will function smoothly. The writer compares the reader in 2033 to an orchestra conductor. Just as a conductor is in control of many different musicians, so the reader in 2033 will control many different gadgets in his or her apartment. This shows that in 2033, we will have organised lives.
6	Candidates should summarise the key positive aspects of life in 2033, according to the article. Any four points from the Additional guidance column (may be in bullet point form or in continuous prose).	Key points: • You will be woken by something nicer than an alarm clock. • You will wake refreshed. • You will wake just when you are ready to. • You can easily control conditions in your apartment. • You can easily skim the day's news. • News will go where you go. • Your breakfast will be perfectly cooked. • Robots will do your housework. • All your data are easily accessible. • You have limitless data storage. • All digital devices will be very high quality (e.g. lightweight, fast, powerful). • Devices can assess your medical needs. • Commute by driverless car. • Your commute will be just as you want it. • Devices can even remind you about social/family events.

The connecting world

Answers to sentence structure questions, page 202

1   How does the sentence structure of the first paragraph suggest that change is inevitable?   2

2   'Whereas they used to bring their daily catch to the market and watch it slowly spoil as the day progressed, now they keep it on the line, in the river, and wait for calls from customers' (paragraph 1). How does the structure of this sentence emphasis the idea that life has already improved for African fisherwomen?   2

3 How does sentence structure in the second paragraph make clear what the writers mean by 'basic–feature phones'? 2

4 What is the function of the dash in paragraph 7? 2

5 How does the sentence structure of the final paragraph show that the writers are reaching their conclusion? 2

Q	Expected response	Additional guidance
1	Candidates should identify a feature of sentence structure for 1 mark and explain, for a further mark, how it suggests the inevitability of change.	Feature: repetition of 'no' + suitable explanation, e.g. very definite.
2	Candidates should identify a feature of sentence structure for 1 mark and explain, for a further mark, how it suggests that the fisherwomen's lives have already improved.	Feature: 'Whereas …' vs 'now' + suitable explanation, e.g. divides sentence into past and present.
3	Candidates should identify a feature of sentence structure for 1 mark and explain, for a further mark, how it clarifies the meaning of the phrase.	Feature: parenthesis/use of dashes + suitable explanation, e.g. gives extra information/ explanation of what these basic features are.
4	Candidates should give a clear explanation of the function of the dash.	Introduces list/explanation/examples of how we will make more effective use of our time.
5	Candidates should identify a feature of sentence structure for 1 mark and explain, for a further mark, how it implies the writers are reaching a conclusion.	Feature: 'Without question' at start of pararaph + suitable explanation, e.g. shows they are summing up.

Answers to summarising questions, page 203

6 Referring to the whole article, **in your own words** list ways in which the writers suggest that a technological change will bring benefits for developing countries. 4

7 Referring to the whole article, **in your own words** list ways in which the writers suggest that a technological change and increasing connectivity may have disadvantages. 4

Q	Expected response	Additional guidance
6	Candidates should summarise the key benefits of technological change for developing countries, according to the article. Any four points from the Additional guidance column (may be in bullet point form or in continuous prose).	Key points: • Such change will transform these countries. • Customers can order produce by phone when needed, saving waste, etc. • Data can be collected more easily. • Data can be used more easily. • Gathering/having accurate data will benefit growth and development. • Governments can measure success. • Media and NGOs can check facts. • 3D printing will allow cheap local production of useful items.
7	Candidates should summarise the key disadvantages, according to the article. Any four points from the Additional guidance column (may be in bullet point form or in continuous prose).	Key points: • We will have less control of our personal information. • Our pasts will be well documented and may affect our prospects. • We will not be able to control or influence what other people think of us. • Other people will be able to get into our online identities and share or change them. • Our valuable identity will mostly exist online. • The government may seek to control that identity. • There will be an illegal trade in stolen or fake identities. • Repressive governments will be more able to control their citizens.

Children are sent to school too young in the UK

Answers to questions on page 206

1 'It's an eye-catching statistic.' **In your own words** explain how examples given in the first paragraph illustrate this idea. 2

Q	Expected response	Additional guidance
1	Candidates should show that they understand the meaning of the phrase by referring to examples that illustrate the idea. Any two ideas from the Additional guidance column for 1 mark each.	At least some attempted own words gloss of: • 'Almost 20% of schoolchildren in the UK are registered as having special educational needs …' • '… five times higher than the EU average.'

2   Look at paragraph 2. **In your own words**, explain some of the
suggested solutions to the problem.   3

Q	Expected response	Additional guidance
2	Candidates should demonstrate an understanding of some solutions. Any three ideas from the Additional guidance column for 1 mark each.	At least some attempted own words gloss of: • 'more intense' • 'more rigorous' • 'longer hours at school' • 'more testing' • 'more competition' • 'schools that are more strict' • 'conformist'

3   Show how the context of paragraph 3 helps you to understand
the meaning of 'discrepancy' as used in this paragraph.   2

Q	Expected response	Additional guidance
3	Candidates should demonstrate understanding of the meaning of the word and provide contextual evidence of how they arrived at this for 1 + 1 marks.	Meaning: difference, mismatch, etc. Context: quotation of or reference to comparison of Britain vs. rest of Europe.

4   Referring to paragraph 4 in your answer, **in your own words**
explain how starting school at a later age may be better for
students.   2

Q	Expected response	Additional guidance
4	Candidates should show an understanding that the example of Finland appears to support later schooling. Any two points from the Additional guidance column for 1 mark each.	At least some attempted own words gloss of: • 'Finland has the best educational outcomes in the EU …' • '… the highest age for beginning formal education …' • '… a full three years later than many children here.'

5   How does the first sentence of paragraph 5 act as a link at this
stage in the writer's argument?   2

Q	Expected response	Additional guidance
5	Candidates should, by quotation and explanation, show what idea is being linked back to, and what new idea is being introduced.	'… too early an age' links back to the early age British children start school as mentioned in paragraph 4. '(There are) many reasons' introduces some of the problems children have at school, mentioned from paragraph 5 onwards.

6 What are some of the reasons why 'gifted' children underachieve? Refer to paragraph 6 in your answer, **using your own words.** 4

Q	Expected response	Additional guidance
6	Candidates should identify reasons why gifted children underachieve. Any four points from the Additonal Guidance column for 1 mark each.	At least some attempt at own words gloss of: • 'inability to manage time' • 'disorganisation' • 'frequently losing things' • 'lack of motivation to succeed' • 'problems with friendships' • 'bullying' • 'disruptive' • 'confrontational' • 'disrespectful' • 'difficulty concentrating' • 'poor handwriting' • 'poor presentation of work' • 'perfectionist personality type'

7 How does the writer's use of repetition in paragraph 8 help to show the problems faced by gifted children? 2

Q	Expected response	Additional guidance
7	Candidates should identify one example of repetition and explain how this shows the problems of gifted children. 1 mark for example, 1 mark for explanation.	Repetition: 'disorder' + suitable explanation, e.g. it makes these children seem as if they have something wrong with them/ they are described as being mentally ill.

8 Choose one of the following images from paragraph 9:
  • 'a ghastly vision'
  • 'the straightjacket that has been laced around their intellect'
  • 'like fireworks'
Explain what your chosen image means and examine its effect. 3

Q	Expected response	Additional guidance
8	Full analysis of the image – 3 marks. Clear analysis of the image – 2 marks. Weak analysis of the image – 1 mark. Misunderstanding of the image – 0 marks.	For 3 marks, candidates should state the comparison and show how it is linked to the example used in the passage. This would be considered a full analysis: The writer compares the idea of children being wrongly diagnosed with learning difficulties to a ghastly vision. Just as a ghastly vision is horrible to see or even imagine, so the idea of children being wrongly labelled this way is a terrible one.

		This shows how awful it is for children to be mistakenly described as having learning difficulties.
		The writer compares sending children to school young to putting then in straightjackets. Just as a straightjacket stops free movement, so going to school too young is restrictive and cruel. This shows early education is a bad idea.
		The writer compares enjoying your education to fireworks. Just as fireworks are sudden and exciting so some children can suddenly realise how much they love the excitement of learning. This shows that education can be a fantastic experience.

9   Read paragraph 10. Explain **two** ways in which the writer makes clear her disapproval of starting school at an early age.   4

Q	Expected response	Additional guidance
9	Candidates should identify and explain two things the writer does.	Possible answers: • Use of short sentences + suitable explanation of effect. • 'little understanding' + suitable explanation of effect. • Contrast of/difference between thriving and non-thriving children + suitable explanation of effect. • 'inappropriate' + explanation of effect. • Rejects idea that some children necessarily have learning difficulty + suitable explanation of effect.

10 How does the writer's quotation of Pasi Sahlberg in paragraph 11 support her overall argument?   2

Q	Expected response	Additional guidance
10	Candidates should demonstrate an understanding of how the argument is supported. Any two ideas from the Additional guidance column for 1 mark each.	• She is described as an 'expert'. • She is from Finland, which the writer has said has good educational outcomes. • She uses statistics to support her ideas. • What she says backs up the writer's point that Finland is good at identifying special needs.

11 Referring to the whole article, **in your own words** list the key disadvantages the writer believes are caused by starting formal education at too early an age. 4

Q	Expected response	Additional guidance
11	Candidates should summarise the disadvantages of starting formal education early, according to the writer. Any four points from the Additional guidance column (may be in bullet point form or prose).	Key points: • It is not good for children academically. • It is not good for them psychologically. • They do not do as well as children in other countries where education starts later. • The brightest children (may) do least well. • Natural curiosity is stifled by formal learning. • Talented children are not spotted. • Talented children are often labelled as having learning difficulties. • Children who do not get much stimulation at home will be excited by being at school, then put off when they are made to conform. • Early education may have a worse effect on boys than on girls.

Chapter 7

'Trio'

Answers to questions on page 230

1 The author gives this poem a sense of reality. Show how this is achieved in the first 8 lines. ('Coming up … sees this but!') 2

Expected response	Additional guidance
2 marks can be awarded for two ways in which a sense of reality is created. Only 1 mark should be awarded for one way in which this is created. Other examples from the first eight lines may be acceptable.	Real place: 'Buchanan Street'. (1) Detail of weather: 'sharp winter evening'. (1) Precise detail of who was seen: 'a young man and two girls'. (1) Use of present tense, e.g. 'coming', 'carries', 'are laughing', 'rises', 'pass'. (1) Use of dialogue: 'Wait till he sees this but!' (1) Use of Glaswegian dialect: 'Wait till he sees this but!' (1)

2 In lines 9–11 ('The chihuahua has ... sprig of mistletoe')
   Morgan describes what the young people are carrying. What
   mood or atmosphere is created by the writer and how does
   he use language effectively to create this mood?   3

Expected response	Additional guidance
Statement of acceptable mood or atmosphere for 1 mark. Example/quotation of writer's use of language for 1 mark. Comment for 1 mark. Other examples from lines 9 to 11 may be acceptable.	Possible answers include: Mood or atmosphere: • Loving, safe, protective, etc. Writer's use of language: • 'tartan coat' protects/warms dog • 'teapot-holder' suggests keeping dog warm, protecting it • 'white shawl' protects/warms baby • 'fresh sweet cake' implies birthday/marriage/other loving celebration • 'milky plastic cover' protects guitar • 'milky' suggests protection and nurture of milk • 'mistletoe' suggests love. Mood or atmosphere: • welcoming, inclusive, etc. Writer's use of language: • 'chihuahua' as foreign dog in Scottish 'tartan' coat – those from abroad are safe and welcome here Mood or atmosphere: • alert, excited, etc. Writer's use of language: • 'bright eyes' suggests alertness of baby

3 Many of the main ideas in the poem come across clearly in
   lines 12–18 ('Orphean sprig!... this march of three'). Identify at
   least **one** of Morgan's main ideas from these lines. Show how **one**
   example of the poet's language in these lines helps to clarify or
   illustrate his meaning.   3

Expected response	Additional guidance
1 mark can be awarded for one main idea or concern shown in lines 12–18. Example/quotation of writer's use of language for 1 mark. Comment for 1 mark. Other examples from lines 12–18 may be acceptable.	Possible answers include: Main idea: • Happiness can be found in/sadness can be banished by ordinary things. Writer's use of language: • Exclamation marks suggest excitement, shouting for joy. • 'The vale of tears is powerless before you.'

- Word choice of 'abdicates'.
- Line layout of 'under the Christmas lights'.
- Reference to or quotation of all or part of lines 16–18.

Main idea:

- Power of music to charm, even rescue us.

Writer's use of language:

- Allusion to myth of Orpheus.

Main idea:

- Human life and love are sacred, with or without religion.

Writer's use of language:

- 'Whether Christ is born or is not born …'.

4   Show how two examples of the poet's use of language in lines 19–23 ('And the three… this winter's day') help to clarify or illustrate his ideas in these lines.

4

Expected response	Additional guidance
4 marks can be awarded for two examples of language helping to clarify or illustrate meaning. Example (1) plus comment (1) – any two will gain 4 marks. Only one use of language will gain a maximum of 2 marks. Other examples from lines 19–23 are acceptable.	Possible answers include: Idea: • The trio should be protected as something rare and precious. Writer's use of language: • Use of dash parenthesis to surround and contain the encounter. • (Ambiguity of) 'ringing round them'. • '… like a guard'. Idea: • The effect of the trio is a lasting one. Writer's use of language: • Repetition in 'vanished … not vanished'. • Self-contradiction in 'vanished … not vanished'. Idea: • Power of the trio. Writer's use of language: • 'in their arms they wind …' Idea: • power of laughter/happiness Writer's use of language: • 'laughter ringing round them (like a guard)'

Answer to question on page 231

5 With close textual reference, show how the ideas and/or language of this poem are similar to another poem or poems by Morgan that you have read. 8

Please note: due to constraints of space, detailed teaching and commentary here only covers two Morgan poems, 'Trio' and 'Good Friday'. The mark scheme therefore demands reference to only one other poem. However, SQA mark schemes expect stronger candidates/more successful answers (those earning 5 or more marks) to refer to 'Trio' and at least two other poems. The most natural third poem to refer to along with these would be 'In the Snack Bar'.

Expected response	Additional guidance
Candidates should show awareness of the ideas and/or language of the wider works or Morgan, and be able to relate this awareness to 'Trio'.	**8–7 marks** Candidates should identify at least three features/ideas in the poem and be able to comment on these in at least one other poem. The discussion should be supported by detailed quotation from the poems being discussed. Skilled discussion of other Morgan poetry in relation to 'Trio'. (8) Still skilled, but lacking some assurance. (7)
	6–5 marks Candidates should identify at least two features of ideas and/or language in the poem and be able to comment on these in at least one other poem. The discussion should be supported by several quotations from the poems being discussed. Confident discussion of other Morgan poetry in relation to 'Trio'. (6) Slightly less confident discussion. (5)
	4–3 marks Candidates should identify two features of ideas and/or language common to one other poem. There should be at least two quotations from at least one other poem to support the candidate's discussion. Some discussion attempted of other Morgan poetry in relation to 'Trio'. (4) Weaker discussion. (3)

	2–1 marks
	Candidates should identify at least one feature of ideas and/or language of other Morgan poetry in relation to 'Trio', with at least one quotation. (2)
	Acknowledgement of common feature(s) with general reference. (1)
	0 marks
	No reference to any similarity/common feature with any other poem.

'Good Friday'

Answers to questions on page 231

1 The author gives this poem a sense of reality. Show how this is achieved in the first three lines. *('Three o'clock … Bath Street?')* 2

Expected response	Additional guidance
2 marks can be awarded for two ways in which a sense of reality is created.	Real place: 'Bath Street'. (1)
	Detail of weather: 'sun'. (1)
Only 1 mark should be awarded for one way in which this is created.	Exact time: 'three o'clock'. (1)
	Use of present tense, e.g. 'lurches', 'flops', 'are laughing', 'rises', 'pass'. (1)
Other examples from the first three lines may be acceptable.	
	Use of dialogue: 'D's this go', 'right along Bath Street'. (1)

2 How does the writer's use of language in lines 6 to 16 ('I've had a wee drink … see what I mean?') show the man's need to communicate? 3

Expected response	Additional guidance
3 marks can be awarded for three examples/quotations of language showing a desire to communicate or to be understood.	'ye understand' (1)
	'ye'll maybe think' (1)
	'ye see' (1)
Other examples from these lines may be acceptable.	'I'm no boring you eh?' (1)
	'see what I mean?' (1)
	repetition of 'ye understand' (1)
	repetition of 'ye see' (1)

3 With close reference to lines 6 to 23 ('I've had a wee drink … bliddy ignorant. Well –') explain how the poem shows at least one belief Morgan has about Easter and/or the church **3**

Expected response	Additional guidance
1 mark for a reasonable belief Morgan may be expressing about Easter and/or the church.	Possible belief:
	• That Easter means different things to different people.
1 mark for reference or quotation.	Support from text:
1 mark for comment.	• 'I've got to get some Easter eggs for the kiddies.'
Other properly evidenced answers may be acceptable.	• 'I like to celebrate when I'm no working …'.
	Possible belief:
	• That the church has not done a very good job of explaining things.
	Support from text:
	• The man does not know 'what today's in aid of'.
	Possible belief:
	• That the church is not good at reaching ordinary working people.
	Support from text:
	• The man in the poem says he is 'bliddy ignorant' about Easter.
	• Morgan the poet knows the story in enough detail to be able to refer in his opening lines to the detail about the darkness and the third hour.

4 Show how two examples of the poet's use of language in lines 23 to 26 ('The bus lurches … steady legs') create an effective ending to the poem. **4**

Expected response	Additional guidance
4 marks can be awarded for two examples of language helping to create an effective ending.	Possible answers include:
	Example:
Example (1) plus comment (1) – any two will gain 4 marks.	• 'the bus brakes violently'
	Comment:
Only one use of language will gain a maximum of 2 marks.	• Brings poem to a definite stop.
	Example:
Other examples from lines 23–26 are acceptable.	• 'swings down – off'
	Comment:
	• Working man leaves bus (and poem) and encounter ends.

	Example: • 'into the sun' Comment: • Sense of moving on to new place/idea of near resurrection. Example: • rhyme of 'eggs' + 'legs' Comment: • Gives poem sense of punchline/ending. Example: • line layout Comment: • Shows how man moved/undermines idea of man moving steadily.

5 With close textual reference, show how the ideas and/or language of this poem are similar to another poem or poems by Morgan that you have read.   8

Marking scheme as above for 'Trio', bearing in mind the warning that SQA specimen papers generally demand better candidates/ stronger answers to refer to the focus poem and **at least two** other poems, not one as referred to here.